M

PREP SCHOOL

How to Improve Your Kitchen Skills and Cooking Techniques

James P. DeWan

S
SURREY
BOOKS

AN **AGATE** IMPRINT

CHICAGO

Chicago Tribune
Tony W. Hunter, Publisher
Vince Casanova, President
Gerould W. Kern, Editor
R. Bruce Dold, Editorial Page Editor
Bill Adee, Vice President/Digital
Jane Hirt, Managing Editor
Joycelyn Winnecke, Associate Editor
Peter Kendall, Deputy Managing Editor

Library of Congress Cataloging-in-Publication Data

DeWan, James P.
Prep school : how to improve your kitchen skills and cooking techniques / James P. DeWan and Chicago Tribune Staff.
    pages cm
Includes bibliographical references and index.
Summary: "A collection of articles from the Chicago Tribune column of the same name describing and illustrating cooking techniques and advice"-- Provided by publisher.
ISBN 978-1-57284-148-2 (hardcover) -- ISBN 1-57284-148-6 (hardcover) -- ISBN 978-1-57284-415-5 (ebook) -- ISBN 1-57284-415-9 (ebook)
1. Cooking. I. Chicago Tribune (Firm) II. Chicago tribune (Chicago, Ill. : 1963) III. Title.
TX651.D49 2013
641.5--dc23
                            2013019126

Surrey Books is an imprint of Agate Publishing. Agate books are available in bulk at discount prices.
For more information visit agatepublishing.com.

This book is dedicated to Elaine, Violet and Seamus, from whom I learn the very best things in life, to Carol Haddix, whose brilliant idea Prep School was in the first place, to Joe Gray, who keeps the column going, and to my students and colleagues at Kendall College, who understand that our own education doesn't stop until we're dead. And maybe not even then...

CONTENTS

CONTENTS

CONTENTS

ABOUT THIS BOOK

This book was created from the Chicago Tribune's popular feature, "Prep School," by James P. DeWan. DeWan is a chef, culinary instructor and award-winning food writer. He has served on the culinary faculty at Kendall College in Chicago. DeWan lives in Chicago.

KITCHEN
TIPS ▶

PRESENTS FOR THE COOK

On the off chance you would like a little help, here are a few gift suggestions for anyone who likes to cook. The items we've suggested include some places to buy them. You can shop online, too. While you're shopping, you can conduct a little research on the many brands available. Many department stores also carry these tools.

Mandoline (photo 1)

This is a slicing implement, essentially a plane with a straight- or V-blade in the middle. Run your food down the plane across the blade and out pops perfectly even, perfectly thin, perfectly perfect little slices of potato, carrot, radish—just about any fruit or vegetable.

You want a mandoline for a couple of reasons. First, it's so fast: The pieces of food come flying off. Second, all those pieces are exactly the same size, which means they look terrific and, more importantly, they'll all cook at the same rate. Mandolines come in a variety of styles and prices.

Classic mandolines are generally stainless steel and have folding legs. For maximum versatility, look for one with a fully adjustable blade rather than preset widths. It should also include separate blades or attachments for gaufrettes, batonnets, julienne strips.

Also gaining popularity now are Japanese or Asian mandolines. These are generally cheaper, often made of plastic, and not as versatile. However, for basic slicing, they're great.

Photo 1

Protective gloves

One thing about all mandolines, though, is they are sharper than David Letterman. Be very, very careful. I've sliced myself. My colleagues and students have sliced themselves. One thing you might want to accessorize with is a protective glove. It will protect your hand, plus you'll look totally fierce. They're not cheap, but then again, neither is finger reattachment surgery.

Food mill

This tool always seems so old-fashioned to me, but I love it. Turn boiled or baked potatoes into puree, then add hot cream, butter, salt and pepper for the lightest, creamiest mashed potatoes ever. Or use it with any cooked legumes—black beans, navy beans, chickpeas—and the strainer will catch the outer skins, leaving your puree perfectly smooth.

Chinois and ladle (photo 2)

A chinois is a conical fine-mesh strainer. Pass your sauces and pureed or cream soups through one of these babies and your finished product will be the culinary equivalent of silk pajamas.

The 2-ounce ladle is handy for thicker products, say, a butternut squash soup. Fill the chinois about two-thirds of the way, then drop the ladle in as far as it will go. With a rapid wrist motion, pogo the ladle repeatedly and rapidly up and down an inch or two, and the liquid will come shooting out of the bottom of the chinois. For ultra fine results, repeat this process two or three times.

Microplane grater (photo 3)

This crazy little piece of equipment is great for zesting citrus, grating fresh Parmesan or creating decorative chocolate shavings. The filament-thin strands off a Microplane float like eiderdown onto your plate. The visual and textural qualities are like nothing you can make with a knife or box grater. In terms of inexpensive kitchen gadgets, I would have to say that this is just about my favorite.

COOKING TIPS TO MAKE LIFE BETTER IN THE KITCHEN

Here is a little holiday present in the form of useful kitchen tips. We know, you didn't get us anything. Just consider this to be a thank you for reading.

WHY YOU NEED TO LEARN THESE

The first six ideas ought to become part of your kitchen routine. They'll make your whole operation run more smoothly. The last is a simple suggestion that we included for no better reason than it's so yummy.

Secure your cutting board

If your cutting board slips and slides on the counter, it can lead to uneven cuts or bloodied fingers. Fold a damp kitchen towel in half, and place it between the board and the counter with no edges peeking out.

You know what else works great? The rubber webbing stuff that keeps your rugs from sliding. Buy a little piece at a home improvement store and cut it to the dimensions of your board.

Mise en place

This is one of the single most fundamental concepts in cooking. It's a French term meaning that all of your prep is completed and all of your tools are at hand before you begin cooking.

You've seen it on cooking shows: Any ingredient the chef adds to the pot is already cut and measured out. That's mise en place. Small plastic or metal bowls are perfect. Ramekins work, too, though they are breakable, making them taboo in professional kitchens (photo 1).

Photo 1

Clean as you go

Whether you're cutting vegetables, measuring out canned chicken broth or pureeing soup in a blender, as soon as you're done, clean up. Wipe down your board, your tools and your work station.

If you're cutting strongly flavored or colored ingredients such as garlic or parsley, and especially if you're cutting meat or other raw proteins, wash your board and tools thoroughly before continuing.

Keep knives sharp

Start the new year by having your knives sharpened professionally. Look in the yellow pages under "cutlery" or ask your local kitchenware shop to recommend someone. Sharp knives make all the difference. Plus, they're safer to use because they are less likely to slip. Even if you do happen to nick yourself, a sharp knife will make a clean cut that heals quickly while a dull knife makes more of a slow-healing tear. Yuck.

Once your knives are sharp, hone them with a steel before each use, holding the knife at a 20- to 30-degree angle to the steel. The knife edge, while it looks straight and unbroken, is in fact a series of microscopic teeth that get bent over during use. Honing with a steel pushes those bent teeth back up, realigning the edge and returning it to its full sharpness.

Towels

Keep a supply of clean, dry kitchen towels within easy reach. They're great for wiping down your board or mopping up spills, and they render unnecessary those bulky, single use pot holders. (Use only dry towels to grab hot pots. Moisture conducts heat and you can burn yourself using a damp towel.)

SHARP KNIVES MAKE ALL THE DIFFERENCE. PLUS, THEY'RE SAFER TO USE BECAUSE THEY ARE LESS LIKELY TO SLIP.

Parchment paper

Sheets or rolls of parchment paper (also called baking paper) are available at some supermarkets and many kitchen supply shops. Place a sheet on the bottom of baking trays or roasting pans to catch drips and spills, making cleanup easy. Parchment is also great for cooking, and bakers use it for everything from lining cake pans to folding cones for piping.

Bacon

After all the practical stuff, here's one idea we include just because it tastes so good:

Instead of sauteing or sweating your vegetables in oil or butter, try using bacon fat. Cut a couple slices of bacon into 1-inch-long strips and cook them over medium heat. As they cook, the fat renders. When the bacon is done to your satisfaction (we like ours crispy), remove it and pour out all but a couple tablespoons of the fat. Use the remaining fat to saute your vegetables for soups, sauces or side dishes.

You'll be impressed by the depth of flavor a little bacon can bring. Use the reserved bacon for garnish.

6 ESSENTIALS TO MAKE YOU A BETTER COOK

Back in the day, if you'll recall, we ended the school term with a review of the most important concepts—the stuff that would be on the final. Prep School salutes that model by recapping six essential ideas that will make you a better cook. And, yes, this will be on the final.

As an additional advantage to you, excellent reader, you can combine everything in this column to make a wonderful dinner: sauteed chicken breast with pan sauce and rice pilaf. Yum.

WHY YOU NEED TO LEARN IT

For years, I've been boring my friends to tears with the admonition, "You have to understand method and technique." In cooking, techniques are the things you do to ingredients to prepare them for cooking, such as separating a chicken into eight pieces or dicing an onion. Methods are the steps you take to cook those ingredients, as in braising, or the pilaf method for cooking grains. Know techniques and understand methods, and you're well on your way to really knowing how to cook.

STEPS TO FOLLOW

As with anything, the more you practice, the better you'll get. One thing to remember, we're not strict with ingredient amounts, so it's very important to taste as you go.

1. Mise en place. This French term means that all your prep work is complete and all your tools are ready before you begin cooking. It's what keeps you from burning your onions while you're chopping your garlic. Any ingredient the chef adds to the pot is already cut and measured out. That's mise en place.

2. Holding a chef's knife. You can't cook without using a knife. Pinch the blade between the index finger and thumb of your dominant hand (knife hand), just in front of the handle. Wrap your remaining three fingers around the handle (photo 1). Your other hand, the guide hand, holds the food and guides your knife. Grip food with your thumb, ring finger and pinkie, then stretch your index and middle fingers (your guide fingers) out in front so that their middle sections are perfectly vertical while the nails sections are bent slightly backward. This is called the "claw" position. When you cut, place the blade of the knife directly against the vertical middle sections. This allows you to cut safely and accurately.

3. Onion dice. Cut off the stem end, then halve the onion vertically from root end to trimmed stem and remove peel. Place halved onion cut-side down with cut stem end facing your knife hand. Make a series of horizontal cuts 80 percent of the way back

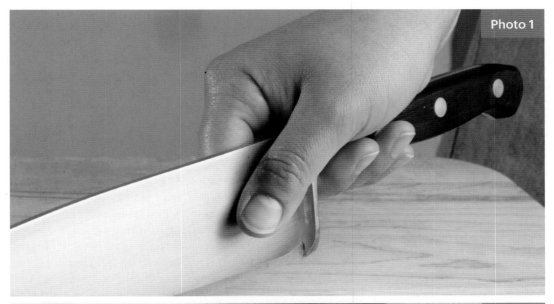

Photo 1

Photo 2

toward the root. Rotate the onion 90 degrees so the stem end is now facing you, then make a series of vertical cuts across the top, again going only 80 percent of the way back. The onion should still (mostly) hold together. Rotate it back to its original position and cut vertical slices down through the onion. Beautiful dice will fall off onto your board (photo 2).

6 ESSENTIALS TO MAKE YOU A BETTER COOK *(continued)*

4. Pilaf. Sweat your onion dice (cook over a medium flame in a little fat so that they wilt and release moisture without browning). When they're translucent, add long- or medium-grain rice and stir to coat with fat (photo 3). However much rice you've added by volume, add twice as much liquid. Water works fine, but stock or broth is more flavorful. Season with salt, then bring to a boil, cover and reduce heat to a gentle simmer. Cook 20 minutes. Remove from heat; let stand, covered, 10 minutes. Fluff with a fork.

5. Saute. Sauteing is perfect for naturally tender cuts of meat: steaks, chops and chicken breasts. Start with a skillet just large enough to hold whatever you're cooking, and place it over medium-high heat. When the pan is hot, add just enough fat (vegetable oil is perfect) to coat the bottom. Place your meat in the pan serving-side down and don't touch it. When it forms a nice, golden brown crust and is cooked about halfway through, flip it over and finish cooking. Remove from heat, rest 5 minutes and serve.

6. Pan sauce. After you've removed your meat from the pan, pour out any excess fat. Throw in some onion dice and/or chopped garlic and sweat. Deglaze with wine, juice, beer or stock (this means pour a little into the pan and scrape up any brown bits that are on the bottom so they become part of the sauce). Add any flavoring ingredients, such as a spoonful of Dijon mustard, chopped tomatoes, sauteed mushrooms or bottled chutney, then add a little stock. Reduce liquid and remove from heat. Stir in a little butter, check the seasoning, then serve with your sauteed meat and rice pilaf.

Photo 3

ORDER IN THE KITCHEN? THE FRENCH HAVE AN ANSWER TO COOKING CHAOS

Have you noticed that when a television chef says, "Add some chopped onions," you never actually see him chop the onions? He just grabs a little bowl that is somehow miraculously filled with chopped onions and tosses them in. This is what the French call mise en place.

Mise en place translates roughly as "set up," and refers to the practice of having all your ingredients prepared and all your pans and utensils ready before you start cooking.

WHY YOU NEED TO LEARN IT

We've all done it: Say your recipe calls for you to saute garlic in butter for 30 seconds and then deglaze with white wine. Easy: Throw in the garlic, and use the 30 seconds to grab from the fridge the wine left over from last night's dinner. Unfortunately, at the exact moment your fingers grasp the handle of the refrigerator door, you remember that you finished that bottle last night. No problem, you've still got 20 seconds to run downstairs, grab a fresh bottle and open it before the garlic burns. Fifteen seconds later you're back in the kitchen, rifling the drawers for the corkscrew.

"Honey," you yell upstairs to your spouse, "where's the corkscrew?"

"What?" your spouse yells back unhelpfully.

"I said, 'Where's the … ' Oh, never mind," you scream, positioning a pencil onto the cork and pounding it with a skillet, forcing the cork down into the bottle.

Meanwhile, great clouds of acrid smoke are billowing from the charred crisps of garlic.

If only you'd had your mise en place.

STEPS TO FOLLOW

Remember, the key is getting everything ready BEFORE YOU TURN ON THE STOVE.

1. If you're using a recipe, read it all the way through.

2. Read it again, this time visualizing the steps. If you're not using a recipe, visualize the steps you'll go through once you start cooking.

3. Set up your station:

- Place your cutting board on a damp towel to keep it from slipping.

- Set out some clean, dry towels to wipe down your station.

▶

ORDER IN THE KITCHEN? *(continued)*

- Set your knives and utensils on a clean towel next to your board.

- Set out a large, clean bowl for peelings and other scraps.

- Set out a selection of clean bowls of various sizes. Ramekins are great for holding small items like spices, garlic, shallots, oil, liquor, etc.

4. One at a time, cut your ingredients to the sizes called for in the recipe and place them in separate containers. After you've prepped one ingredient, wipe down the board and countertop before moving on. (Cleaning as you go saves time and effort at the end.) Ingredients that are added to the cooking pan at the same time, such as onions and peppers, may be placed in the same bowl.

5. Measure out the liquids—oil, broth, wine, etc.—into individual bowls.

6. Measure herbs and spices into ramekins. Again, if they're all going into the pan together, measure them into one dish.

7. Finally, when everything is cut and chopped and measured and poured, put all the ingredients on a sheet tray in the order in which they'll be added, and set the sheet tray as close as you can to the stove.

8. Start cooking.

One final word: This all may seem obvious or incredibly and unnecessarily detailed. However, once you get into the habit of doing this EVERY TIME YOU COOK, you will begin to notice that you're spending less time in the kitchen, and quite possibly your food is going to start tasting more consistently wonderful.

KNIFE SKILLS ▶

SHARPENING YOUR KNIFE SKILLS

WHY YOU NEED TO LEARN IT

One of the most important aspects of cooking is the ability to use a chef's knife. Proper knife technique ensures the accuracy of cuts, the freedom to move quickly through food preparation, and above all, safety. (We here at Prep School have a credo: No Blood.)

PUTTING YOUR SKILLS TO WORK

Sauteed zucchini with cherry tomatoes, garlic and basil (pg. 24)

STEPS TO FOLLOW

By following the steps below and paying strict attention to the accompanying photos, you can begin getting comfortable with your knife. Remember that knife work, like anything, takes practice. Pay attention to how the knife feels, not only in your hand but against your guide fingers as well. Go slowly. Be patient. And remember, No Blood.

The knife hand

Hold the blade between the thumb and index finger. Keep your thumb straight, and your index finger curled against the blade, up and out of the way. Do not extend it along the spine. Curl your three remaining fingers around the handle, holding it snugly to your palm.

Awkward as it may seem, this is the correct way to hold a knife. Practice it.

The guide hand

We will use a medium zucchini—halved lengthwise with the ends cut off—to show you what to do with your other hand.

Resting your middle and index fingers on the top edge of the zucchini, grip it in back between your thumb and your ring finger and pinkie.

Notice that the middle sections of your index and middle fingers are vertical, perpendicular to the cutting board. It is against these two sections that you will rest the flat part of your knife blade, guiding it as you work. Notice, too, that the tips of your index and middle fingers are curved back, away from the blade and out of harm's way. It may seem uncomfortable, scary even, to rest the knife against your fingers, but with the ends of your guide fingers curled away from the blade, it is very, very safe. Trust us.

Zucchini half-moons

Start from the rest position. Then, keeping the forward part of the knife edge in constant contact with the board, draw the blade up

Photo 1

and back until the end of the knife blade is just on the other side of the zucchini. Your knife should now be at about a 30-degree angle.

Holding your gripping fingers steady, move your guide fingers back ¼ inch, keeping the flat of your blade flush against them. You've now exposed the part of the zucchini you're going to slice.

Slice smoothly down and forward through the zucchini until you have returned to the rest position (photo 1). There should be a ¼-inch wide half moon laying on your cutting board (or stuck to your knife blade—either way is OK). Bravo.

Now, repeat this motion until the zucchini has been fully dispatched.

Some things to remember

- Slicing is a forward motion. When you pull back on the knife, it is only to get it ready for the next cut.

- Keep the flat edge of your blade in constant contact with your guide fingers.

- Your gripping fingers (thumb, ring and pinkie) stay relatively steady as the guide fingers move back toward them, exposing more and more of the zucchini.

- Go SLOWLY.

- Practice, practice, practice.

SAUTEED ZUCCHINI WITH CHERRY TOMATOES, GARLIC AND BASIL

An easy and delicious side, prepped with one of your new skills.

PREP TIME: 15 MINUTES

COOK TIME: 5 MINUTES

YIELD: 4 SERVINGS

2 tablespoons olive oil

2 medium zucchini, cut into half-moons

2 cloves garlic, crushed

¼ cup cherry tomatoes, halved

2 tablespoons chopped fresh basil

½ teaspoon salt

Freshly ground pepper

1. Heat a 10-inch skillet over medium-high heat; add the olive oil, swirling to coat the pan. Add zucchini; cook, stirring often, until slightly browned, about 2 minutes.

2. Add the garlic; cook, stirring, until just fragrant, about 30 seconds. Add the tomatoes; stir until softened, about 1 minute. Stir in the basil, salt and pepper to taste.

NUTRITION INFORMATION PER SERVING: 65 calories, 91% of calories from fat, 7g fat, 1g saturated fat, 0mg cholesterol, 1g carbohydrates, 0.4g protein, 292mg sodium, 0.2g fiber

STEELING YOURSELF: LEARNING HOW TO HONE YOUR KNIVES WILL KEEP YOUR CUTS SAFE AND TRUE

You've probably got a steel in your knife block. That's that long, thin, solid tube of textured metal with a black handle. Contrary to many people's beliefs, the steel is not used for sharpening a knife. To sharpen a dull knife, you need a sharpening stone. But the steel is used for another necessary task: honing.

If you're like most people, though, your steel probably gets less use than your appendix. My friends, this will change.

STEPS TO FOLLOW

Most of us think of knives as being one long continuous blade. True enough, I suppose, though in fact the edge of that blade is made up of gazillions of teeny-tiny individual teeth, all lined up in a row. Every time you use your knife—every time—those teeth can get bent over a little bit. As you can imagine, this would make even the sharpest knife a little less efficient in the cutting department.

Honing knocks those teeth back straight up, so your blade works as well as it can. Thus, every time you get out your knife, get out your steel, too, and put it through the paces. Your knife will work better, and therefore you will work better.

Oh, and one more thing. There's more than one way to hone a knife. Here's one of them:

1. Take the steel in your guide hand. Hold it out in front of you, parallel to the ground, as if it were the safety bar on a roller coaster.

2. Hold your knife in your knife hand and place the heel of the blade at the tip of the steel, on the side of the steel that's farthest from you. The steel will be between the blade and your body (photo 1, next page).

WHY YOU NEED TO LEARN IT

A sharp, well-honed knife cuts truer and easier. This means you can work more quickly and accurately. More importantly, it means you can work more safely.

STEELING YOURSELF *(continued)*

3. Keep the blade of your knife at about an 18-degree to a 22-degree angle to the steel. Move the blade down the steel. You'll finish with the tip of the blade down at the handle of the steel (photo 2).

4. Now do the same thing with the other side of the blade on the other side of the steel, the side closest to you (photo 3). As before, keep the blade at an 18-degree to a 22-degree angle to the steel. Once again, start with the heel of the knife at the tip of the steel and move it down.

5. Alternate strokes so that you hone both sides of the blade evenly. Give each side half a dozen strokes or so every time you use your knife.

Final note: Remember, honing does not sharpen a dull knife. If you haven't sharpened your knives recently, take them to your local hardware or a specialty cutlery store (phone first) and have them sharpened professionally. Then, get yourself a sharpening stone (that's a whole 'nother Prep School), and keep your knives as sharp as they were when you got them. You'll be astounded at the difference a sharpened, honed knife makes.

Photo 1

Photo 2

Photo 3

LEARNING THE BEST CUTS

Here's a simple rule: Big things cook slow; little things cook fast. Think about what that means when you're cooking vegetables.

STEPS TO FOLLOW

We'll start off easy, with two of the larger cuts. Other cuts listed at the end use the same technique; only the dimensions are different.

For all cuts, remember to steady the food with your guide hand. The middle section of your index and middle fingers must remain vertical, and the blade of the knife will rest against them.

Batonnets

1. Peel a carrot, trim off the ends, and cut it into 2-inch cylinders (photo 1).

Photo 1

WHY YOU NEED TO LEARN IT

For any given vegetable, it's important that all the pieces be the same size. Otherwise, some pieces will end up perfectly cooked, larger pieces will be crunchy and underdone, and smaller ones will be burned or reduced to a pulpy mush.

Below you'll find easy directions for producing beautiful, even vegetable cuts. Before you begin, please remember one thing: The directions may be simple, but the task itself is not. As with most things in life, knife cuts require practice and patience.

Since you have to eat anyway, though, practice your cuts whenever you use your knife. You'll get better and faster, and soon you'll be knocking out dishes that look as wonderful as they taste.

You'll need a chef's knife, a cutting board, a ruler and a big carrot. (Potatoes, rutabagas—any hard vegetable works just as well.)

LEARNING THE BEST CUTS *(continued)*

2. Turn the cylinder into a box by cutting straight down on four sides (photo 2). Your goal is to make perfect right angles, resulting in a perfect rectangle. Again, we do not expect perfection on the first or even the 10th try. Remember: practice and patience.

3. Cut a ¼-inch wide plank lengthwise from the box and set it aside (photo 3). Repeat until the entire box has been turned into ¼-inch thick planks.

4. Lay one plank down in front of you. (Later, with practice, you can stack the planks for speed.) Cut the plank lengthwise into ¼-inch pieces (photo 4). In theory, you will now have a piece of carrot 2 inches long and ¼-inch square.

Of course, we know better than to expect perfection on the first attempt. If you look at one of your batonnets from the end, you should see a perfect square. More likely, you'll see a four-sided shape with uneven lines and angles, what mathematicians call a "skew quadrilateral." That's OK. This is hard. Just keep practicing until it's right.

Small dice

Start with batonnets (2-by-¼-inch square). Lay the batonnets perpendicular to the blade of the knife and cut off ¼-inch lengths, giving you ¼-inch cubes. These pieces are your "small dice."

You now have the ability to practice a number of different cuts whose only differences are their dimensions (see chart).

Small vegetable cuts

THE CUTS	THE MEASUREMENTS (in inches)
Batonnets	2 x ¼ x ¼
Julienne	2 x ⅛ x ⅛
Fine julienne	2 x ¹⁄₁₆ x ¹⁄₁₆
Small dice	¼-inch cubes (start with batonnets)
Medium dice	½-inch cubes (start by cutting ½-inch planks)
Large dice	¾-inch cubes (start by cutting ¾-inch planks)
Brunoise	⅛-inch cubes (start with julienne)
Fine brunoise	¹⁄₁₆-inch cubes (start with fine julienne)

IF YOU LOOK AT ONE OF YOUR
BATONNETS FROM THE END, YOU
SHOULD SEE A PERFECT SQUARE.

TWICE THE DICE: USING TWO KNIVES CAN DOUBLE EFFICIENCY AND MINIMIZE PREP TIME

Nuts. Herbs. Garlic. All so lovely, and all such a potential pain to chop, especially in any quantity. Here, you'll learn how two knives are better than one.

WHY YOU NEED TO LEARN IT

It doesn't take Pythagoras to figure out that using two knives should allow you to go—well, let's see—twice as fast. And, like so many kitchen techniques, once you get the hang of it, you will feel, and look, really, really tough.

STEPS TO FOLLOW

I'm sure I don't need to remind you about the proper way to hold a knife, but on the off chance that you've come down with a touch of the amnesia, we'll start with that.

We'll be using two equal-size chef's knives for this; the length (8-inch, 10-inch) is up to you.

One knife: Refresher

1. Pinch the blade of the knife between the thumb and index finger of your knife hand. Make sure that the tip of your index finger is well above the edge of the blade. If it were to slip below the edge, you could very easily slice off a little piece, and believe me, none of us want to see that.

2. Curl your remaining three fingers around the handle so that the thumbward side of your middle finger is brushing against the heel of the knife.

If you're new to this style of holding a knife, practice it and get comfortable with it before moving on to the next section. This grip is the one favored by the vast majority of professional chefs and provides the most control over the blade.

Two knives: Now it gets cool

1. Pinch the blade of one knife between the thumb and index finger of your knife hand (photo 1). Rest the edge of the blade on a cutting board to give yourself some stability.

2. Place the second knife's handle between your index and middle fingers so that it becomes parallel with the first knife. Grip the blade of the second knife with your index and middle fingers (photo 2).

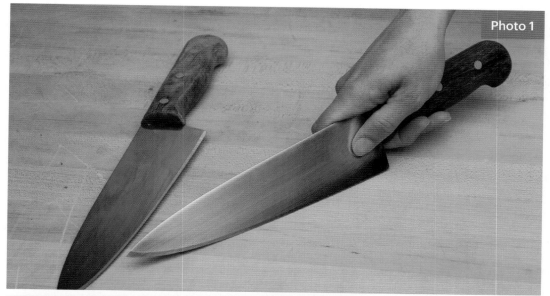

Photo 1

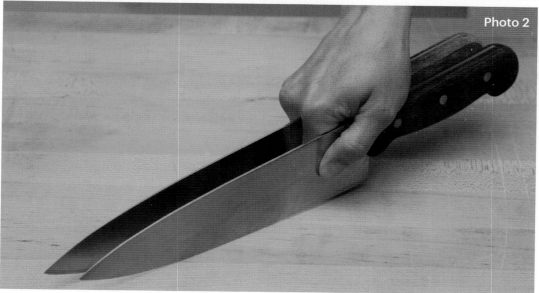

Photo 2

3. Wrap your remaining two fingers around the handles of both knives. Undoubtedly, this will feel awkward at first, but, while both knife blades are still on the cutting board, steady them with your guide hand and then relax the muscles in your knife hand and fingers so that they settle into the most comfortable position possible. Practice lifting the knives and setting them down several times until you can do it without them going off the parallel.

TWICE THE DICE *(continued)*

Using the knives

You can do this with nuts, herbs, anything that needs to be reduced to a small size in a short period of time. We'll use some fresh parsley.

1. Mound the parsley loosely in the center of your cutting board. Holding both your knives, set the blades down, to one side of the pile. Use the palm of your guide hand to anchor the tips of the knives. Keep the fingers of your guide hand splayed and up and away from the board and the knives. I don't think I need to tell you why...

2. Lift up on the knife handles while using your guide hand to keep the tips on the board, as if you were using a paper cutter (photo 3). Using a steady up and down motion, start chopping without stopping. As you cut, pivot the knives slowly from their tips so that the blades sweep across the parsley, chopping as you go.

For some reason, I only chop in one direction, and then when I get to the far edge of the pile, I start over from my original point. Other people go back and forth across the parsley. You do what you want.

3. Keep chopping and pivoting until the parsley (or nuts or garlic) is reduced to the state of fineness you need.

Photo 3

MASTERING THE PERFECT DICED ONION

Over the centuries, France's contributions to human culture have been enormous. None of them, however, compare with this technique for dicing an onion.

STEPS TO FOLLOW

1. Cut the stem end off the onion. The stem end is the one that's a bit pointy; the root end has the little oniony "hairs" growing out of it.

2. Set the onion on this newly flattened stem end. Cut straight down through the root end to divide the onion in two (photo 1). Peel the onion halves, making sure the outermost layer is moist and firm. If it's brown, dry or loose, remove the layer(s) until you have nothing left but beautiful, firm onion.

3. Set one of the onion halves cut side down with the flat stem end facing your knife hand. Place the palm of your guide hand directly on top of the onion with your fingers lifting up and away from the sharp knife blade, out of harm's way. This might be the time to re- mind you of our motto here at Prep School: NO BLOOD!

WHY YOU NEED TO LEARN IT

Time—or, more correctly, the lack of time—is an obstacle to good cook- ing. Improving your knife skills will cut down drasti- cally on preparation time, leaving you more time to experiment with newer or more complex recipes.

PUTTING YOUR SKILLS TO WORK

Red onion compote (pg. 36)

Photo 1

MASTERING THE PERFECT DICED ONION *(continued)*

4. Starting at the bottom of the onion, with the knife blade parallel to the cutting board, make three or four horizontal cuts through the onion back to, but not through, the root. The size of your dice will be determined by the distance between these cuts. Fewer cuts spaced wider apart will give you bigger dice. More cuts, closer together, will give you smaller dice. Don't cut through the root end because that's what holds the onion together while you're dicing it.

5. Turn the onion 90 degrees so that the stem end is facing you. Hold your knife with the blade perpendicular to the cutting board and the tip pointed back toward the root end of the onion. Make a series of downward cuts, keeping the side of the blade against your guide hand fingers as they glide backward across the surface of the onion (photo 2).

6. Rotate the onion back until the stem end is once more facing your knife hand. Steady the onion between your thumb and your ring finger and pinky, with the index and middle fingers of your guide hand on top. Again, keeping the side of the blade against the index and middle fingers, make a series of forward slices down through the onion (photo 3). There's your dice. Now, go make something yummy.

A couple of tips

- If your knife is as it should be, and by that we mean good and sharp, in Step 5 you can cut straight down through the onion with a chopping motion. As you practice, this ultimately will be quicker than using a back-and-forth sawing motion.

- A sharp knife will cut through the onion cleanly. A dull knife smashes as it cuts, releasing into the air around you more of that oniony vapor that brings tears to your eyes.

Photo 2

Photo 3

RED ONION COMPOTE

This is a wonderfully piquant accompaniment, hot or cold, to grilled or roasted meats, buttered or marinated vegetables, even salads. Use it as you would any other relish.

PREP TIME: 5 MINUTES

COOK TIME: 30 MINUTES

YIELD: 1¾ CUPS

2 tablespoons butter, plus 1 tablespoon chilled butter, optional

1 large red onion, diced

1 cup balsamic vinegar

1 bay leaf

1 sprig fresh thyme

½ teaspoon salt

Freshly ground pepper

1. Melt 2 tablespoons of butter in a skillet over medium-high heat; add the onion. Reduce heat to medium-low; cook, stirring often, until onion just begins to brown, about 10 minutes.

2. Add the balsamic vinegar, bay leaf and thyme to the mixture. Heat mixture to a boil over medium-high heat; reduce heat to a simmer. Cook until the vinegar is reduced to a syrupy glaze, about 15 minutes. Whisk in the tablespoon of chilled butter, if desired; season with salt and pepper to taste. Serve hot or cold.

NUTRITION INFORMATION PER TABLESPOON: 15 calories, 51% of calories from fat, 1g fat, 0.5g saturated fat, 2mg cholesterol, 2g carbohydrates, 0.1g protein, 50mg sodium, 0.1g fiber

THERE'S ANOTHER WAY TO SLICE IT: IN WHICH WE RETURN TO THE NOBLE ONION

Let's get excited about chopping onions. By the way, I've heard this technique referred to as both emincer and julienne. You choose.

STEPS TO FOLLOW

I know I don't need to tell you this, but, please, make sure your knife is good and sharp. Thank you.

1. Trim off the root and stem ends of the onion, then peel it.

2. Set the onion on one of the cut ends and slice it in half straight down through the center. Be sure to keep your guide hand in the claw position (photo 1).

3. Set one half of the onion on the cutting board, flat side down with one of the cut ends facing you. The striations which go across the onion should be pointing toward you.

WHY YOU NEED TO LEARN IT

What's cool about this technique is that it's counterintuitive. Most people are inclined to slice onions perpendicular to the striations. This gives you slices, all right, but they're of radically different lengths. Try it our way—along the striations—and see how much more evenly all the pieces turn out.

Photo 1

THERE'S ANOTHER WAY TO SLICE IT *(continued)*

4. Place your knife on top of the onion parallel to the striations, about a quarter of the way in on your knife hand side (photo 2). With your guide hand in the claw position, cut straight down, removing one quarter of the onion in a wedge shape.

5. Flip that wedge onto its other flat side, then rotate it 180 degrees. The "cliff face" of the wedge should now be facing the thumb of your guide hand.

6. Hold the onion with your guide hand in the claw position. Place your knife on top of the onion at the "bottom of the hill." Remember that the blade of your knife is going to be flat against the middle section of the index and middle fingers of that guide hand. If you need to read that sentence over again, please do. We're not just going for accuracy, but speed and safety too. Believe me, no one wants to see you cut your fingers less than me. Except for you, of course.

7. Lift the knife blade about an inch or so off the top of the onion, keeping the flat side of the blade flush against your guide fingers. Now bring it straight down in a chopping motion to cut a slice about ⅛-inch thick (photo 3). If your knife is nice and sharp it should cut easily through the onion all the way down to the cutting board. (If your blade is dull—well, get it sharpened, of course, but in the meantime, instead of a straight up-and-down chopping motion, use more of a forward-and-down slicing motion, keeping the tip of your knife on the cutting board.)

8. As you lift the blade up for the second chop, keep its flat side against your guide fingers as they move slowly and steadily backward "up the hill" toward your anchored thumb. Make another downward chop, and then repeat until you've cut that whole wedge into ⅛-inch strips.

9. Now attend to the remaining three quarters of the onion. Place your guide hand in the claw position on top of the onion, with your guide fingers poised at the "top of the cliff." Again, keeping the flat side of the blade against your guide fingers, chop straight down, one ⅛-inch from the edge of the cliff.

10. Draw your guide fingers slowly and steadily back toward your anchored guide thumb, and stop when you've chopped all but the last quarter of the onion.

11. Knock over the remaining quarter onion onto its other flat face. The "cliff" will now be facing your guide hand. Cut this piece exactly like the one in step 6.

Photo 2

Photo 3

TRICKS FOR TACKLING RIPE SUMMER FRUIT

In midsummer, when local harvests are just starting to come in, fruit is perfect simply as is. Fat and juicy and ripened from the sun, it's eaten leaning forward, the juices bypassing the shirt on their way down the chin. As the weeks go by, though, we can tire of this ritual and begin to search for new and delicious recipes.

WHY YOU NEED TO LEARN IT

We've only got a few short weeks to enjoy locally grown seasonal fruit. The more prep tricks you know, the faster you can make many different dishes. Here are two ways to handle fruit.

PUTTING YOUR SKILLS TO WORK

Cantaloupe salad with mascarpone and pancetta (pg. 44)

STEPS TO FOLLOW

One technique is useful for peeling melons, citrus, mangoes and pineapples. We've used cantaloupe here.

(It also works great for eggplant, though it is best, after trimming off the two "poles" (ends), to cut eggplants in half along the equator and work with them one half at a time.)

1. Cut just enough off the north and south poles of the cantaloupe to expose a bit of the golden flesh.

2. Set the cantaloupe on one of its cut ends on a cutting board. Securing it with your guide hand, place a knife edge on the flattened top, where the rind meets the flesh (photo 1). Using forward slicing motions, cut a strip of rind from top to bottom, following the natural curve of the melon (photo 2).

Photo 1

Photo 2

TRICKS FOR TACKLING RIPE SUMMER FRUIT *(continued)*

3. Rotate the line of newly bared cantaloupe flesh toward you about an inch or two (the width of the slice of rind you just removed). Place the edge of the knife back at the top. Cut another strip of rind from the melon, using the exposed vertical edge of the rind as your guide (photo 3). Repeat this process until the entire melon has been freed from its rindy restraints, leaving you with golden goodness.

4. From here, split the cantaloupe in half, scoop out the seeds (photo 4) and cut into slices, julienne or dice as the recipe or your whim suits.

A second technique is good for peaches, plums, nectarines and other stone fruits.

1. Skins of stone fruits can be removed using a technique called blanching and shocking. First, plunge the fruit into boiling water for about 15 seconds. Remove immediately and submerge in a bowl of ice water. As soon as they cool, the skins should slip off fairly easily.

2. Use a sharp knife, starting at one pole, to cut through the flesh to the pit, all the way around the fruit. Twist the halves in opposite directions to separate. Use your fingers or a knife or spoon to pry out the pit.

Photo 3

Photo 4

CANTALOUPE SALAD WITH MASCARPONE AND PANCETTA

Pancetta is an Italian bacon sold at Italian markets and some specialty markets; regular bacon can be substituted.

PREP TIME: 20 MINUTES

COOK TIME: 8 MINUTES

YIELD: 6 SERVINGS

3 ounces pancetta, cut into ¼-inch dice

¼ cup plus 1 tablespoon olive oil

6 tablespoons balsamic vinegar

1 tablespoon brown sugar

1 large ripe cantaloupe

6 ounces mascarpone cheese

1 head Boston lettuce

1 small bunch fresh mint, finely chopped

½ teaspoon salt

Freshly ground pepper

1. Heat 1 tablespoon of the oil over medium heat in a skillet. Cook the pancetta until crispy, about 8 minutes; drain on a paper towel.

2. Meanwhile, heat the vinegar and brown sugar in a saucepan over medium heat; cook until reduced by half to a light syrup consistency, about 5 minutes. Remove from heat; set aside to cool.

3. Remove the rind from the cantaloupe; cut in half. Refrigerate one half for another use. Scoop out the seeds in the other half. Cut into julienne; place in a large bowl. Sprinkle with a little coarse salt; toss. Whisk together the balsamic vinegar syrup and the remaining ¼ cup of olive oil. Season with salt and pepper to taste.

4. Place a lettuce leaf on each of 6 salad plates. Divide mascarpone among plates, placing in the center of the lettuce; sprinkle with a little of the pancetta. Top mascarpone with a small mound of cantaloupe. Sprinkle each with a little more pancetta and mint. Drizzle the dressing in a crisscross pattern over each salad and around the plate.

NUTRITION INFORMATION PER SERVING: 104 calories, 76% of calories from fat, 9g fat, 3g saturated fat, 16mg cholesterol, 4g carbohydrates, 2g protein, 127mg sodium, 0.5g fiber

SHARPENING YOUR SKILLS ON A WHOLE BIRD

Call me a barbarian, but I find the process of breaking down a chicken to be peculiarly satisfying. Many people find the task daunting—if not disgusting—and worry about destroying the chicken in the process. If you let the chicken's anatomy be your guide, though, the process is easy.

STEPS TO FOLLOW

For the legs, use a thin, stiff boning knife. For the breasts, use a heavier chef's knife.

The legs and thighs

1. Place the chicken on its back with the legs toward you. One at a time, pull the legs out from the body and cut through the skin, closer to the leg than to the breast (photo 1). We want the lean breast meat to have plenty of juicy skin covering it.

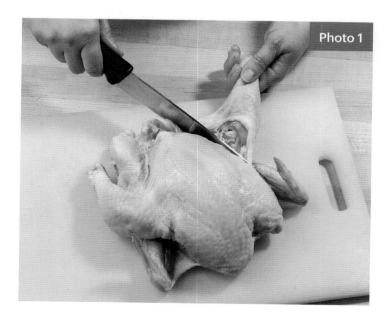

Photo 1

WHY YOU NEED TO LEARN IT

Whole birds tend to be only slightly cheaper than cut-up pieces. However, birds sold cut up usually do not include the backs (which are excellent to save for making home-made stock) nor the giblets (delicious cooked up on their own or when used to flavor other dishes). Also, in the spirit of understanding your food, and therefore understanding your world, seeing the bird closer to its true form contributes to the appreciation of what exactly it is you're eating.

PUTTING YOUR SKILLS TO WORK

Sylvie's chicken (pg. 50)

SHARPENING YOUR SKILLS ON
A WHOLE BIRD *(continued)*

2. Here's the rough part: Set down your knife and place one hand under each leg, grasping them with your thumbs. Place the tips of your fingers at the joint where the legs join the body. Now, suppressing your revulsion, rotate your forearms from the elbows, pulling back on the legs with your thumbs as you push up with your fingers, popping the leg joints out of the body.

3. Turn the chicken over and locate the two "oysters," the small but meaty circles of flesh at the outside center of the back. With a little practice, you can include these when you remove the legs: Using the tip of your knife, free the oysters from the carcass, leaving them attached to the skin. To remove the legs, cut behind the oyster and between the thigh bone and carcass.

4. Place the legs/thighs skin side down on your board. Pull the skin back to expose the joint connecting the leg and the thigh; you'll see a thin white line of fat. Place the blade of your knife immediately to the leg side of that line (photo 2) and cut straight down. Your knife will go right through, separating the two pieces. If you hit solid bone, line up the blade again and try again.

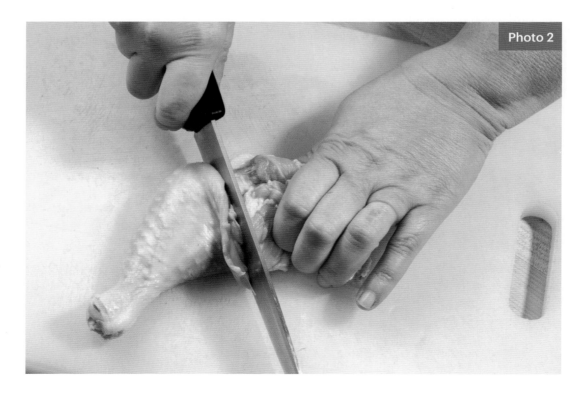

Photo 2

The wings and breast

1. With the carcass still on its back, extend the wings one at a time and place your knife blade on the joint connecting the wing tip. Cut straight down to remove it, leaving the other two wing sections attached to the carcass.

2. To remove the wing, first move it back and forth to locate the joint where it attaches to the carcass. Slice through that joint (photo 3) and don't worry if you take some of the breast meat along with the wing. A little breast meat can make a wing portion seem more substantial.

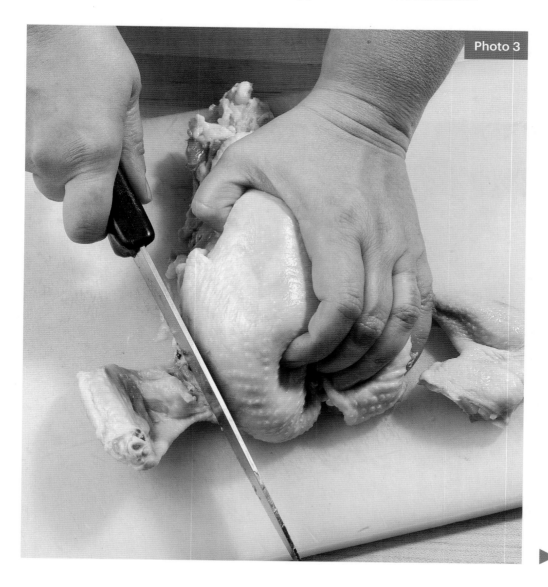

Photo 3

SHARPENING YOUR SKILLS ON
A WHOLE BIRD *(continued)*

3. Set the carcass on end with the thin ends of the breast pointing up. Use your heavy chef's knife to cut straight down between the breast and the back (photo 4). Expect to hear a little bone crunching as your knife goes through. Save the back portion along with the wing tips to make a quick chicken stock or to enhance canned broth.

4. Place the whole breast on your board, skin side up. With your chef's knife, split the breast in half through the keel (breast) bone (photo 5). If breast halves are too large for one portion, split them into quarters.

Photo 4

Photo 5

SYLVIE'S CHICKEN

My Parisienne friend Sylvie Hornus made this when she stayed at our house a few years back. I marveled then at its flavor, today at its simplicity. Serve with noodles or rice.

PREP TIME: 20 MINUTES

COOK TIME: 37 MINUTES

YIELD: 4 SERVINGS

1 chicken, 3½-4 pounds, cut up

½ teaspoon salt

Freshly ground pepper

2 tablespoons vegetable oil

2 shallots, minced

⅓ cup white wine or dry vermouth

⅔ cup chicken stock or canned low-sodium chicken broth

½ teaspoon dried thyme or 1 teaspoon minced fresh thyme

3 tablespoons cold butter

1. Season the chicken with salt and pepper. Heat a large skillet over medium-high heat. Add the oil; heat 30 seconds. Add the legs and thighs, skin side down; cook until golden brown, about 5 minutes. Turn the pieces over; add chicken breasts, skin side down. (The breasts cook more quickly and therefore demand less time in the pan.)

2. Cook, turning, until all of the pieces are brown on all sides, about 12 more minutes; reduce heat to medium. Cover the pan, leaving a small opening for steam to escape. Cook the chicken until a meat thermometer inserted into the thigh or leg reads 165 degrees, about 15 minutes.

3. Remove chicken to a warm plate. Pour out any excess fat, leaving any browned bits or juice. Turn up the heat; add the shallots. Cook, stirring to prevent them from burning, 30 seconds.

4. Deglaze the pan by adding the white wine and scraping up any brown bits. When the wine has nearly evaporated, add the chicken broth; continue stirring. Heat to a boil; cook to reduce the mixture slightly, about 5 minutes. Remove the pan from the heat.

5. Add the thyme; whisk in the cold butter to emulsify the sauce. Taste for seasoning. Serve the chicken pieces with the sauce.

NUTRITION INFORMATION PER SERVING: 577 calories, 57% of calories from fat, 35g fat, 10g saturated fat, 186mg cholesterol, 2g carbohydrates, 59g protein, 489mg sodium, 0g fiber

SPATCHCOCKING MAKES COOKING A BIRD QUICKER

Here's a great technique with a cool name: spatchcocking. The Oxford English Dictionary traces the term to 18th century Ireland, where it was simply a shortened version of "dispatch the cock."

WHY YOU NEED TO LEARN IT

By removing the backbone and the keel bone of a chicken, the bird resembles a butterfly, a presentation that cooks more quickly and is easier to carve.

After you have flattened your bird, rub it with spices or marinate it. Grill it over indirect heat or on a grill pan, or roast it in a hot oven (425 degrees) until the skin is crispy and golden brown.

One note: The breast side of the chicken is the meaty side. The back is bony, and the backbone runs the length of the bird from the neck to the tail.

PUTTING YOUR SKILLS TO WORK

Grill-roasted spatchcocked chicken (pg. 56)

STEPS TO FOLLOW

1. Remove any extraneous fat. Place the chicken on the cutting board back-side up with the tail end at the top. Locate the oysters, the meaty ovals just below where the thighs meet the body. Many people consider the oysters to be the most succulent part of the bird, and you'll want to leave them attached.

2. Grasp the bird at the top with your guide hand, just to one side of the tail. Place the blade of a boning or chef's knife next to the tail on the other side and cut down through the bird using the backbone as a guide (photo 1). You'll be cutting through rib bones here, so expect crunching sounds. When you get to the oyster, turn your blade in slightly toward the backbone and go around the oyster, leaving it attached to the body.

3. Open the chicken up and place skin-side down so the backbone is next to your knife hand. Steadying the chicken with your guide hand, cut the backbone free, again leaving the oyster attached (photo 2, next page).

4. Now remove the keel bone, the dark piece of bone that separates the two breast halves. Hold the chicken, skin-side down, with both hands so your fingers meet underneath, directly below the keel bone. With your thumbs on top, on either side of the keel bone, bend the two halves back, pressing up with your fingers (photo 3, next page). You may hear a wet snap as the keel bone breaks free.

5. Grasp the keel bone in one hand and strip it away from the breast meat. If it breaks, pull the pieces out with your fingers or, if they're really stuck, cut them out with your knife. Behold, the spatchcocked chicken.

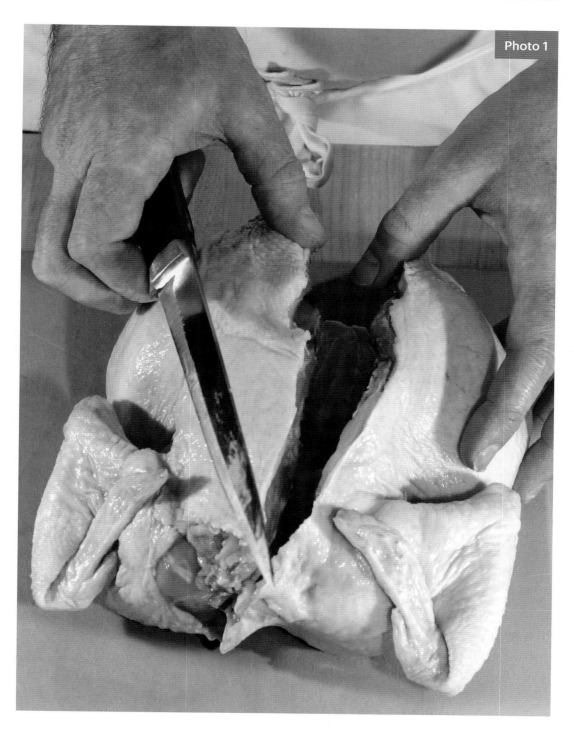

Photo 1

SPATCHCOCKING MAKES COOKING
A BIRD QUICKER *(continued)*

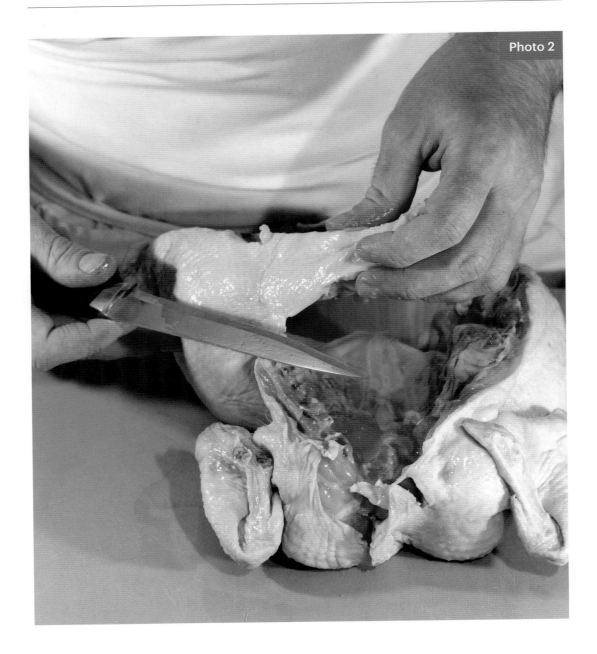

Photo 2

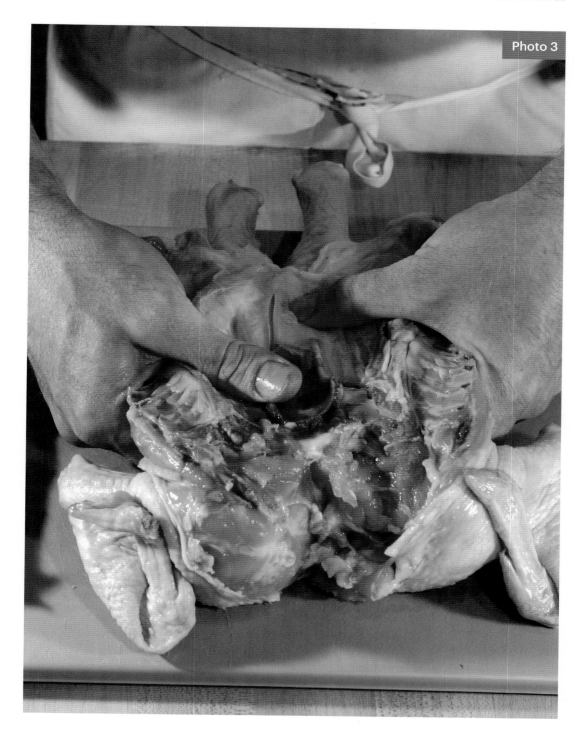

Photo 3

GRILL-ROASTED SPATCHCOCKED CHICKEN

A spatchcocked chicken is a perfect choice for indirect grilling over charcoal.

PREP TIME: 20 MINUTES

COOK TIME: 45 MINUTES

YIELD: 4 SERVINGS

1 teaspoon hot paprika

1 teaspoon coarse salt

1 teaspoon ground white
   pepper

1 teaspoon ground black
   pepper

1 whole fryer, about 3
   pounds

1. Place a drip pan on one side of a charcoal grill bottom. Light a full chimney of charcoal briquets in the grill; wait until covered with white ash. Pile the charcoal on the other side of the grill. Brush the grill with oil or spray it with pan spray.

2. Combine black and white peppers, paprika and salt; set aside. Spatchcock the chicken, according to the accompanying instructions. Sprinkle the pepper mixture over the skin.

3. Place the chicken skin-side up on the grill over the drip pan. Cover grill; grill until the skin is golden brown and crispy and a thermometer inserted into the thickest part of the thigh reads 165 degrees, 40-60 minutes.

NUTRITION INFORMATION PER SERVING: 398 calories, 55% of calories from fat, 24g fat, 6.6g saturated fat, 134mg cholesterol, 1g carbohydrates, 42g protein, 710mg sodium, 0.4g fiber

CHICKEN TAKES A ROMANTIC TURN

Here's a great technique for chicken that results in the "airline breast." The provenance of that term is unclear, though Richard Lobb, a spokesman for the National Chicken Council, says that the name comes from its popularity among airlines in the early days of commercial aviation.

WHY YOU NEED TO LEARN IT

This is a beautiful and relatively simple technique that's perfect for a romantic dinner for two.

The lone wing bone, stripped of meat, gives the breast a really cool look, a look that makes you realize that the cook prepared this breast him- or herself, that it didn't come from the meat department at the supermarket.

Start with a whole bird, and save the legs for another use and the carcass and wing ends for stock. Better yet, freeze the carcass and wait to make stock until you've collected four or five more if you have room. That should be enough to make a good gallon of stock.

Airline breasts are easiest when roasted in the oven. Treat it as you would a regular boneless, skinless breast. Wrap the bone in foil before cooking to prevent it from charring and then remove it for serving.

STEPS TO FOLLOW

Use a thin, stiff boning knife, then move to a chef's knife and a paring knife for the last two steps.

First, remove the leg/thighs:

1. Place the bird breast-side up with the legs toward you. Pull the legs out from the body and cut through the skin close to the leg. This leaves plenty of juicy skin to cover the lean breast.

2. Bend the legs back to pop the thighbones out of the joint attached to the bird.

3. Slice through the joint to remove the leg/ thigh. Set the leg/thighs aside for another use.

Remove the breast meat:

4. Locate the keel bone, the hard ridge that separates the right and left halves of the breast. Make an incision along the entire length of that ridge (photo 1).

Photo 1

CHICKEN TAKES A ROMANTIC TURN *(continued)*

5. Use the tip of your boning knife to scrape the breast meat away from one side of the bone. As you do this, use your guide hand to gently pull the meat away from the bone (photo 2). Make sure your knife is always scraping the bone, not cutting through meat. Keep scraping and pulling until the breast is attached only at the bottom of the carcass.

6. Starting at the end opposite the wing, run your knife along the bottom edge of the carcass, pulling on the breast to separate it. Stop at the wing.

7. Grasp the breast and wing in your guide hand and pull gently away from the carcass. Place your knife on the carcass above the wing and follow the bone down to the wing joint. Cut straight down through this joint, leaving the wing attached to the breast.

8. Place a heavy chef's knife between the drumette and the middle section of the wing and cut through. Set the middle section/wing tip piece aside for another use.

9. Use the chef's knife to chop off the very end of the drumette, the end farthest from the breast.

10. Use a paring knife to scrape the flesh on the drumette back toward the breast (photo 3). Make the bone as clean as you can, then wipe it dry with a clean towel.

11. Lay the breast skin-side up on the cutting board and smooth out the skin. The drumette bone should be sticking up smartly, saluting you for a job well done.

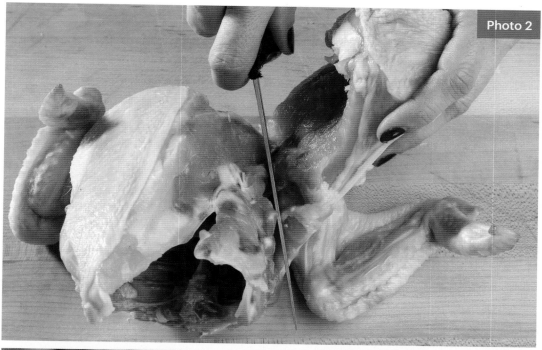

Photo 2

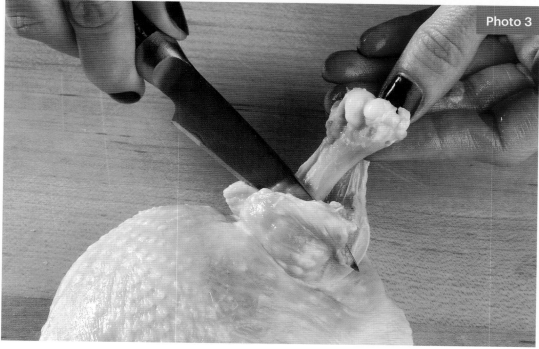

Photo 3

ORANGE SUPREMES ADD ELEGANT TOUCH

Here's a great technique for citrus fruit that is relatively easy. The result is called "orange supremes," which is merely the name for the segments of fruit once the rind and membrane have been removed.

WHY YOU NEED TO LEARN IT

This step-by-step process makes great-looking garnishes for salads, desserts—anything that could use a splash of citrus.

PUTTING YOUR SKILLS TO WORK

Orange supremes in orange syrup (pg. 65)

Although these instructions entail the use of a chef's knife, some chefs prefer to use a paring knife for this technique.

Peeling the orange

Along with citrus, this is a great way to peel large objects such as melons, mangoes, pineapples, even eggplants that you've split along the equator.

1. Cut off each end of the orange, just enough for the flesh to show (photo 1).

2. Set the orange on the cutting board on one of its flattened ends. Secure it with your guide hand, placing your thumb and your ring finger and pinky on the sides and your index and middle fingers on top. Place the knife edge on top of the orange where the peel meets the exposed flesh. Remove a strip of peel from end to end, using forward slicing motions and following the natural curve of the orange to avoid taking too much of the juicy flesh.

3. Rotate the cut side of the orange toward you about an inch (the width of the slice of peel you just removed). Place the edge of the knife back at the top where the peel meets the flesh. Cut down along the exposed edge of the peel, using that edge as your guide (photo 2). Repeat until the entire orange has been peeled.

▶

Photo 1

Photo 2

ORANGE SUPREMES ADD ELEGANT TOUCH *(continued)*

Cutting the supremes

4. Hold the orange in your guide hand with one of the ends pointing toward you. Focus on one orange section and identify the left membrane, the right membrane, and the orange flesh in the center. Place the knife edge—about three-fourths of the way toward the tip—on top of the section just to the inside of one membrane (photo 3). Rather than using a sawing motion, simply slice forward, letting the weight of the knife take the blade down through the orange. The blade should stop where the section ends at the center of the orange.

5. Remove the knife and move it to the other side of the section, so that it is just to the inside the other membrane. Repeat the forward slicing motion until the blade meets the cut made from the first side, freeing up the section. Use the blade to lift up and remove the section (photo 4).

6. Rotate the orange in your hand just enough to have a new section directly in front of you. Repeat the process until all of the sections are removed and only the "membrane skeleton" is left.

7. Squeeze juice from the membrane skeleton into a cup. Toast your success, or reserve the juice for later.

Photo 3

Photo 4

ORANGE SUPREMES IN ORANGE SYRUP

A simple and attractive display for a dessert or appetizer buffet.

1. Cut oranges into segments (supremes) over a bowl; strain any of the juice through a fine sieve.

2. Put juice into a measuring cup; add enough bottled juice to measure about 1½ cups. Pour into a small saucepan; stir in sugar to dissolve. Cook over medium-high heat until reduced to about ⅓ cup, about 15–20 minutes. Remove from heat; stir in brandy, if desired. Set aside.

3. Arrange orange supremes in a circle on a serving dish. Drizzle orange syrup over them; dust with cinnamon. Garnish with mint leaves.

NUTRITION INFORMATION PER SERVING: 86 calories, 2% of calories from fat, 0.2 g fat, 0 g saturated fat, 0 mg cholesterol, 22 g carbohydrates, 1 g protein, 0 mg sodium, 3 g fiber

PREPARATION TIME: 30 MINUTES

COOK TIME: 20 MINUTES

YIELD: 4 SERVINGS

4 oranges

Bottled orange juice

2 tablespoons sugar

1 to 2 tablespoons brandy, Armagnac or orange liqueur, optional

Ground cinnamon, fresh mint leaves

FILLET YOUR WAY TO DINNER: BUTTERFLYING A WHOLE FISH PUTS YOU IN CONTROL OF YOUR FOOD AND SAVES MONEY

It took years to learn to love fish. The meatless Fridays of a Roman Catholic childhood left me with the impression that "fish equals penance." Now that I've disabused myself of such ridiculous notions, I can devour fresh seafood to my healthy heart's content.

Moreover, I can introduce a little economy into this otherwise pricey commodity by buying whole fish and filleting it myself.

WHY YOU NEED TO LEARN IT

Everyone should know how to fillet a fish. Buying whole fish will save you some dough. More importantly, though, the more dependent we are on processed food, whether in the form of fish fillets, chicken parts, canned tomato sauce or frozen pizza, the more control we surrender over our diet and, consequently, our health and even our very lifestyle. So grab your boning knife and start practicing. And as always, remember: Patience.

PUTTING YOUR SKILLS TO WORK

Shrimp-stuffed trout (pg. 70)

STEPS TO FOLLOW

Start with a whole, drawn trout. Drawn trout have been scaled, slit along the bottom and freed of all entrails. If you open it up you can see all the bones from the inside.

To butterfly your trout, you'll need a sharp boning knife, a pair of kitchen shears or chef's knife, and some needle-nose pliers. (Note: If you're stuffing the butterflied trout, you may want to leave the head on for presentation. If that look is a little too real for your taste, you can remove the head easily with a chef's knife.)

1. Take the kitchen shears or chef's knife and cut away the fins and any tough cartilage to which they may be attached.

2. If the slit down the belly stops before the tail, lay the trout on its side and use your boning knife to extend the opening all the way back. Take care not to poke the tip of your knife through the top side.

3. Lay the fish on its back and spread it apart so you can see the backbone and ribs easily. Cut through the rib bones on one side right where they connect to the back bone, taking care not to cut all the way through the back of the fish (photo 1).

4. Stick the tip of your knife underneath the rib bones where you've just cut through. Making short strokes, feel the tip brush against the bones as you peel them slowly back away from the meat (photo 2). Repeat steps 3 and 4 on the other side of the backbone.

Photo 1

Photo 2

FILLET YOUR WAY TO DINNER *(continued)*

5. Angling the tip of your knife down and in, cut down alongside and underneath one side of the backbone. Repeat on the other side. You'll hear and feel a light crunching as your knife goes through another set of bones called the pin bones.

6. Use your shears to snip the backbone both where it joins the tail and also where it joins the head. The entire backbone can now be lifted straight out of the fish (photo 3).

7. Run the tip of your finger along the length of the fillets, just about an inch to either side of the center. You'll feel the pin bones sticking up. Use the pliers to grab the ends of the pin bones and pull them out (photo 4). Try not to rip up the fillet in the process, but don't worry if you do: The fish will be presented skin side up. The fish is now ready to be stuffed whole.

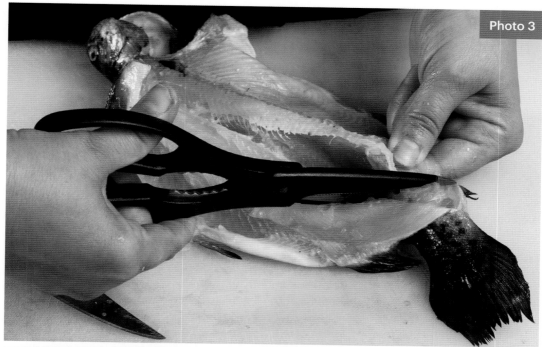

Photo 3

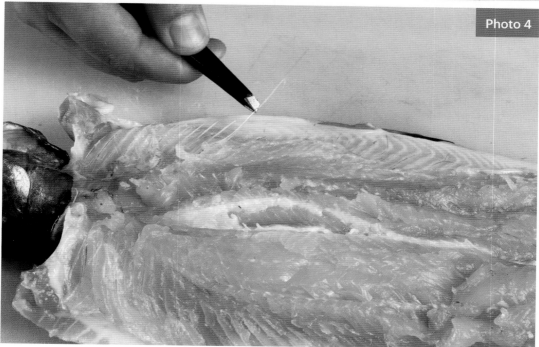

Photo 4

SHRIMP-STUFFED TROUT

This simple concept has countless variations. Corn bread stuffing, crabmeat stuffing, wild rice, dried fruit—the possibilities are endless.

PREP TIME: 30 MINUTES

COOK TIME: 35 MINUTES

SERVES: 2 AS AN ENTREE, 4 AS AN APPETIZER

3 tablespoons butter

½ onion, cut into small dice

1 rib celery, cut into thin slices

2 cloves garlic, minced

¼ pound peeled, deveined shrimp, cut into medium dice

1 tablespoon brandy, optional

½ cup bread crumbs

1 teaspoon chopped fresh herbs such as thyme or oregano, or ½ teaspoon dried herbs

½ teaspoon salt

Freshly ground pepper

2 butterflied trout

4 slices bacon

1. Heat oven to 425 degrees. Melt 1 tablespoon of the butter in a skillet over medium-high heat. Add onion and celery; cook, stirring, until limp, 2 minutes. Add garlic; cook 30 seconds. Add shrimp; cook until just cooked, about 2 minutes.

2. Add brandy; carefully tilt pan just enough to ignite over burner flame or light with a long handled match. Shake pan until flames subside.

3. Add bread crumbs and herbs; stir to combine. Add remaining 2 tablespoons of the butter; let melt. Stir just to moisten mixture; add the salt and pepper to taste.

4. Lay each butterflied trout skin-side down on a baking sheet. Mound half of the stuffing evenly along one fillet of each trout; fold other fillet over stuffing. Wrap 2 slices of bacon around the middle of each trout. Place in oven; cook until bacon is cooked, about 30 minutes.

NUTRITION INFORMATION PER SERVING: 738 calories, 47% of calories from fat, 37g fat, 17g saturated fat, 296mg cholesterol, 26g carbohydrates, 71g protein, 1,425mg sodium, 3g fiber

MORE THAN ONE WAY TO CHOP A NUT

There's a lot to be said for cooking, much of it bad: It's hard. It's time consuming. It's messy. AND WHAT IF SOMETHING GOES WRONG!?

Nuts, particularly the chopping thereof, have given pause to more than a few home cooks. How do I keep the pieces from flying everywhere? How do I chop them evenly? Here are the answers.

STEPS TO FOLLOW

Depending on how you're using the nuts, the size of the pieces can be anywhere from the large and uneven to the small and uniform. Consider the look and the mouthfeel: If the nuts are covering a frosted cake, for example, you might want a smooth layer of finely chopped nuts. If they're garnishing a dish of candied yams, you might want larger pieces with more substance. Remember, there's no right or wrong; there's only what you're looking to create.

Also, accept the fact that bits of nut will be flying about your kitchen. This is why the gods have given us brooms.

Finally, remember that, like all things culinary, if you haven't done this before, don't let the unfamiliarity of the task put you off. Don't worry about doing it "incorrectly." Just do it, and remember that next time it will be that much easier.

Having said that, there are a number of ways to proceed.

Food processor

The food processor is the easiest way to go and works terrifically as long as you follow a few guidelines. The power and speed of food processors can quickly take your nuts too far and turn them to dust before you know it.

First: Don't overload the bowl of the processor. Work in batches of about 1 cup at a time.

Second: Don't just turn on the machine and go out for a stroll in the garden. Pulse them, just for half a second at a time, until they're the consistency and size that you want.

WHY YOU NEED TO LEARN IT

Chopping nuts is one of those tasks that seems more complicated, more treacherous than it really is. Thus, this lesson is twofold: first, how to chop nuts, and second, how to translate this experience into other aspects of cooking.

MORE THAN ONE WAY TO CHOP A NUT *(continued)*

One knife

Use this technique for a rough cut of nuts.

1. Pile the nuts in the center of the board.

2. Hold the knife, blade edge down, next to the pile.

3. Place the palm of your guide hand over the tip of the knife. Keep the fingers on this hand spread out and arched up, out of harm's way.

4. Holding the tip to the board with your guide hand, lift the knife handle and bring the blade down repeatedly over the nuts, like you're working a pump handle or a paper cutter. As you bring the blade up, pivot slightly on the tip, moving the blade back and forth over the nuts.

Two knives

Use this technique for a finer cut (works best with knives the same length).

1. Spread the nuts in a single layer on your cutting board. Place the side of a chef's knife flat on top of the nuts and give a rap with your balled fist. This will break the nuts into smaller, more manageable pieces.

2. Gather the nuts again in a small pile in the center of the board. This time, take two chef's knives and place them side by side with their handles flush against one another. Grab both handles with your knife hand, holding them firmly together so that the knives can work in unison (photo 1).

3. Proceed exactly as above, starting at No. 2.

Photo 1

PREPARATION AND COOKING TECHNIQUES ▸

YOU'LL FLIP FOR THIS SAUTEING SKILL: COOK FOOD EVENLY—AND LOOK COOL DOING IT

Few things in the kitchen give more immediate satisfaction than grabbing a pan off the fire, giving it a couple of flicks, and watching the food turn cartwheels as all sides are exposed evenly to the heat.

WHY YOU NEED TO LEARN IT

It works great, it looks great, and it makes you feel like you know what you're doing.

The word saute comes from the French sauter, to leap or jump. It means cooking pieces of food over medium to medium-high heat, stirring or tossing to allow them to brown evenly. As a general rule, it is done with a small amount of fat (butter, oil, etc.), usually just enough to coat the bottom of the pan. Using only a small amount prevents the dish from becoming greasy and keeps unwanted showers of grease from splattering your stove.

The tossing technique is simple, but it requires practice and a reliance on muscle memory. In other words, you need to do it until your hands feel it, until it becomes as automatic as brushing your teeth.

STEPS TO FOLLOW

Follow these simple directions and soon you'll be like some culinary Isaac Newton, employing the laws of physics (using momentum and friction) to achieve the perfect saute.

To practice, use a 9-inch saute pan (the kind with sloped sides), and add to it about a quarter cup of uncooked rice. (Cornmeal will work too, as will dried beans, couscous, just about anything small, dry and evenly shaped).

As this is practice, we will NOT be doing this over an open flame. You might even consider doing it over a wide space like a dining room table.

Then practice, practice. Wasn't it the Wicked Witch of the West who said, "All in good time, my little pretty"?

1. Hold the pan nearly horizontal with just a slight downward slope toward the front edge (photo 1).

2. Move it firmly about six inches straight ahead and stop suddenly WITHOUT PULLING BACK ON THE PAN. After the pan stops moving, notice how the momentum of the rice continues to carry it forward and part way up the sloped front side of the pan (photo 2).

Photo 1

Photo 2

YOU'LL FLIP FOR THIS SAUTEING SKILL *(continued)*

3. Lift the pan so that you're tilting the front edge very slightly upward. Pull it back quickly to where you started and stop, again without reversing direction. Notice once more how the momentum of the rice carries it back across the flat surface after the pan has stopped (photo 3).

4. Practice the forward and backward moves several times until the pan begins to feel a bit more natural in your hand. Until you've achieved some consistency, come to a full stop between the forward and backward motions.

5. Now, put the two moves together, and do the forward and backward motion back to back ONE TIME without stopping in between. Move the pan forward, then pull back immediately while the rice is still traveling forward under its own momentum. Because of the wonderful world of physics, the rice will now come off the sloped front of the pan with a little more force, some of it actually "jumping" into the air a little bit before falling back.

6. Practice this many, many times, stopping between each attempt, until the forward and backward movements, not only of your hand, but also of the pan and, more importantly, the rice within the pan, are the same every time.

7. Finally, make your forward and backward motions continuous. Find the rhythm and watch as the rice cascades in beautiful arcs over the surface of the pan as you flip it (photo 4).

Photo 3

Photo 4

COME INTO THE FOLD: FRENCH TECHNIQUE INTENSIFIES FLAVOR, EASES CLEANUP

The French word papillote generally refers to paper, but it is related to the word for "butterfly," papillon. Food cooked en papillote is wrapped in parchment paper or aluminum foil and baked in a hot oven or sauteed with oil.

Parchment paper can be found at many supermarkets and kitchen supply shops and often comes in sheets about 24-by-16 inches.

WHY YOU NEED TO LEARN IT

Food prepared en papillote has two wonderful qualities wholly apart from how good it tastes. First, it comes in its own disposable cooking vessel, making cleanup a snap. It also creates a wonderful presentation, particularly when using parchment, which, when buttered, puffs up and browns in the oven.

To use foil, simply place the food in the center of a large sheet, then fold the sides up and over, crimping it directly over the food. For parchment, follow these directions.

PUTTING YOUR SKILLS TO WORK

Salmon with julienned vegetables (pg. 80)

STEPS TO FOLLOW

1. Fold a sheet of parchment paper in half, short side to short side.

2. Take a pencil and, starting at the bottom of the crease, draw half of a heart shape to cover most of the parchment. Once you get the hang of cutting out these shapes, the drawing step can be eliminated.

3. Using regular scissors or kitchen shears, cut along the pencil line (photo 1). Be sure to cut through both sides of the paper. Open up the paper into a complete heart shape.

4. With the point of the heart facing you, place the food directly in the center of the right half of the heart so that the crease is to the left (photo 2). Fold the left half over the food.

5. Starting at the crease at the top of the heart, fold down toward the center a strip of paper that's about ½-inch wide and anywhere from 2 to 4 inches long (photo 3), then crease it. Make sure you include both the top and bottom halves of the paper in your fold.

6. Make a second fold to create another strip, one half inch by several inches, that begins in the center of the first crease. The two folds should have a pleated look.

7. Continue making folds and creasing, all the way around the perimeter of the heart, until it is completely sealed. The series

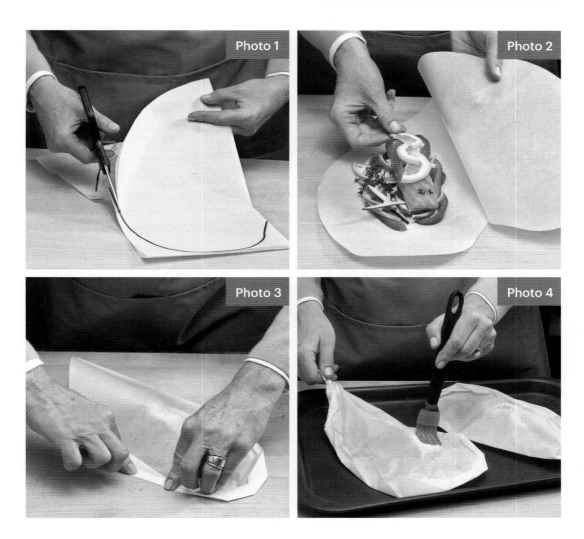

of overlapping creases will create a sturdy seal, keeping in the steam and the juices. The point at the bottom of the heart can then be twisted to lock it.

8. Brush the paper with oil or butter and place on a sheet tray in a hot oven (photo 4). When the paper is puffy and golden brown, after about 8 to 12 minutes, remove from the oven. Make a small slit in the paper to keep it from deflating as it cools. Place on a plate and serve.

You may be able to fit several servings in each package, depending on the size of the item and the size of your parchment heart. For the most exciting presentation, use just one serving per package and let all your guests open their own. Be sure to remind everyone, however, that the parchment itself IS NOT EDIBLE.

SALMON WITH JULIENNED VEGETABLES

PREP TIME: 30 MINUTES

COOK TIME: 9 MINUTES

YIELD: 4 SERVINGS

2 tablespoons melted
    butter

1 red bell pepper

1 green bell pepper

1 zucchini

1 yellow squash

½ red onion

2 cloves garlic, minced

½ teaspoon minced fresh
    thyme or other herb

3 tablespoons extra-virgin
    olive oil

½ teaspoon salt, freshly
    ground pepper

Freshly ground pepper

4 skinless fillets of salmon,
    about 4 ounces each

2 lemons, sliced into thin
    rounds

½ cup dry white wine

1. Heat oven to 425 degrees. Cut out four parchment hearts; brush the right side of each with melted butter.

2. Cut peppers, zucchini, yellow squash and onion into 2-inch-by-⅛-inch julienne strips. Combine in a bowl with the garlic, herb, olive oil, salt and pepper to taste.

3. Place one-fourth of the julienned vegetables in the center of the right half of each parchment heart. Place a salmon fillet on top; season with salt and pepper to taste. Top each fillet with 3 overlapping pieces of lemon. Drizzle 2 tablespoons of the wine over each fillet.

4. Seal the hearts with a series of overlapping pleats; place two hearts each on two baking sheets. Bake until the paper is puffed and brown, about 8–12 minutes. Cut a small slit in each heart to prevent it from collapsing. Place hearts on serving plates for each diner to open.

NUTRITION INFORMATION PER SERVING: 304 calories, 55% of calories from fat, 18g fat, 3g saturated fat, 72mg cholesterol, 8g carbohydrates, 27g protein, 350mg sodium, 2g fiber

STIR-FRYING PUTS SOME SIZZLE IN A COOK'S REPERTOIRE

Stir-frying offers a great opportunity to use the Prep School techniques you've been ac-quiring: knife cuts, blanching and shocking (quick simmering followed by a dip in an ice bath), and that vegetable toss used in sauteing. Have you been practicing?

Bear in mind that all the ingredients in stir-fries need to be cut into bite-sized pieces: They cook very quickly and they're eaten (typically) with chopsticks.

STEPS TO FOLLOW

For a stir-fry that is perfectly cooked, remember these three sim-ple rules: high heat, low-fat and no overcrowding the pan.

High heat cooks food quickly, leaving vegetables crisp and beau-tiful. (Cooking vegetables over lower heat is a technique called "sweating." This draws out moisture, leaving vegetables soft and wilted with a duller color.)

Low-fat means your dinner won't be greasy.

Overcrowding lowers the temperature of the pan. This causes the vegetables to sweat, turning your stir-fry mushy and drab. If you have lots to stir-fry, do it in batches. At the end, return every-thing to the pan just long enough to reheat.

Here's a general method. Be prepared for different recipes to mix things up a bit.

1. Prepare your mise en place (photo 1, next page). This essential step means your liquids are measured and your vegetables are cut and waiting in separate bowls. Your meat—if you're using it— is sliced and possibly marinating.

2. Place a wok or large skillet over the highest heat. Just as it starts to smoke, add only a tablespoon or two of oil. (Peanut oil, the traditional choice, works very well because of its high "smoke point"—the temperature at which oil starts to break down. Corn oil's smoke point is similar and works just as well.)

WHY YOU NEED TO LEARN IT

Stir-frying is all about the proper cooking of the vegetables. Cooked quickly over high heat, they maintain their crunch and vibrant colors. When you've mastered the tech-nique, the incredible vari-ety of flavoring ideas will astound you. Oyster sauce, chili-garlic paste and hoisin sauce are three delicious options readily available in most supermarkets. Browse through cookbooks or surf the Web for doz-ens—if not thousands—of other great ideas.

PUTTING YOUR SKILLS TO WORK

Broccoli and beef in oyster sauce (pg. 84)

STIR-FRYING PUTS SOME SIZZLE IN A COOK'S REPERTOIRE *(continued)*

Photo 1

3. If marinating meat, drain it, reserving the marinade. Add the meat to the pan. You'll hear a loud sizzle and see some steam. Let the meat sit for several seconds to bring the pan back up to temperature. Stir the meat, exposing all sides to the heat. Beef and meaty fish like salmon can be cooked to medium. For chicken, pork or shellfish, stir-fry until just cooked through. When done, remove it to a bowl.

4. Add vegetables in reverse order of how quickly they cook. Onions generally are first. (Some cooks start with aromatics like garlic and ginger, but those are easy to burn. Try adding them when the onions are about 30 seconds short of being done.)

If you're using a large amount of vegetables, cook in batches until crisp-tender, then remove them to a bowl. Keep the pan as hot as you can, and let each vegetable have adequate contact with the pan so that it stir-fries rather than sweats (photo 2).

5. Return all the cooked ingredients to the pan along with any vegetables (such as broccoli, green beans or cauliflower) that you blanched and shocked ahead of time. (Blanching and shocking is not mandatory—that's a French technique—but it will help to cook some vegetables perfectly while maintaining their texture and color.)

6. Add the sauce and flavoring ingredients (photo 3). For a thicker sauce, make a cornstarch slurry (a tablespoon of cornstarch dissolved in a little cold liquid) and add it to your pan. It will thicken immediately upon boiling. Taste for seasoning and serve.

BROCCOLI AND BEEF IN OYSTER SAUCE

Here's a classic combination that's easily adaptable. Use other meats or vegetables as you see fit and serve with steamed rice.

PREP TIME: 30 MINUTES

COOK TIME: 10 MINUTES

YIELD: 2 SERVINGS

Sauce:

1 tablespoon cornstarch

⅔ cup canned beef broth

3 tablespoons oyster sauce

1 tablespoon roasted sesame oil

1 teaspoon chili-garlic paste, optional

Stir-fry:

1 tablespoon soy sauce

1 tablespoon dry sherry

1 tablespoon brown sugar

1 strip steak, about 8 ounces, sliced into thin strips

1 medium head broccoli, broken or cut into florets

2 tablespoons peanut oil

¼ medium red onion, cut into julienne strips

2 small cloves garlic, minced

1. For sauce, stir cornstarch into 2 tablespoons of the broth in a small bowl; set aside. Stir together remaining broth, oyster sauce, sesame oil and chili-garlic paste in another small bowl; set aside.

2. Mix together the soy sauce, sherry and brown sugar in a large bowl. Add the sliced beef; toss to combine. Set aside.

3. Meanwhile, heat a large pot of salted water to a boil over medium-high heat. Add the broccoli; cook until bright green and tender-crunchy, about 2 minutes. Drain; transfer broccoli to a bowl filled with ice water to stop cooking. Drain; set aside.

4. Place a large wok or skillet over high heat until almost smoking. Drain the beef; reserve marinade. Add 1 tablespoon of the peanut oil to the skillet; add beef. Stir-fry until beef is browned, about 2 minutes. Transfer to a bowl or platter.

5. Heat remaining 1 tablespoon of the oil in the wok over medium-high heat. Add onion; stir-fry 1 minute. Add the garlic; stir-fry until fragrant, about 30 seconds. Add the beef, broccoli, reserved marinade and the oyster sauce mixture. Cook until the liquid comes to a boil; drizzle the cornstarch mixture into the pan. Cook, stirring, until thickened and heated through, about 2 minutes.

NUTRITION INFORMATION PER SERVING: 487 calories, 51% of calories from fat, 29g fat, 6g saturated fat, 62mg cholesterol, 27g carbohydrates, 35g protein, 1,069mg sodium, 10g fiber

BUILDING A BETTER BURGER

With all due respect to my vegan and vegetarian readers, you might want to skip this Prep School. Here, we're talking burgers.

WHY YOU NEED TO LEARN IT

This is another step on the road to thinking—and cooking—like a chef. It's easy to take burgers for granted, but as with everything else, the more we know, the better the end product will be.

PUTTING YOUR SKILLS TO WORK

Southwestern turkey burger with corn and Cheddar (pg. 89)
Blue cheese, spinach and bacon-stuffed hamburgers (pg. 90)

STEPS TO FOLLOW

First, notice that I'm using the term "burger" instead of "hamburger." Hamburgers are made of beef, but from this day forward, remember that great burgers come from many sources: lamb, pork, turkey, even salmon or crab.

Think of the meat as a neutral ingredient you can flavor a billion different ways. Then, using your experience and knowledge, start putting together combinations, and taste as you go. Season judiciously, and periodically take a little piece of the mixture out and drop it in a hot saute pan to see how it tastes.

Beyond that, here are a few other things to think about:

1. It helps to understand meat. Meat is comprised of muscle, connective tissue and fat. Most people prefer burgers made from meat that has 15 to 20 percent fat, such as beef chuck. Grinding is perfect for these fattier cuts because they also have lots of tough connective tissue that grinding breaks into chewable bits. Burgers made from leaner meats like turkey can dry out very easily and should be augmented with moisture-adding ingredients.

2. Don't just think about what goes "on" your burger. Think about what goes "in" your burger too. We want the entirety of the burger, not just the top, to be seasoned and flavored. Then, think of all the great flavor combinations you've had in the past, and imagine them in a burger:

Consider ethnic ingredients: Make a Mexican burger by adding ingredients like chipotle or other chilies, Mexican cheese, cilantro and sauteed onions and garlic. Or a Greek burger with ground lamb, chopped fresh mint and crumbled feta cheese. Or an Italian burger of ground beef and hot Italian sausage with little chunks of provolone. One thing: Any vegetable you add, such as onions, garlic, shallots, celery, etc., should be softened first by sauteing or sweating.

Think of other classic combinations you could mix into ground meat: hamburgers infused with crumbled bacon, shredded Cheddar and caramelized onions; salmon burgers with capers and parsley; pork burgers with bacon and sauteed apples.

Bottled condiments such as steak sauce, chili sauce or barbecue sauce are easy to use. When adding liquid, you may want to increase the burger's structural soundness by adding an egg or bread crumbs.

And no matter what, be sure to season with salt. Figure about a teaspoon per pound of meat, but start with less and taste as you go.

3. When mixing ground meat, make sure it's cold and keep the mixing to a minimum. If the meat gets too warm—this can result simply from the heat of your hands—the fat melts and turns everything into a gloppy mess. The best idea is keep the meat, bowl and utensils in the fridge until mixing time. Then, place your mixing bowl inside another bowl filled with ice.

4. Don't ignore what goes on the burger. Ketchup and mustard are classic, but try to match your condiments accordingly. If you're serving an Asian-themed salmon burger mixed with soy sauce, ginger and sesame seeds, spread it with a little mayo mixed with wasabi. For an Italian sausage burger, consider a simple marinara.

5. Take notes. Chances are, no matter how good your idea sounds, most things won't be perfect the first time around. If you write down what you did, though, you can tweak the recipe.

SOUTHWESTERN TURKEY BURGER WITH CORN AND CHEDDAR

Serve these burgers on a hamburger bun or corn bread with your favorite salsa or chipotle mayonnaise. To make chipotle mayo stir pureed chipotle pepper (which are smoked jalapeno peppers sold in small cans or jars as chipotle in adobo sauce) to taste into jarred mayo.

1. Heat a skillet over medium-high heat; add the oil. Add corn and onion; cook, stirring, until the onion softens and corns cooks through, about 5 minutes. Transfer to a large bowl; set aside to cool. Add the ground turkey, egg, bread crumbs, cheese, cilantro, chili powder, cumin, salt and pepper to taste, mixing together with hands.

2. Heat a grill or broiler. Meanwhile, cook a small piece of the mixture in the skillet, turning, 1 minute. Transfer to a paper-lined plate; taste for seasoning. Adjust seasoning; form the remaining mixture into 4 burgers.

3. Place burgers on grill or under broiler; cook, turning once, until just cooked through, 5-7 minutes per side.

NUTRITION INFORMATION PER SERVING: 428 calories, 52% of calories from fat, 25g fat, 7g saturated fat, 150mg cholesterol, 21g carbohydrates, 30g protein, 874mg sodium, 2g fiber

PREP TIME: 25 MINUTES

COOK TIME: 10 MINUTES

YIELD: 4 SERVINGS

2 tablespoons vegetable oil

Kernels from 2 ears corn

½ onion, diced

1 pound ground turkey

1 egg

½ cup bread crumbs

½ cup shredded sharp Cheddar cheese

¼ cup chopped cilantro

1 tablespoon chili powder

½ tablespoon cumin

1 teaspoon salt

Freshly ground pepper

BLUE CHEESE, SPINACH AND BACON-STUFFED HAMBURGERS

PREP TIME: 20 MINUTES

COOK TIME:10 MINUTES

YIELD: 4 SERVINGS

6 slices bacon, cut into ¼-inch pieces

2 cloves garlic, minced

½ pound spinach

1 tablespoon white wine

1¼ teaspoons coarse salt

Freshly ground pepper

1 pound ground chuck

¼ pound blue cheese, crumbled

1. Set a skillet over medium heat; cook the bacon slowly until the fat has been rendered and the bacon is crisp. Remove the bacon; transfer to a plate lined with a paper towel.

2. Discard all but 2 tablespoons of fat; return the pan to medium-high heat. Add the garlic, spinach and white wine; cook, just until the spinach wilts, about 1 minute. Season with ¼ teaspoon of the salt and pepper to taste. Remove the spinach; set aside to cool.

3. Heat a grill or broiler. Season the ground chuck with the remaining 1 teaspoon of the salt and pepper to taste. Divide into 8 equal portions; form into ¼-inch patties.

4. Squeeze most of the moisture from the spinach. Divide the spinach into 4 portions; place 1 portion on each of 4 patties. Evenly distribute bacon and blue cheese over spinach, keeping stuffing at least ½ inch from the edge of the patties. Top each of the 4 "stuffed" patties with an unstuffed patty. Press down gently to seal.

5. Transfer to a grill or under a broiler. Cook, turning once, until meat is just cooked through, 5-7 minutes per side.

NUTRITION INFORMATION PER SERVING: 264 calories, 54% of calories from fat, 16g fat, 8g saturated fat, 77mg cholesterol, 3g carbohydrates, 28g protein, 1,309mg sodium, 1g fiber

STUFFING PORK CHOPS IN NO TIME: ENDLESS VARIATIONS FOR ELEGANT DINNER

On average, we eat almost a pound of pork every week, according to the USDA. That breaks down into a handful of ribs, some succulent roasts, and lots and lots of chops.

STEPS TO FOLLOW

One key to spectacular stuffed chops is creating big pockets with small openings. Here's how:

1. Set the chop on your board with the bone away from you and steady it with your guide hand. Hold a paring knife or small boning knife horizontally with the spine toward the bone and the tip pointing into the meat (photo 1). Make sure the blade is equidistant from the top and bottom of the chop. An even thickness on both sides promotes even cooking.

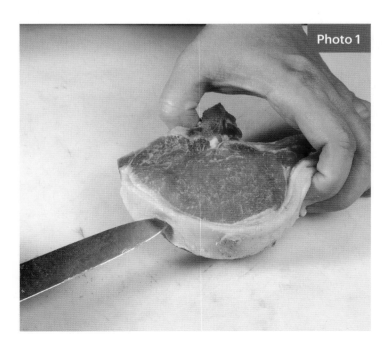

Photo 1

WHY YOU NEED TO LEARN IT

Stuffing a chop doubles the elegance factor while increasing the prep time only slightly. Once you get the hang of carving out a pocket, the possibilities are endless. Chopped nuts, cooked rice, sausage or chopped meat, blanched vegetables, cheese, fruit—all are fair game.

PUTTING YOUR SKILLS TO WORK

Apple, currant and blue cheese-stuffed pork chops (pg. 94)

STUFFING PORK CHOPS IN NO TIME *(continued)*

2. Before you begin, lay the blade on top of the chop to map out your plan. You'll puncture the meat and insert the blade with the spine against or close to the bone. Go straight in as far as you can without emerging from the other side (photo 2). Don't let the tip tear a hole in the meat. (When you do make that mistake, don't worry. Use slightly less stuffing to prevent leakage, and then put the chop on the plate with the torn side down.)

3. With the blade inside the chop and the spine facing the bone, pivot the knife from the entry hole and cut through the center of the chop to the opposite side. Keep your guide hand on the meat to feel the motion and location of the knife underneath. Try not to enlarge the entry hole, and don't let the knife tip poke through the meat.

As you slice through the interior of the chop, bring the knife tip to within about a half-inch of the edge of the chop. Remember, the goal is to create a large, sturdy pocket with a small opening.

4. When you think you've got a nice pocket, remove the knife. Take one finger and insert it into the pocket to check your handiwork (photo 3).

5. To stuff, give the chop a gentle squeeze around its waist to open the hole a bit. Use your fingers to push the stuffing inside (photo 4).

6. If you're making dinner for a group, you may find it quicker to fill the chops using a pastry bag with a large tip.

Some notes on stuffings

- Remember that the stuffing is an accompaniment to the chop and, as such, its purpose is to highlight and accentuate the flavor of the pork, not hide or overpower it.

- If you're using aromatics such as onions, celery, garlic, etc., saute them before combining with other ingredients.

- Spinach can be placed in boiling water for a minute, then transferred to an ice bath, then chopped.

- If you're including a starch such as rice or bread crumbs, consider adding some melted butter or bind the stuffing with a beaten egg or egg white.

- Finally, make sure to season the stuffing along with the outside of the chop.

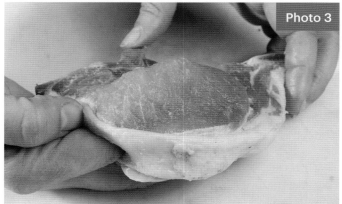

REMEMBER, THE GOAL IS TO CREATE A LARGE, STURDY POCKET WITH A SMALL OPENING.

APPLE, CURRANT AND BLUE CHEESE-STUFFED PORK CHOPS

We used 1 ounce blue cheese in the stuffing but if you prefer, up to 3 ounces can be used.

PREP TIME: 30 MINUTES

COOK TIME: 26 MINUTES

YIELD: 4 SERVINGS

2 tablespoons butter

2 tart apples, such as Granny Smith, peeled, chopped

1 shallot, minced

2 tablespoons Cognac, brandy or Calvados

1 ounce blue cheese, crumbled

¼ cup dried currants, raisins or cranberries

1 teaspoon salt

Freshly ground pepper

4 rib pork chops, about 1-1½-inches thick, pockets cut for stuffing

1 tablespoon olive oil

1. Heat oven to 425 degrees. Heat an ovenproof skillet over medium-high heat. Add the butter; melt. Add the apples; cook, stirring, until apples turn golden-brown, about 8 minutes. Add the shallot; cook, stirring, until softened, about 1 minute. Add the Cognac; carefully light the mixture with a kitchen match. Remove pan from the heat; let the flames go out. Transfer mixture to a large bowl; cool 5 minutes.

2. Stir blue cheese and dried fruit into mixture; season with ½ teaspoon of the salt and pepper to taste. Stuff the chops until the centers are slightly bulging; season both sides with remaining ½ teaspoon of the salt and pepper to taste. Set aside.

3. Wipe out the skillet. Heat over high heat; add the oil. Heat until oil just begins to smoke, about 30 seconds. Add pork chops; cook, turning once, until seared on both sides, about 3 minutes per side.

4. Transfer the skillet to the oven. Cook until chops are cooked through, about 5-10 minutes, depending on the amount of stuffing and thickness of the chop.

NUTRITION INFORMATION PER SERVING: 312 calories, 57% of calories from fat, 20g fat, 9g saturated fat, 73mg cholesterol, 16g carbohydrates, 18g protein, 772mg sodium, 1g fiber

BRAISE AWAY THE WINTER BLUES: ROLL UP WARM RELIEF IN THE FORM OF A CLASSIC ITALIAN BRACIOLA

Accursed winter remains, I'm afraid, leaving me hungry for warmth. Bless braising, then, for providing the perfect excuse to turn on—and leave on—the oven. And braciola (brah-TCHO-lah), the famous Italian rolled beef, is a perfect braise. Pounded and stuffed, its long cooking in a slow oven infuses its bath of tomato sauce with meaty richness, leaving it fall-apart tender in the process.

STEPS TO FOLLOW

Some people like flank steak. Some people like thin slices off the round. You don't even have to use beef, of course. Pork, lamb, yak—whatever happens to look good and not cost an arm and a leg. The thing to remember is you want a cut that takes well to braising. Avoid the expensive cuts from the loin or ribs of the animal; use tougher cuts instead, the ones that come with a bit of connective tissue. That long, slow cooking in liquid will tenderize tough muscle, dissolving the connective tissue into gelatin, which then imparts wonderful body to your sauce.

1. Start with your filling. You can think in terms of layers of individual components, or as a homogenous mixture, like any common bread crumb stuffing.

For layers, think of things that pile up nicely, with different colors and textures, like prosciutto, provolone, slices of hard-cooked egg, roasted bell peppers, crumbled bacon ... I could go on.

For a stuffing, just prepare something good, like ricotta with chopped, cooked spinach, or crumbled sausage. Or if you're using pork, maybe sauteed apples tossed with bread crumbs, fresh sage and melted butter.

Don't sweat it. Taste the filling as you make it. If it tastes good, your braciole (the plural form of the word) will be terrific.

WHY YOU NEED TO LEARN IT

Braising is one of the classic methods for the preparation of tougher cuts of meat.

PUTTING YOUR SKILLS TO WORK

Braciole with prosciutto and roasted peppers (pg. 98)

BRAISE AWAY THE WINTER BLUES *(continued)*

2. Pound small cuts of meat into pieces about ¼-inch thick, and maybe 4 to 6 inches square (photo 1). You definitely want them thin, but you can play with the overall size all you like. To flatten the cuts of meat, put them between two sheets of plastic wrap and whack them with a meat mallet or the bottom of a small pan.

3. Cover the flattened cuts of meat with your filling. Leave half an inch or so around the edges so the filling doesn't leak out.

4. Roll the braciole up like a jellyroll or a rug (photo 2), and tie them loosely with string to keep them from falling apart.

5. In a very hot pan, preferably one with straight sides, sear the braciole in a small amount of oil, turning to brown on all sides (photo 3).

6. Remove the braciole to a plate, pour out the grease, and deglaze the pan with a little red wine: That means pouring the wine into the pan and heating it to a boil, then scraping up the brown bits that are stuck to the bottom.

7. When the wine has almost evaporated, add crushed canned tomatoes or a simple tomato sauce. You want enough to just cover the braciole, which you're now going to put back in. Be sure to pour any juices from the plate they were resting on into the pan.

8. Heat the sauce to a boil, then turn down the heat and cover. You can leave it on a low flame on the stove or put it in a 325-degree oven. Either way, they should go at least 90 minutes, possibly more. You want the meat to yield easily to your fork.

9. When the braciole are nearly done, heat a big pot of salted water to a boil and make some pasta.

10. Remove the braciole to a serving platter and toss the sauce with the pasta. Now that, my friend, is some good, good eating.

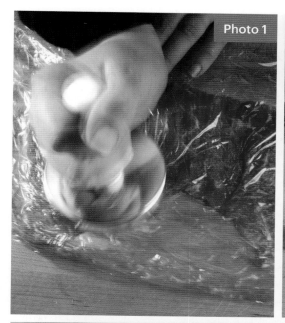

Photo 1

Photo 2

Photo 3

BRACIOLE WITH PROSCIUTTO AND ROASTED PEPPERS

PREP TIME: 20 MINUTES

COOK TIME: 2-3 HOURS

YIELD: 4 SERVINGS

1 pound flank steak, cut into 4 even pieces, butterflied

1 teaspoon salt

Freshly ground pepper

8 thin slices prosciutto

16 leaves fresh basil

2 hard-cooked eggs, quartered lengthwise

1 roasted red pepper, cut into 8 lengthwise slices

3 tablespoons vegetable oil

½ cup dry red wine

1 onion, diced

1 green bell pepper, cored, trimmed, diced

4 cloves garlic, minced

1 can (28 ounces) crushed tomatoes

½ pound pasta, cooked to package directions

1. Place a steak piece between two sheets of plastic wrap; pound with a meat mallet or the flat side of a pan until ¼-inch thick. Repeat with remaining meat.

2. Season each piece of the meat with ¼ teaspoon of the salt and pepper to taste; cover each piece with 2 prosciutto slices; top each piece with 4 basil leaves. Divide egg quarters and pepper strips among the pieces. Roll up each; tie securely with string.

3. Place a large skillet over high heat; add the oil. Heat 30 seconds; add the braciole. Cook, turning, until seared, about 3 minutes. Transfer to a platter; set aside. Add red wine to the skillet; cook, stirring, to deglaze the pan, about 5 minutes.

4. Add the onion and green bell pepper to the pan; cook, stirring, until softened, about 3 minutes. Add the garlic; cook, stirring, until garlic becomes fragrant, about 30 seconds. Add the tomatoes; heat to a boil. Return the meat rolls to the skillet; lower the heat to a simmer. Cover; cook until fall-apart tender, 2-3 hours.

5. Transfer the braciole to a platter. Set aside. Add the cooked pasta to the skillet; toss with the sauce. Cut the strings from the braciole; serve with the pasta.

Note: You can ask your butcher to butterfly the steak, or to do it at home: Carefully slice the steak in half horizontally, cutting almost but not completely through. Then open it like a book—or butterfly.

NUTRITION INFORMATION PER SERVING: 637 calories, 33% of calories from fat, 23g fat, 6g saturated fat, 163mg cholesterol, 66g carbohydrates, 43g protein, 1,362mg sodium, 8g fiber

PRAISING BRAISING: SLOW-COOKING TECHNIQUE BRINGS OUT THE BEST IN MANY CUTS OF MEAT

It's hard to say enough about braising. Tough and stringy meat cuts are seared, then cooked long and slow in a small amount of flavorful liquid. Not only does the drawn-out cooking impart the richness of the meat to the liquid, but it breaks down the meat's connective tissue into gelatin, adding body to the sauce while leaving the meat fall-apart tender.

WHY YOU NEED TO LEARN IT

Braising is an extremely versatile technique, and the leisurely cooking time gives you a wide margin of error. Meats from legs and shoulders are good for braising, though other cuts work as well. Poultry legs, veal or lamb shanks, beef short ribs, chuck roast and brisket—the choices are endless.

PUTTING YOUR SKILLS TO WORK

Braised lamb shanks (pg. 104)

STEPS TO FOLLOW

1. Heat a large covered pan or Dutch oven over a high flame. Season the meat with salt and pepper, then dredge it in flour, shaking off the excess. Add a tablespoon of vegetable oil to the pan, then add the meat. Brown the meat deeply on all sides (photo 1), then remove it and set aside, leaving the pan on the flame.

2. If the pan is a bit dry, add another tablespoon of oil. Throw in some aromatic vegetables (onions, carrots, celery, garlic, etc.) that you've cut into rough medium dice (½-inch cubes). These vegetables are mainly to flavor the sauce and can be strained out later, which means you don't need to obsess over perfect dicing. Toss the vegetables in the hot fat until they caramelize, turning a nice golden brown.

3. Deglaze the pan with a flavorful liquid, such as wine, beer or stock, even fruit juice: Turn up the flame to high, then add a couple ounces of liquid to the pan (photo 2). As the liquid boils and evaporates, use a wooden spoon to scrape up the flavorful brown bits that have attached themselves to the bottom of the pan.

▶

Photo 1

Photo 2

PRAISING BRAISING *(continued)*

Photo 3

4. Return the meat to the pan. Add enough liquid to come halfway up the side of the meat (photo 3). Again, nearly any flavorful liquid will do: stock or low-sodium canned broth, wine, beer, canned tomatoes with their juice.

5. Add whatever spices or flavoring ingredients you wish to use, then heat the liquid to a simmer and cover the pan. At this point, you can either turn the heat down to a bare simmer and finish cooking on the stove top, or place the whole thing in a 325-degree oven. Different meats cook at different rates, depending on the amount of connective tissue, the age of the animal, etc. In general, though, tougher meats take longer, and you want the finished product to be falling off the bone or easily pulled apart with a fork.

Photo 4

6. When the meat is done, remove it from the pot. Strain the liquid through a fine-mesh strainer (called a chinois) into a clean saucepan (photo 4). If the sauce is too thin, reduce it over high heat until it coats the back of a spoon. Alternately, you could puree the strained vegetables and stir them back in, or add a cornstarch slurry or whisk in a tablespoon or two of beurre manie—equal parts flour and softened butter, mashed together into a smooth paste. If using a beurre manie, let the sauce simmer for a few minutes to cook out any starchy taste. Be sure to taste the sauce for seasoning.

7. When the sauce is ready, return the meat to the pan. At this point, and this is a great point, you can refrigerate it and hold it overnight or for two or three days. Simply reheat and you're ready for company.

BRAISED LAMB SHANKS

Here's a basic but delicious braise. All braises are simply variations on this theme. Serve with mashed potatoes, noodles or couscous.

PREP TIME: 30 MINUTES

COOK TIME: 2 HOURS

YIELD: 4 SERVINGS

4 small lamb shanks

½ teaspoon salt

Freshly ground pepper

2 cups flour

2 to 3 tablespoons vegetable oil

½ each, cut into medium dice: onion, carrot, celery rib

2 cloves garlic, minced

½ cup dry red wine

2 cans (14½ ounces) beef broth

2 bay leaves

1 teaspoon dried thyme or herbes de Provence

8 sprigs fresh parsley

1 tablespoon cornstarch, optional

1. Heat oven to 325 degrees. Heat a large Dutch oven over medium-high heat. Season the lamb shanks with salt and pepper; coat in flour, shaking off the excess. Add 2 tablespoons of the vegetable oil to the hot pan; add 2 of the lamb shanks. Brown on all sides, about 8 minutes. Remove; set aside. Repeat with remaining 2 shanks.

2. Add 1 tablespoon of the oil to the pan if needed. Add the onion, carrot and celery; cook, stirring often, until golden brown, about 10 minutes. Add the garlic; cook 1 minute.

3. Add the wine, stirring to scrape up any browned bits. Cook until wine almost disappears, about 5 minutes. Return the lamb shanks to the pan; pour in enough of the beef broth to come halfway up the sides of the shanks. Add the bay leaves, thyme and parsley. Heat to a simmer; cover.

4. Place the pan in the oven. Braise, turning the lamb shanks over in the sauce every 30 minutes, until the shanks are tender and meat can be pulled easily from the bone, about 1½–2 hours.

5. Remove shanks to a platter. Strain the sauce through a fine mesh sieve into a clean saucepan; discard the solids. Heat sauce over medium-high heat. To thicken the sauce, if desired, mix 1 tablespoon of cornstarch with 2 tablespoons of cold liquid: broth, water or wine. Stir half the mixture slowly into the boiling sauce; add remaining mixture if needed. Adjust seasoning. Return the shanks to the sauce to warm the meat, about 3 minutes.

NUTRITION INFORMATION PER SERVING: 521 calories, 49% of calories from fat, 28g fat, 11g saturated fat, 128mg cholesterol, 24g carbohydrates, 40g protein, 1,092mg sodium, 1g fiber

TAKE ONE ROAST, TIE UP IN KNOTS: TRUSSING A ROAST MAKES A NEAT PACKAGE FOR MORE EVEN COOKING— AND IS EASIER TO MASTER

One casualty of our fastener-filled modernity is a familiarity with rope. We've gone from knot-handy to not-handy-in-the-least. Let's reclaim some of our lost dexterity and tie up a roast.

WHY YOU NEED TO LEARN IT

Trussing a roast is one of those techniques, like flipping veggies in a saute pan or creaming garlic, that is so surprisingly fun that you'll be looking for excuses to use it. There are billions of stuffed and rolled dishes that need to be trussed. Also, trussing helps oddly or unevenly shaped items hold a compact form for more even cooking.

PUTTING YOUR SKILLS TO WORK

Mint pesto-stuffed leg of lamb (pg. 110)

STEPS TO FOLLOW

To practice, we recommend using something relatively small and evenly shaped, like a boneless pork loin roast (we used a leg of lamb because of the accompanying recipe, perfect for Easter). Start with a length of kitchen string about five or six times the length of the roast.

1. Set the roast fat side up on the board with one end facing you. Loop one end of the string around the roast about an inch from the end; tie a knot (photo 1).

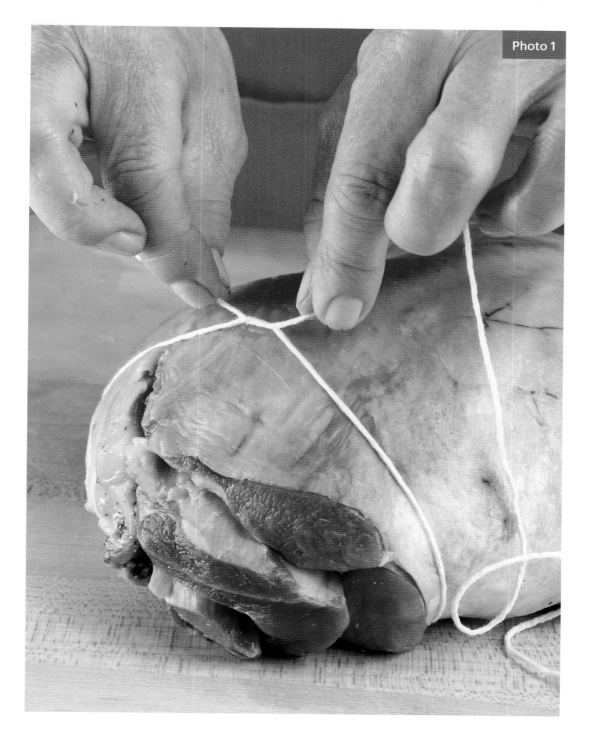

Photo 1

TAKE ONE ROAST, TIE UP IN KNOTS *(continued)*

2. Pinch the string 1 or 2 inches past the knot. Loop the remaining string around and under the roast. Bring the end of the string up and under the portion where you are pinching the string (photo 2). Pull the string up and forward to tighten the loop around the meat. Repeat this procedure until you have a series of loops all the way down the roast (photo 3).

3. When you reach the far end, hold the string over the edge and flip the roast onto its top. Straighten the loops along the bottom of the roast to give them a neat appearance.

4. Pull the loose end of the string gently and lay it over the last loop. Tuck it under the loop, then back toward you; pull straight up to tighten. Repeat with each loop (photo 4).

5. When you reach the end, flip the roast back over and tie the loose end of the string to the original knot.

Photo 2

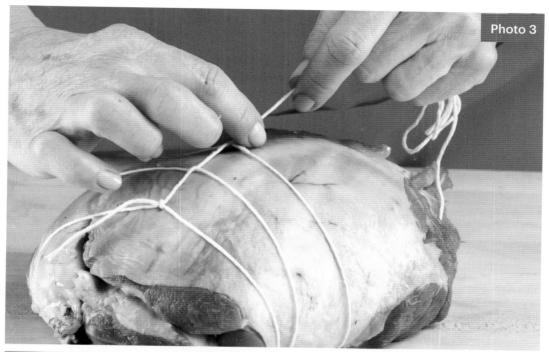

Photo 3

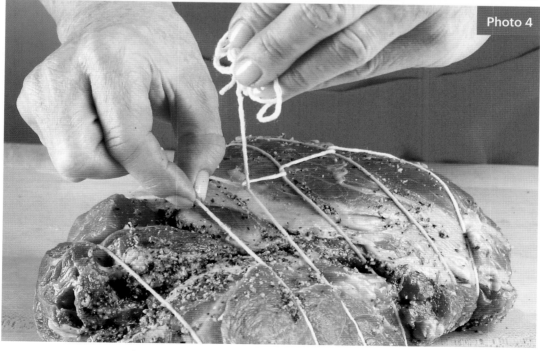

Photo 4

MINT PESTO-STUFFED LEG OF LAMB

PREP TIME: 40 MINUTES

COOK TIME: 1 HOUR,
15 MINUTES

RESTING TIME: 15 MINUTES

YIELD: 10 SERVINGS

2 cups flat-leaf parsley sprigs

1 cup fresh mint leaves

⅓ cup chopped walnuts, toasted almonds or pine nuts

4 to 6 cloves garlic

Juice of 1 lemon

½ cup extra-virgin olive oil

1 boneless leg of lamb, about 3-4 pounds

1 teaspoon coarse salt or to taste

Freshly ground pepper

1. Heat oven to 375 degrees. Process the parsley, mint, walnuts, garlic and lemon juice in a food processor just to combine, about 10 seconds. With the motor running, drizzle in the olive oil slowly; process to a smooth paste. Set the pesto aside.

2. Open the boneless leg of lamb; season with ½ teaspoon of the salt and pepper to taste. Spread the pesto evenly across the surface; roll the lamb back up and place the leg, seam side down, on the cutting board with the seam away from you. Truss the leg just tightly enough to hold its shape; season the outside with the remaining ½ teaspoon of salt and pepper to taste.

3. Place the leg on a rack in a roasting pan; roast until a meat thermometer registers 140 degrees for medium-rare, about 1 hour, 15 minutes, or to desired degree of doneness.

NUTRITION INFORMATION PER SERVING: 366 calories, 68% of calories from fat, 27g fat, 8g saturated fat, 85mg cholesterol, 2g carbohydrates, 27g protein, 309mg sodium, 1g fiber

SMOKY SENSATION: EASY, AGE-OLD TECHNIQUE YIELDS AN OUTDOOR FLAVOR

Long before electricity and gas burners, cooking was done over open fires. The smell and taste of smoke permeated every facet of life.

Nowadays, smoke is more of a nuisance, something to be dry cleaned from our clothes. Let's reclaim some of what we lost in our race to modernity.

STEPS TO FOLLOW

We'll focus on "hot smoking." Unlike "cold smoking"—a longer process that takes place at roughly room temperature—hot smoking cooks the food as it smokes. Some items, like salmon fillets, can be cooked to a perfect medium-rare in the time it takes to get a nice smoky flavor. Other items may need to finish cooking in a hot oven, a skillet or on the grill.

The smoker itself is little more than an enclosed container with a tight-fitting lid. Think of it as a steamer, only instead of an inch of water at the bottom of the pan you've got a handful of smoldering wood chips or some other fragrant fuel. You can purchase a bona fide "stovetop smoker" at kitchen-supply stores, or you can use a wok or any large cast-iron, stainless-steel or heavy-gauge aluminum pot with a lid. You also can use a disposable roasting pan and cover it with more foil. You might want to line your pot with foil to ease cleaning later.

1. Prepare your food: Meat, fish, vegetables—anything can be smoked. Have it prepped and ready before you turn on the stove. Often this means setting it in a marinade, brine or rub.

2. Prepare your smoker. (If you're using a commercial smoker, follow the manufacturer's instructions.) For a pot or disposable aluminum container, place four wadded balls of aluminum foil around the bottom. (If using a wok, you'll just need a circular wire rack that can rest a couple inches from the bottom.)

WHY YOU NEED TO LEARN IT

Smoke adds a dimension unattainable through conventional cooking methods. Though unfamiliar to most home cooks, stove-top smoking is an eminently accessible skill. If you share our love of all things smoky, it will make you very, very happy.

PUTTING YOUR SKILLS TO WORK

Smoked salmon fillets (pg. 113)
Smoked, grilled squash topped with tomato Parmesan (pg. 114)

SMOKY SENSATION: EASY, AGE-OLD TECHNIQUE YIELDS AN OUTDOOR FLAVOR *(continued)*

3. Turn on your ventilation hood, open some windows, or both. (There's no getting around it: Smoke is smoky, and your kitchen may retain some of the aromas for a day or two.) Alternately, you can do this outside on a grill. Set your smoker on the grate directly above the coals.

4. Mound a handful of wood chips on the bottom. Place smoker on the stove with the chips directly over the burner. Turn heat to high.

5. While the chips are heating up, get your food ready. If it's in a marinade, remove it and pat it dry. Place it in a single layer on a wire rack that fits the pan. Make sure the pieces are not touching each other.

6. When the chips start smoking, put the wire rack with the food atop the aluminum balls, making sure it's elevated a few inches. Cover the pan. If using a wok or pot, you can reduce the amount of escaping smoke by stretching aluminum foil across the open top. When you replace the lid, crimp the foil down over the sides. With the lid in place, reduce the heat to medium-low.

7. Smoke the food for the desired amount of time. Remember, the longer you leave the food in, the more it cooks and the more smoke flavor it absorbs.

SMOKED SALMON FILLETS

The marinade is an extra step that you can ignore if you're in a hurry. Or you can change or augment the marinade to suit your tastes. It won't affect the smoking time.

1. Whisk together the wine, soy sauce, brown sugar and mashed garlic in a medium bowl. Place salmon fillets in a large plastic bag; add the marinade. Seal the bag; shake to coat fillets. Refrigerate 1 hour.

2. Place 2 tablespoons of the wood chips on the bottom of smoker. Set uncovered smoker on burner over high heat. Remove salmon from marinade; pat dry. Season the fillets with salt and pepper to taste; place on smoking rack. When wood chips are smoking, place rack in smoker. Cover; turn heat to low. Smoke until salmon is medium-rare and flakes with a fork, about 15-20 minutes.

NUTRITION INFORMATION PER SERVING: 284 calories, 40% of calories from fat, 12.3g fat, 1.9g saturated fat, 107mg cholesterol, 1.9g carbohydrates, 39g protein, 502mg sodium, 0g fiber

PREP TIME: 10 MINUTES

MARINATING TIME: 1 HOUR

COOK TIME: 15-20 MINUTES

YIELD: 4 SERVINGS

2 tablespoons white wine

1 tablespoon soy sauce

1 tablespoon brown sugar

1 small clove garlic, mashed

4 salmon fillets, about 6 ounces each

2 tablespoons mesquite or other hardwood chips

½ teaspoon coarse salt

Freshly ground pepper

SMOKED, GRILLED SQUASH TOPPED WITH TOMATO PARMESAN

A student of mine, Brian Ward, made these in class. They were outstanding, and I asked Brian to share his recipe. Grilling the squash is optional.

PREP TIME: 20 MINUTES

COOK TIME: 15 MINUTES

YIELD: 4 SERVINGS

2 zucchini or yellow squash, sliced lengthwise into about four ¼-inch slices

2 small plum tomatoes, diced

2 tablespoons freshly grated Parmesan cheese

2 tablespoons olive oil

¼ cup minced red onion

1 tablespoon fresh, minced basil

1 tablespoon fresh, minced chives

½ teaspoon salt

¼ to 1 teaspoon ground red pepper, optional

1. Heat grill or grill pan over medium-high heat; grill squash until grill marks form, about 1 minute per side.

2. Combine the tomatoes, cheese, oil, onion, basil, chives, salt and ground red pepper in a small bowl; spoon mixture onto grilled squash.

3. Place squash on a rack in a stove-top smoker; smoke over low heat until squash is just tender, about 10 minutes.

NUTRITION INFORMATION PER SERVING: 87 calories, 78% of calories from fat, 7.8g fat, 1.6g saturated fat, 2.5mg cholesterol, 2.9g carbohydrates, 1.9g protein, 295mg sodium, 0.7g fiber

TO BRINE IS DIVINE: A SIMPLE SOAK LOCKS MOISTURE AND FLAVOR INTO LEAN MEATS

If you've eaten corned beef, you've eaten brined meat. Traditionally, brining—soaking in a salt solution—was used as a preservative in those dark centuries before electricity. With today's electrical appliances keeping our food well chilled or frozen, brining is primarily a flavor enhancer.

WHY YOU NEED TO LEARN IT

It's too easy to overcook meat to an unpleasant dryness, especially lean meats such as pork chops or chicken breasts. Also, even when the outside is salted, the interior of the meat often seems bland and unseasoned.

Brining solves both of these problems through the bothersome miracles of science. (Discussions biological and chemical still knot my stomach just like they did in high school, so I'll try to make this painless for all of us.)

First, brining makes cooked meat juicier. The brine solution contains more moisture than is found naturally inside the meat cells. Placing meat in the solution, then, causes it to soak up the liquid, not unlike a sponge. Since meat loses up to 30 percent of its moisture during cooking, this additional liquid can make a big difference in the finished product. In fact, brining can reduce total moisture loss by half.

As for the problem of seasoning, remember that the brine solution is very salty while the interior of the meat is not. Through a process called "osmosis" (here's where my stomach starts to tighten), the salt in the solution passes through the cell walls of the meat until the fluid on the inside of the cells has the same amount of salt as the fluid on the outside. Thus, the inside of the meat gets seasoned, and every bite is delicious through and through.

PUTTING YOUR SKILLS TO WORK

Spiced, brined pork chops with dried fruit sauce (pg. 118) .

STEPS TO FOLLOW

Brining times depend upon the size of the items being brined. Smaller things like shrimp or pork chops go rather quickly, in an hour or less, while larger items—whole turkeys, for example—may take an entire day or more.

1. Figure out how much solution to make: Place your meat in a non-reactive container (plastic, glass, stainless steel or even a large plastic bag) and add water to cover. Remove meat and measure the amount of water. That's the amount of brining solution you'll need.

2. Figure about ¼ cup of regular table salt per quart of water. Some people include other ingredients as well, such as spices or fruit juices. Many recipes call for sugar, which encourages browning of the meat during cooking.

3. To make the brine, dissolve the salt (and any other soluble ingredients like sugar) in as small an amount of hot water as you can (photo 1). Once it is dissolved, add the remainder of the cold water and stir to dissolve the salt.

4. Put whatever you're brining directly into the cold solution (photo 2). Cover it with plastic wrap; place in the refrigerator. Food safety rules demand that brining be done below 40 degrees.

5. Figure on about two hours per pound. Remember, you're going by the weight of the individual pieces, not by the total. If your pork chops weigh about ½ pound each, brine all of them together for about an hour. One 12-pound turkey, on the other hand, would need 24 hours.

6. Remove items from brine and pat dry. If you're brining whole birds or skin-on pieces, you may want to set them, uncovered, on a rack in the refrigerator for several hours to allow the skin to dry completely. This will produce a crisp skin when you cook it.

Photo 1

Photo 2

SPICED, BRINED PORK CHOPS WITH DRIED FRUIT SAUCE

These flavorful chops with the sweet and tangy sauce go great with simple couscous and a green salad. You also can substitute a whole pork tenderloin for the chops; just roast it at 425 degrees for about 20 minutes.

PREP TIME: 10 MINUTES

BRINING TIME: 1 HOUR

COOK TIME: 16 MINUTES

YIELD: 4 SERVING

4 brined pork loin chops, about 8 ounces each, see note

1 tablespoon paprika

1 teaspoon ground cumin

1 teaspoon coriander

1 teaspoon ground pepper

1 teaspoon garlic powder

½ teaspoon ground cinnamon

¼ teaspoon ground cloves

¼ teaspoon allspice

1 cup red wine vinegar

¼ cup sugar

¼ cup chopped dried fruit such as cherries, raisins

1 tablespoon butter

Couscous, cooked according to package directions

1. Heat broiler or grill. Remove pork chops from brine; dry thoroughly with paper towels. Combine paprika, cumin, coriander, pepper, garlic powder, cinnamon, cloves and allspice in a small bowl. Rub enough spice mixture onto both sides of chops to coat evenly; set aside.

2. Stir together the vinegar, sugar and dried fruit in a medium saucepan over high heat; cook until syrupy, about 4 minutes.

3. Meanwhile, broil or grill pork chops to medium, about 6 minutes per side. Remove from heat; set aside 5 minutes. Remove sauce from heat; whisk butter into the sauce.

4. Place a small mound of couscous in the center of each plate; lean a pork chop against it. Drizzle sauce around the plate.

Note: To brine pork chops, dissolve ¼ cup of salt and ¼ cup sugar in 1 cup of hot water. Pour into a non-reactive container. Add 3 more cups of cold water. Place pork chops in brine; cover. Refrigerate 1 hour.

NUTRITION INFORMATION PER SERVING: 447 calories, 47% of calories from fat, 23g fat, 9g saturated fat, 127mg cholesterol, 21g carbohydrates, 37g protein, 719mg sodium, 3g fiber

RUNNING HOT AND COLD: BLANCHING AND SHOCKING SERVE MANY KITCHEN NEEDS

Blanching refers to a quick cooking in liquid, most often water. Usually the water is boiling before the items are immersed. I love this type of blanching (the type discussed here) for fresh vegetables like green beans, asparagus, broccoli or cauliflower. It's also great for loosening the skins of stone fruits or tomatoes, making for easy peeling.

Another blanching method starts in cold water that then is brought to a quick boil. Pork ribs, for example, are blanched in this fashion to remove excess fat and impurities before roasting or barbecuing.

A third type of blanching refers to a preliminary cooking in oil before the final prep at service time. French fries may be blanched in oil until limp, then cooled and held until they're deep-fried to a golden brown.

Shocking is the aptly named technique in which a food, immediately after blanching, is plunged into an ice bath.

WHY YOU NEED TO LEARN IT

Blanching is helpful when peeling tomatoes but also, as in this lesson, is perfect for prepping vegetables in advance. Once they're blanched and shocked, vegetables can be held for several days in the refrigerator, then warmed quickly in butter or oil at mealtime or eaten cold in salads or appetizers.

One other concept we should address, by the way, is called "carryover cooking." An item cooks, whether in the oven, in water or on the stove top, from the outside in. When it's removed from the heat source, the heat on the outside of the item continues flowing to the inside, "carrying over" the cooking. This is why the interior temperature of a roast rises 5 to 10 degrees after it is removed from the oven. It also is why we shock vegetables after they're blanched to the perfect degree of doneness. Otherwise, they can overcook while sitting in the colander.

PUTTING YOUR SKILLS TO WORK

Green beans Provencale
(pg. 125)

STEPS TO FOLLOW

Blanching

1. Heat a large pot of water to a boil. Because the immersion of cold vegetables will cool down the water, the more veggies you have, the more water you'll need. Ideally, the water should return to boiling within seconds. Lowering the water temperature too much will slow the cooking and may have an adverse effect on the color and texture of the vegetables.

2. When the water reaches a rolling boil, add a generous amount of salt. Harold McGee, author of the seminal "On Food and Cooking: The Science and Lore of the Kitchen," suggests two tablespoons of table salt (or three to four tablespoons of kosher salt) per quart of water. This sounds like a lot, but you want the water to taste like the ocean (most of that salt will not be absorbed by the vegetables and therefore will not lead to high sodium content).

3. Add the vegetables (photo 1). Don't cover the pot, especially with green vegetables. Acids leech from the vegetables into the water as they cook. If the pot is covered, these acids return to the water as the steam condenses on the lid. Increased acidity contributes to that awful olive color that plagues overcooked green vegetables.

Photo 1

RUNNING HOT AND COLD *(continued)*

4. Remove the vegetables when they're al dente, literally "to the tooth." An al dente vegetable, while very definitely cooked out of its raw stage, still has a bit of a bite; it's firm, not mushy. If you're planning on reusing the blanching liquid—either for more vegetables or perhaps for pasta—remove the finished vegetables with a metal spoon, tongs or a skimmer. Otherwise, pour the entire contents into a colander.

Shocking

5. While the vegetables are blanching, prepare an ice bath: Fill a large bowl halfway with ice, then fill the bowl with cold water.

6. Add the drained vegetables to the ice bath (photo 2). Press them down to submerge them. The idea is to stop the cooking immediately.

7. When the vegetables have chilled—this will take several minutes—remove them to a dry towel, then set them aside until ready to use.

Photo 2

GREEN BEANS PROVENCALE

Blanch your beans beforehand and this delicious dish can be prepared in less than 10 minutes. Substitute other vegetables—asparagus, cauliflower, fresh peas—for easy variations.

1. Place the oil and garlic in a large skillet over medium-high heat. Cook, stirring, just until the garlic begins to become aromatic, about 30-60 seconds; stir in the tomatoes. Cook, stirring, until tomatoes are just softened, about 30 seconds.

2. Add the beans; toss with the tomatoes and garlic. Cook until beans are just warmed through, about 2 minutes. Season with salt and pepper to taste. Toss with fresh herbs.

NUTRITION INFORMATION PER SERVING: 54 calories, 36% of calories from fat, 2g fat, 0.3g saturated fat, 0mg cholesterol, 8g carbohydrates, 2g protein, 198mg sodium, 4g fiber

PREP TIME: 15 MINUTES

COOK TIME: 10 MINUTES

YIELD: 6 SERVINGS

1 tablespoon olive oil

2 cloves garlic, minced

4 tomatoes, peeled, seeded, chopped, or ½ pint cherry or grape tomatoes, halved or quartered

1 pound green beans, blanched, shocked

½ teaspoon salt

Freshly ground pepper

1 tablespoon minced fresh basil and thyme or other combination of fresh herbs

FRENCH ELEGANCE, ON THE DOUBLE

Fillets of fish a la meuniere: The name for this beautiful presentation probably refers to the flour in which the fish is dredged before sauteing. La meuniere means "the miller's wife."

The preparation can be used with whole fish or steaks, but attains another level of perfection altogether with simple fillets. Sole would be very French, very traditional, but any thin fillet would be lovely.

WHY YOU SHOULD LEARN IT

This is a dish that helped change the course of American cookery. On Nov. 3, 1948, Julia Child and her husband, Paul, just off the boat from America, stopped for a typically French lunch on their way to Paris. According to Child's biographer, Noel Riley Fitch, the meal they enjoyed included sole a la meuniere. Child, until then a rather uninspired home cook, later remarked of that repast, "The whole experience was an opening up of the soul and spirit for me. ... I was hooked, and for life, as it has turned out."

Also, the dish is easy, elegant and delicious. Total time from preparation to table is about 10 minutes.

STEPS TO FOLLOW

1. Heat a large skillet or saute pan over medium heat. Toss in 1 tablespoon or so of clarified butter or oil to heat.

2. Meanwhile, season 1 or 2 fillets of fish per person with salt and pepper. Coat with flour. Shake the excess flour from the fillets.

3. Place fillets bone side down in the pan (photo 1). Cook the fillets until golden brown, about 1-2 minutes, depending on the thickness.

4. Use a fish or regular spatula to flip each fillet very carefully in the pan (photo 2) so that the bone side—which is the presentation side—is now up. The second side requires less cooking time; as soon as it's browned, remove fillets to a plate.

5. Discard the fat in the pan and toss in 2 tablespoons of whole butter. While it melts, sprinkle the fish generously with chopped fresh parsley.

▶

Photo 1

Photo 2

FRENCH ELEGANCE, ON THE DOUBLE *(continued)*

6. When the butter has turned a lovely nut brown color (called beurre noisette) (photo 3), pour it over the fish (photo 4). You'll hear the parsley crackle beneath the hot fat. Now, squeeze some fresh lemon over it and ... wow, this is so good. Yum.

Plating idea

Place a mound of rice in the center of the plate. Lean the fish against the rice. Top with the parsley, beurre noisette and lemon. Serve with something green, like fresh green beans.

To make clarified butter

Melt 2 sticks of butter in a saucepan over low heat. Let it cook gently 20-30 minutes, until the solids have fallen to the bottom and are just beginning to turn a little brown. Strain the liquid through cheesecloth into a container. It will keep in the refrigerator for weeks.

A last note

Skinless fillets are typically served "bone-side up" and "skin-side down." The skin side is flatter and can be identified by a series of slanted lines running to the edge from the center of the fillets, like branches on a Christmas tree. The bone side tends to have a bit more topography to it and more elevation.

Photo 3

Photo 4

DON'T FEAR THE MUSSELS: CLEANING, COOKING THESE TASTY BIVALVES IS A SNAP

A number of years ago I found myself in Galway, on the west coast of Ireland. Every night, a gentleman would make the rounds among that city's dozens of pubs toting trays of mussels, fresh from Galway Bay, steamed and shucked into small paper cups. After a night of Guinness, a couple of cups of mussels at a pound a pop seemed just the thing.

STEPS TO FOLLOW

Mussels are so easy to prepare that most of what we're going over here is the steps leading up to cooking.

Storing and cleaning

1. Refrigerate mussels as soon as you get them home. Store them in a self-draining, breathable container, never in water; we need to keep them alive until we cook them. They'll keep this way for two to three days.

2. Just before cooking, rinse the mussels under cold running water. If they're gritty, scrub them with a brush (photo 1, next page). Discard any with broken or cracked shells. Mussels that feel unusually heavy are probably filled with mud and should be tossed. Tap any whose shells are open with a knife. If the shell closes, the mussel is alive and therefore good. Discard any that won't close.

Now, many cookbooks and chefs alike advocate soaking mussels in tap water for an hour or so before cooking. The idea is that they'll take in the clean water and eject any sand or grit that's hiding inside their shells. Some sources suggest adding flour, cornstarch or cornmeal to the water to encourage the purging. Others suggest these additions will fatten the mussels or whiten their flesh in the process.

However, knowing that mussels are ocean creatures, and me being generally suspicious anyway, I decided to consult three

WHY YOU NEED TO LEARN IT

Mussels are too much the rarity in home kitchens. After all, they're relatively inexpensive; they're lean and loaded with more heart-healthy omega-3 fatty acids than any other shellfish; plus, with their shells agape, bathed in a bowl of steaming broth, they're as visually arresting as they are delicious.

PUTTING YOUR SKILLS TO WORK

Stout mussels (pg. 132)

DON'T FEAR THE MUSSELS *(continued)*

experts: two marine biologists and one "seafood technology specialist." All three agreed that tap water is the mussel's enemy. At best, the mussel will simply shut its shell, precluding any purging; at worst, it will drown.

While one expert said that mussels soaked in fresh sea water (hard to come by here in the Midwest) will purge themselves of some grit, the other two agreed that farm-raised mussels (and commercially available mussels are nearly all farm-raised) are relatively clean to begin with and don't need purging.

My conclusion: Don't soak. Just rinse, and hope for the best.

3. Remove the thin, stringy strands emerging from the flat side of the mussel. This is the byssal thread, commonly called the "beard." Mussels use it to attach themselves to rocks.

Pinch the beard between your thumb and a knife blade and pull it out (photo 2). If it is too slippery, grab it with a clean, damp towel.

Cooking

4. The simplest way to cook mussels is by steaming: In a covered 4- or 5-quart saucepan, heat to a boil a cup or so of flavorful liquid: beer, wine, fish stock or clam juice. Add some aromatic vegetables (onions, garlic, etc.) or herbs and spices (thyme, bay leaf, etc.). Simmer the liquid for a couple minutes to reduce it and meld the flavors, then add your mussels (photo 3).

Plan on about a pound of mussels per person for an entree, or half a pound for an appetizer. The mussels are done when the shells open. This takes only a few minutes, though it's hard to predict exactly.

5. Remove the mussels and attend to the cooking liquid. You can enrich it by whisking in butter or cream. Also, you can thicken it by whisking in a small amount of beurre manie (equal parts of softened butter and flour mashed into a smooth paste) and heating it to a quick boil. Always taste for seasoning.

6. When the cooking liquid is ready, pour it over the mussels. Serve them with plenty of good, crusty bread for sopping up the flavorful broth.

Photo 1

Photo 2

Photo 3

DON'T SOAK THE MUSSELS. JUST RINSE, AND HOPE FOR THE BEST.

STOUT MUSSELS

The Irish eat like this year-round. Serve with Irish brown bread or any crusty loaf.

PREP TIME: 30 MINUTES

COOK TIME: 17 MINUTES

YIELD: 4 APPETIZER SERVINGS

---

4 to 6 slices bacon, cut into ½-inch pieces

---

1 leek, white part only, chopped

---

2 cloves garlic, minced

---

1 bottle (12 ounces) stout beer

---

1 bay leaf

½ teaspoon dried thyme or 1 teaspoon minced fresh thyme

---

2 pounds mussels, scrubbed, beards removed

---

2 tablespoons cold, un-salted butter

½ teaspoon salt

Freshly ground pepper

---

1 teaspoon fresh lemon juice

---

1. Cook bacon, stirring often, in a Dutch oven over medium heat until crisp, about 5 minutes. Transfer to a paper towel to drain; discard all but 2 tablespoons of fat from the pan.

2. Add leeks to the Dutch oven. Cook, stirring occasionally, until vegetables are limp, about 4 minutes. Add the garlic; cook, stirring, until fragrant, about 30 seconds.

3. Add the beer, bay leaf and thyme; heat to a boil over high heat. Reduce the heat to a simmer; cook 2 minutes. Add mussels; cover. Cook, stirring once halfway through cooking, until all shells are open, about 5 minutes.

4. Turn off heat; transfer the mussels with a slotted spoon to 4 shallow bowls. Whisk the cold butter into the liquid in the Dutch oven; season with salt, pepper to taste and a few drops of lemon juice. Pour over mussels in bowls; garnish with reserved bacon.

NUTRITION INFORMATION PER SERVING: 232 calories, 47% of calories from fat, 12g fat, 5g saturated fat, 64mg cholesterol, 9g carbohydrates, 21g protein, 719mg sodium, 0.5g fiber

CIY (CURE IT YOURSELF): YOU CAN BUY CORNED BEEF, SURE. BUT WHEN YOU MAKE IT AT HOME, YOU WON'T BELIEVE THE FLAVOR AND TEXTURE

Maybe you love a good Reuben sandwich. Or, maybe you just can't wait for St. Paddy's Day because of the excellent pub fare. Whatever your obsession, you ought to consider making your own corned beef.

STEPS TO FOLLOW

Corning is a centuries-old method for preserving meat. (The name comes from an older meaning of "corn," which referred to any grain, and the "corn"-size pieces of salt used in the process.) Of course, what with the discovery of electricity a few short centuries ago and its resultant use in keeping foods cold, there's not much call these days for preserving food in this way.

Still, methods that were used primarily for preservation also resulted in extremely palatable products, and today these methods are employed as much for flavor and texture as they are for preservation.

The process for corning beef is pretty simple: Dissolve some salt along with a handful of other ingredients in water, then completely submerge your meat—typically beef brisket—and leave it in the fridge for a few days. When it's done, you have corned beef. All you need to do is simmer it in water for about three hours, and you're good to go.

Before you try it, though, there are two processes you should understand: curing and brining.

Curing: Consists of covering meat completely in salt for a period of time. Because salt attracts water, it draws moisture from the meat, concentrating the flavors and leaving the meat too dry for bacteria to thrive. At the same time, the salt clinging to meat cells disrupts the metabolic action of any foreign bacteria that happen along, preventing the meat from spoiling.

WHY YOU NEED TO LEARN IT

Corning beef is easy as pie, and the resulting taste and texture will be far superior to most commercial varieties. Plus, it will put you in touch with your human forebears while teaching you something about science.

PUTTING YOUR SKILLS TO WORK

Homemade corned beef (pg. 137)
Cooked corned beef (pg. 138)

CIY (CURE IT YOURSELF) *(continued)*

Along with salt, cures can include sugar and spices for flavor as well as a mixture of sodium nitrite and salt called "tinted curing mixture" (TCM)—aka "pink salt" or "curing salt." TCM is available online or in restaurant supply stores under names like Prague Powder, Insta-Cure or Morton's Curing Salt. It prevents the growth of the bacteria that cause botulism. It also provides flavor and gives corned beef its distinctive red color rather than have it turn a dismal gray.

(Granted, overconsumption of nitrates has been linked to cancer, but we use a relatively tiny amount when curing.)

Brining: Involves soaking meat in a saltwater solution. When meat is placed in the solution, the amount of water and salt inside the meat is less than that in the solution. It is the nature of the universe that, wherever this happens, the salt and water in the meat and in the solution want to even themselves out, to form an equilibrium. Through natural processes called osmosis and diffusion, the water in the solution is carried into the meat along with the salt, nitrites and flavorings. The increased water makes the meat juicier as the salt seasons it inside and out. The salt and nitrites provide a hostile environment for illness-causing microbes.

Injecting: If you have a meat injector (they're available online for about 10 bucks), you can inject the brine into the meat before submerging. To do so, place brisket inside a large bowl. Working around entire perimeter of meat, inject brine horizontally into side of brisket at 2-inch intervals. While this step is not absolutely necessary, it does allow for greater penetration of the solution throughout the meat.

TAKE THE CURE

Once you have a handle on the process, here are a few tips, courtesy of my colleague Pierre Checchi, chef-instructor at Kendall College, who supplied us with the recipes.

- Always start with a proven recipe (such as the one here). Preserving meats, especially when using nitrites, is not conducive to guesswork.

- Distilled water is better than tap water.

- When using nitrites, boil the water with all of the brine ingredients except the nitrites. When the brine cools, add the nitrites.

- Get about 5 pounds of brisket, the thinner the better to make the brine work more quickly. Cut the brisket in half, if you want.

- Make sure meat is completely covered in brine. Use a zip-close bag or some other non-reactive container.

HOMEMADE CORNED BEEF

Adapted from a recipe by chef Pierre Checchi. Look for 2-gallon zip-close plastic bags, or use a large, nonreactive container.

1. Puree garlic and 1 cup water in blender. In a large pot, add puree, remaining water, salt, dextrose, pickling spice and peppercorns (photo 1). Heat to a boil; remove from heat. Stir to dissolve salt and dextrose. Cool to room temperature; cool in refrigerator. Stir TCM into cold brine to dissolve.

2. Place brisket in a sealable plastic bag large enough to hold it and brine. Add brine to bag, making sure brisket is submerged.

3. Place bag inside a large bowl; refrigerate 4 or 5 days. Check periodically to make sure meat is submerged. Flip in brine as needed to ensure complete coverage.

4. When beef is ready, remove from brine, discarding brine. Rinse, pat dry and cook in simmering water (see following recipe).

Note: Dextrose, aka glucose, is a simple sugar commonly available in health-food stores and brewing supply companies. You may use granulated sugar.

PREP TIME: 15 MINUTES

COOK TIME: 10 MINUTES

CHILL: 3 HOURS

CURE: 4-5 DAYS

---

4 cloves garlic, minced

1 gallon water

11 ounces kosher salt

3½ ounces dextrose, see note

½ tablespoon pickling spice

¾ tablespoon whole black peppercorns

1½ ounces TCM (pink salt)

1 piece (5 pound) brisket, fat trimmed to ¼-inch, cut in half

Photo 1

COOKED CORNED BEEF

Adapted from a recipe by chef Pierre Checchi.

PREP TIME: 20 MINUTES

COOK TIME: 3 HOURS

YIELD: ABOUT 9 CUPS

½ pound carrots, peeled, cut into ¼-inch rounds

4 ribs celery, roughly chopped

1 large onion, roughly chopped

½ head garlic (cut horizontally into 2 pieces, use top or bottom)

½ cup pickling spice

1 piece (5 pounds) corned beef

1. Combine all ingredients in a large stockpot; cover with cold water. Heat to a boil; reduce heat. Simmer until meat is tender, about 3 hours. Serve immediately or cool in liquid overnight.

BATHED IN SIMPLICITY: THE BAIN-MARIE IS AN OLD SCHOOL TECHNIQUE TO HEAT FOOD WITHOUT SCORCHING

Even if you have never heard the term before, chances are you have used a bain-marie (bahn mah-REE). Though it comes in many forms, it's basically a container filled with hot water that is used to heat another, smaller container that's placed in or above the water.

Like the double boiler in which you melt chocolate.

Or the water bath in which you bake your cheesecakes.

We'll show you how to improvise a bain-marie quickly and easily. Along with the aforementioned applications, they're terrific for keeping the heat in temperamental foods like sauces and mashed potatoes.

WHY YOU NEED TO LEARN IT

One difficulty in cooking is heat regulation: It's too easy to burn stuff.

However, because water evaporates at 212 degrees, anything inside a bain-marie cannot get any hotter than 212. Plus, because water is a great conductor of heat—much better than air—you can be assured that anything cooked in a bain-marie will be subject to an even temperature.

One more thing I love about the bain-marie is that, in this age of microwaves and electronic ovens, the bain-marie is so old school. It's a pan of hot water. How simple is that? (In fact, it's so totally old school that the name, 'Mary's bath,' comes from alchemy. It's a reference to Moses' sister, who supposedly was an alchemist.)

STEPS TO FOLLOW

Instructions for double boilers and water baths usually are given in recipes, so I won't focus on those. Instead, I'll show you how to improvise a quick bain-marie out of pots and bowls in your own kitchen. This is the best way to keep sauces and mashed potatoes warm. It's also what you would use to make a hollandaise or bearnaise, where too much heat can turn your sauce into scrambled eggs.

The only things you'll need are a saucepan and a metal bowl to set on top. Using a bowl with sloping sides will allow it to nestle snugly into the saucepan.

Now, watch how simple this is.

1. Fill the saucepan with water about a quarter to a third of the way full. Heat the water to a boil, then reduce the heat. You want to keep the water just hot enough so that it continues to evaporate, but not so hot that it's at a rolling boil. It's pretty much just like you would use a steamer.

2. Set the bowl on top of the saucepan. Make sure that the bottom of the bowl is above the water so that the steam heats all surfaces equally.

And there's your bain-marie.

The one thing you want to avoid is allowing the flames to come up around the saucepan to heat the bowl directly. When that happens, the bowl can get so hot that the food inside scorches.

To keep mashed potatoes (or rice or couscous or other starches) warm, simply place them into the bowl as soon as you make them so that they're still piping hot. Cover the bowl with plastic wrap, and make sure the wrap creates a tight seal. Stir the potatoes occasionally to distribute the heat throughout and also to prevent them from drying out where they come into contact with the bowl.

If you're making a hollandaise or bearnaise, hold the bowl with a dry towel or hot pad, and move it on and off the bain-marie. The eggs in the sauce will coagulate at a much lower temperature than the 212 degree limit of the bain-marie; this means you want the steam to warm the bowl extra gently, pulling the bowl off when it approaches the coagulation point. This, of course, takes practice. But, really, doesn't everything?

POACHING PERFECTION: UNDERUSED TECHNIQUE BRINGS OUT THE BEST IN MANY FRUITS

Now that fall is falling, and we can once again stand the thought of heating up our kitchens, we're going to poach some fruit. For some of you, this may seem somewhat unappealing—and believe me, I've gotten my share of odd looks when ordering poached fruit for dessert while my companions scarfed down chocolates and cake.

But trust me, and try it just once.

WHY YOU NEED TO LEARN IT

Poached fruit is so easy to make, so beautiful to behold, so marvelous in flavor and texture, you will, upon creating your first wonderful batch, begin striking yourself in the forehead, cursing yourself for not having enjoyed this treat before. It is perfection by itself—served in its poaching liquid—and it's perhaps even better alongside ice cream. Slice it and layer it onto custards and tarts, or better yet, serve it alongside flavorful meats such as duck, pork or game as a sumptuous, savory accompaniment.

PUTTING YOUR SKILLS TO WORK

Simple poached pears (pg. 146)

STEPS TO FOLLOW

The most common poaching fruits are pears and apples, but literally anything can be poached: peaches, plums, pineapples, cherries—anything you like. Whether or not you adore the final product is simply a matter of taste.

A lot of chefs like slightly underripe fruit for poaching because it can hold its shape better. Sugar in the poaching liquid also will protect against mushiness.

One important thing to remember is that the word "poaching" refers generally to things cooked in a liquid that is between 160 and 180 degrees, well below the boiling point of 212 degrees. The reason we poach fruit rather than boil it is that at that low temperature, the water does not roil about, bashing the fruit into mush; rather, it bathes the fruit in warmth, gently cooking it to a tasty and toothsome tenderness.

Another thing to remember is that the fruit will take on the flavors and color of the poaching liquid.

1. Cut a piece of parchment paper to fit snugly on the inside of your poaching pan. This will act as a malleable lid which keeps your poaching fruit submerged, resulting in a product that is evenly cooked and colored (an important consideration when you're poaching in red wine).

Photo 1

Photo 2

POACHING PERFECTION *(continued)*

2. Heat the poaching liquid to a boil. This can be anything: simple syrup (sugar and water), white or red wine, juice or some combination thereof. The amount of poaching liquid you'll need will vary with the amount of fruit, the size of the pan, etc. Regardless, you'll want the fruit to fit into the pan comfortably, without crowding, with the liquid covering it completely.

Also, remember that you can flavor the liquid with additional ingredients: Vanilla, cinnamon and lemon zest are fairly standard, but imagine giving things a more exotic or savory note with whole peppercorns, cumin, cardamom, even fresh or dried chilies. The possibilities are endless.

3. Prepare your fruit. Most often, but not always, this requires peeling. Fruit can be left whole or cut into halves or even smaller portions. If fruit is poached whole, you'll probably want to remove the core and seeds before serving.

4. Add the fruit to the boiling liquid and reduce the heat to low. You want just the barest amount of movement in the liquid—perhaps a few bubbles on the side of the pan or the odd bubble rising from the center.

5. Cover the fruit with the parchment paper (photo 1, previous page) and poach until done. The amount of time you will need depends on the variety, size and ripeness of the fruit. Some fruits can be done in as little as 5 minutes, while others will take 30 minutes or more.

6. The fruit is done when a sharp knife pushes easily into the flesh (photo 2). When it's ready, turn off the heat and let the fruit cool in the poaching liquid.

7. The poaching liquid may be reserved and used again to poach more items, or it can be reduced to a syrupy consistency and used as a sauce. Make sure you taste the sauce and adjust its seasoning and flavoring as needed.

SIMPLE POACHED PEARS

PREP TIME: 10 MINUTES

COOK TIME: 30 MINUTES

YIELD: 6 SERVINGS

2 cups red wine

2 cups water

1 cup sugar

2 sticks cinnamon

1 teaspoon vanilla

Zest of ½ lemon

6 pears, peeled

1. Combine the wine, water, sugar, cinnamon sticks, vanilla and lemon zest in a Dutch oven; heat to a boil over high heat. Add pears to the poaching liquid; reduce heat to medium-low. If the pears are not completely submerged, add boiling water to cover. Cover pears with a circle of parchment paper; poach until easily pierced, about 30-40 minutes.

2. Turn off heat; let pears cool in the liquid. Serve at room temperature or chilled, whole or cut in half and cored. If desired, heat poaching liquid to a boil; boil until reduced to about 1 cup. Strain the liquid; pour over pears.

NUTRITION INFORMATION PER SERVING: 230 calories, 1% of calories from fat, 0.2g fat, 0g saturated fat, 0mg cholesterol, 59g carbohydrates, 1g protein, 2mg sodium, 5g fiber

FRICASSEE ELEVATES HUMBLE CHICKEN

Statistically speaking, each and every American man, woman and child is responsible for the slaughter of 30 chickens every year. If that thought bothers you, perhaps this topic is not for you. If, on the other hand, it merely produces drooling daydreams of dinners to come, then, my friends, I give you the fricassee.

WHY YOU NEED TO LEARN IT

Fricassees produce meats that are fall-apart tender. With its luxurious finish of cream and optional egg yolk, the sauce has a beautiful ivory hue and a silken texture. This is great company food, but it's also easy enough for a simple family meal.

STEPS TO FOLLOW

Fricassees are most commonly associated with Southern cooking and French cuisine. Here, we'll focus on the French, simply because it is more generally singular in its approach. While the French fricassee is most often considered to be chicken or other white meat simmered in a white sauce, the term in American cookery has been expanded to include just about any form of chicken stew.

The method below is based on that of the father of French classical cuisine, Auguste Escoffier, the original Mr. Know-It-All as far as cooking is concerned. Dedicated Child-o-philes will also recognize a nod to Julia in the mushroom and pearl onion garnish.

For this method, we'll use a 3- to 4-pound chicken cut into eight to 10 pieces (two drumsticks, two thighs, two wings and two breasts that may be cut in half if you like). If you're no stranger to the cute meats, you can also substitute a couple pounds of veal stew meat or even a whole, cut up rabbit.

1. Cut a medium onion into small dice. Melt 2 ounces butter in a large, straight-sided skillet over medium heat. When the foam has subsided (meaning the water has evaporated from the butter), add the onions and cook until they become limp and translucent and exude some moisture.

2. Season the chicken pieces with salt and white pepper and lay them in the pan. Cook them just long enough so that the meat stiffens a bit and loses its translucence but doesn't begin to brown (photo 1). (Remember, this is a white dish.) If you like, add a clove or three of minced garlic and cook it for 30 to 40 seconds. Remove chicken to a plate.

Photo 1

Photo 2

3. Sprinkle everything left in the pan with 2 ounces (about 5 tablespoons) flour and stir to combine it with the fat (photo 2). This creates a roux that will thicken the sauce. Cook this for a couple of minutes, stirring.

4. Add about half a cup white wine and a quart of chicken stock or packaged, low-sodium chicken broth. Whisk or stir the liquid to dissolve the roux. Return chicken to the pan. Increase the heat to bring the liquid to a boil, then reduce the heat. Add a bay leaf, a couple pinches dried thyme and a few sprigs parsley. Simmer 30 to 45 minutes. Prick a thigh to the bone and if the juice runs clear, you're good to go.

▶

FRICASSEE ELEVATES HUMBLE CHICKEN *(continued)*

5. Remove the chicken to a warm plate and pass the sauce through a fine sieve. Whisk two egg yolks with a quarter cup whipping cream in a medium-size bowl and whisk a little of the hot sauce slowly into the cream mixture. This will bring up the temperature of the cream mixture without scrambling the egg yolks. When you've whisked about a cup of sauce into the cream mixture, whisk that back into the sauce.

Note: Omit the yolks if you want. They enrich and thicken the sauce, but they're not necessary.

6. Return the sauce and chicken to a clean saucepan. Reheat slowly until the sauce is hot but not boiling. Adjust the seasoning if necessary.

7. While you're reheating the chicken, you can add cooked mushrooms and pearl onions (photo 3). For the mushrooms, simmer up to a pound of mushrooms in a covered pan in half an inch of water, a knob of butter and a squeeze of lemon juice. You can cook peeled pearl onions the same way, though they'll take more than half an hour as opposed to just a few minutes for the mushrooms. Both of them can be cooked a couple of days in advance.

8. Serve the chicken and sauce with buttered noodles or rice pilaf accompanied by a green vegetable or simple salad.

Photo 3

FRENCHING 101: TECHNIQUE DRESSES UP PORK CHOPS FOR FANCIER DINING

The term "pork chops" doesn't really conjure images of haute cuisine. It's more of simple midweek dinner or family barbecue. No doubt it's because there's no real way to eat pork chops efficiently without picking them up, and that requires getting your hands dirty and greasy. And unfortunately, dirty, greasy hands and haute cuisine do not a happy marriage make.

Ah, but if the bones on the chops have been "frenched" by having all the meat, fat and assorted other bits scraped off, they can be picked up gracefully and gnawed (which, as any stickler for etiquette must allow, is acceptable behavior).

STEPS TO FOLLOW

Start by getting out your paring knife or a small boning knife.

We'll be using a pork rib chop, but you can do this just as easily with lamb or veal chops. (The basics of this technique can be used on chicken wings as well: You can create mini-chicken legs called "drumettes" or "lollipops" out of the wing halves or, by leaving the cleaned and scraped drumette bone attached to the breast, you create what's called an "airline breast.")

When choosing your chops, I'd suggest getting them fresh from the meat counter rather than prepackaged from the meat case: Not all chops are the same, and not all butchering is perfect. Choose chops that have a prominent and uncracked bone. For frenching to be effective, you've got to start with nice materials.

1. Choose the spot on the bone at which you would like to trim. Remember that there's no "right spot." You can trim just an inch or so from the end of the bone, leaving the rest of the chop intact. Alternately, you can get rid of everything but the main piece of meat, called the "eye." This will look terrific, but of course you'll be trimming off more of the meat. But you can chop or grind that meat and use it for a meat loaf, stir-fry or delicious Bolognese sauce.

WHY YOU NEED TO LEARN IT

Frenching creates a very elegant presentation. The little bone handle, scraped free of meat, turns a beautiful burnt-ivory color during cooking. It looks terrific and it gives you a dry, mess-free handle to grab should you want to pick up the chop to get the last couple of succulent bites.

And besides, what more appropriately scary way could there be to celebrate Halloween than by scraping the meat off some bones?

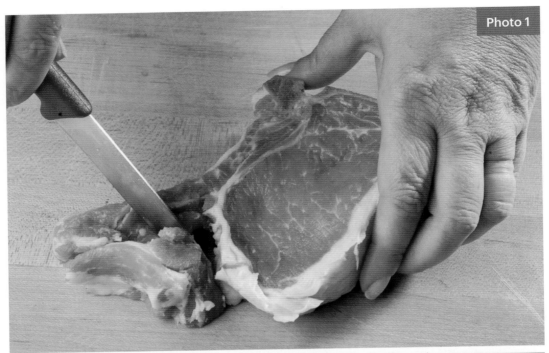

Photo 1

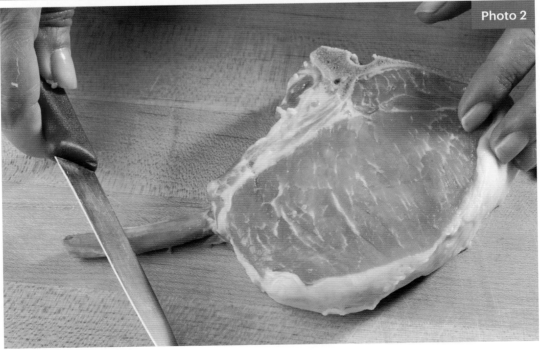

Photo 2

FRENCHING 101 *(continued)*

2. Cut away as much of the meat, fat and tissue as you can easily (photo 1). Don't worry about getting the bone clean yet; we're just getting the big pieces out of the way.

3. When you've got almost everything cut away, flip your knife over and use the spine of the blade to scrape the bone (photo 2). At this point the only thing left will probably be some stringy sinew or connective tissue that's hugging the bone.

4. Slip the point of your knife underneath those last stringy bits. Run the knife along the bone to loosen and separate it from the bone. Cut and remove the connective tissue as far up the bone toward the meat as you can. At this point the bone should be looking pretty dry and free of any tissue.

5. With a clean towel, wipe down the exposed bone to dry it and get any last, stubborn pieces of tissue.

6. Trim any loose ends from the meat and gently push it up toward the eye, just enough to give it a nice shape.

7. Before cooking, wrap the cleaned and exposed bone in foil to prevent it from burning (photo 3). When the chops are done, remove the foil before serving.

Photo 3

A TOAST TO BRINGING OUT FLAVOR

Like classical French cuisine, Mexican food is known for its sauces (or salsas). But unlike the haute cuisine of France, Mexican dishes often are marked by earthy, rustic flavors. Here, we'll examine the common Mexican technique of toasting ingredients. The point of toasting (or broiling) the vegetables is to get a more robust flavor along with a rich color flecked with bits of charred skin.

WHY YOU NEED TO LEARN IT

Anybody can make a quick pico de gallo—a rough cut of fresh tomatoes, onions, peppers, garlic and chilies. But the few extra minutes it takes to toast the ingredients gives you something altogether different, and altogether worth the time.

PUTTING YOUR SKILLS TO WORK

Mahi mahi with orange-scented chipotle-tomatillo salsa (pg. 156)

STEPS TO FOLLOW

The traditional Mexican cooking vessel is the comal—a round, flat metal or terra cotta plate that's placed directly on the fire. Dried chilies, and fresh veggies such as garlic and tomatillos (the small, green tomato-like vegetable encased in a papery husk) are toasted on the comal before being ground into a savory salsa. Because most American cooks don't have a comal at hand, a simple saute pan, skillet or griddle will do. Broiling also works well.

Dried chilies

Set a skillet or saute pan over a medium-high flame. Lay the dried chilies one or two at a time directly on the dry skillet and hold them flat with a spatula. Hold them for 20 to 30 seconds—until you see a few wisps of smoke. Flip the chilies and repeat. The chilies can now be seeded and either pounded into a powder or rehydrated with water to be processed into a sauce.

Fresh chilies

Small chilies such as jalapenos or serranos also can be put in a hot skillet without fat. Let them char on one side. Turn them with tongs until they're blackened fairly equally on all sides (photo 1). They can be seeded, if desired, then chopped or processed whole for a sauce.

Larger chilies, such as poblanos, can be roasted directly over an open flame, like bell peppers. Place them directly on the burners over a medium-high flame. As they char, use tongs to turn them until the whole chili is completely blackened. You also can char them under the broiler or a comal. After they're charred, wrap the chilies in plastic or place in a brown paper bag. The steam emanating from the hot flesh will separate the charred skin, making it easy to peel. When the pepper is cool, unwrap it and rub the charred skin off with your fingers or a clean towel (photo 2).

Roasted large chilies, such as poblanos, can be stuffed for chiles rellenos, cut into strips called rajas, or processed into sauces or soups.

Tomatoes and tomatillos

For larger numbers of whole tomatoes or tomatillos (husk removed and rinsed well), place on a broiling pan lined with foil. Broil until the skin is charred, about six to eight minutes. Use tongs to flip them and broil for another six to eight minutes, until the other side is blackened.

Some chefs remove the blackened skin before processing while others prefer to leave it on. The charred skin will add flavor, texture and color to the finished product, but it is entirely up to you.

Garlic

Break the head of garlic into cloves, but do not peel the individual cloves. You want as much of the papery husk as possible to keep the cloves from burning. Place the whole cloves in a dry saute pan or skillet. When one side blackens, turn each clove to another side. The idea is to just cook the garlic all the way through.

Photo 1

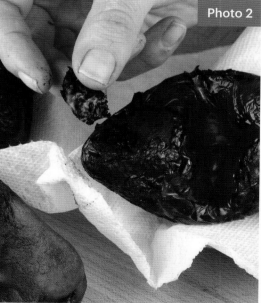
Photo 2

MAHI MAHI WITH ORANGE-SCENTED CHIPOTLE-TOMATILLO SALSA

PREP TIME: 20 MINUTES

COOK TIME: 20 MINUTES

YIELD: 2 SERVINGS

Salsa:

½ pound tomatillos, husks removed, rinsed

2 cloves garlic, unpeeled

½ white onion, cut into large chunks

1 canned chipotle chili in adobo sauce or to taste

½ cup orange juice

½ teaspoon salt

Mahi mahi:

1 teaspoon salt

1 teaspoon paprika

1 teaspoon garlic powder

1 teaspoon black pepper

2 mahi mahi fillets or other firm fish, about 6 ounces each

2 tablespoons vegetable oil

1 orange, cut into segments

1. Line a broiling pan with aluminum foil. Place the tomatillos on foil; broil under high heat until the skin is blackened, about 6 minutes. Turn with tongs to blacken the other side, about 6 minutes. Set aside to cool.

2. Meanwhile, heat a small, heavy skillet over medium-high heat. Add the garlic cloves; toast until the skin blackens, about 2 minutes. Turn to blacken 2 or 3 more sides. Remove from heat; let cool. Peel the cloves; set aside.

3. Place tomatillos, garlic, onion, half of the chipotle chili and half of the orange juice in the bowl of a food processer; process until smooth. If the sauce is not spicy enough, add more chipotle. If it's too thick, add more orange juice. Season with the salt.

4. For the mahi mahi, heat oven to 400 degrees. Combine the salt, paprika, garlic powder and pepper in a small bowl; sprinkle over both sides of the fish. Heat an oven-proof skillet large enough to hold both fillets over medium-high heat; add the oil. Add fillet; cook 2 minutes. Turn; cook 2 minutes.

5. Place the skillet in the oven; roast until the fillets almost flake when tested with a fork, about 2 minutes. Serve with the salsa; garnish with oranges.

NUTRITION INFORMATION PER SERVING: 329 calories, 43% of calories from fat, 15g fat, 2g saturated fat, 160mg cholesterol, 5g carbohydrates, 41g protein, 1,373mg sodium, 2g fiber

LISTEN FOR THE WHISTLING: AND MORE TIPS THAT WILL HELP YOU MAKE THE BEST FRIES EVER

So, you know how Grape-Nuts aren't really nuts? Well, guess what, french fries aren't really French.

"When the Americans went to Belgium to help us out in World War I, they saw military guys cooking potatoes in oil," says Bart Vandaele, Belgian-born chef-owner of Belga Cafe in Washington, D.C., "and because the official language of the Belgian military was French, they called them 'french fries.'" And as Vandaele points out, even the French don't call them french fries; in France, they're pommes frites.

STEPS TO FOLLOW

The first thing you want to do is choose the potato. Starchy potatoes that are lower in water content, such as russet or Idaho, work best. "And older potatoes have a lower moisture content," says Sheagren, "so if you have older potatoes, perfect. If not, not to worry."

Once you've got the spuds, the method, while exacting, is pretty straightforward.

"There are a couple key things that you're looking to accomplish in order to get the best product," Sheagren says, "and the first is to eliminate as much excess starch as you can."

Removing the starch reduces the chances that the fries will stick together, and also, according to Sheagren, gives a crisper fry.

Another important factor is frying the potatoes twice. The first time, called "blanching," involves lower-temperature, longer-duration frying to thoroughly cook the potato. The next step is to brown and crisp the outside at a higher temperature.

Vandaele blanches his fries in 250-degree oil until they are just cooked through. "They whistle to you when they're ready to come out," he says, "because the inside starts to steam, and it whistles like a steam whistle."

After the potatoes come out, they need to rest for an hour or two to come to room temperature before the final frying.

WHY YOU NEED TO LEARN IT

Regardless of their provenance, there's no doubt that this European delicacy is one of America's most popular foods. The problem is, as with so many things, there are more bad examples of french fries than good. And that's why you should know how to make them yourself, because when you're really craving them, you don't want to take any chances.

That's also why we wanted to talk to some experts: Along with Vandaele, we got some tips from Ben Sheagren, executive chef at the Hop Leaf, a Chicago tavern that specializes in Belgian brews and cuisine.

LISTEN FOR THE WHISTLING *(continued)*

Step-by-step

1. Wash your potatoes, and peel them if you like. Leaving the peels on gives a more rustic look, while taking them off will give you a better chance of having all your pieces looking exactly alike. Your call.

2. For perfectly shaped fries, cut the potato into a box shape by first trimming off both ends, then cutting straight down along one side to create a flat surface. Roll the potato onto that surface, and cut straight down on a second side. Do that two more times, and you'll have a nice little oblong potato box. Cut the box into ¼-inch thick planks, then lay the planks down and cut them into sticks that are as long as the potato and ¼-inch square on the ends (photo 1). These are your fries.

3. Place the fries in a large bowl of cold water. This rinses away some of the surface starch, making it more likely that the fries will not stick together while cooking.

4. Fill a large, heavy pot halfway with vegetable oil and heat it to 250 to 300 degrees. It's important to use a frying thermometer because it's vital that the first frying is done at a lower temperature than the second.

5. Add your fries in batches that will not overcrowd the pot (photo 2). Fry them gently until they are cooked through but not browned at all, about 6 to 8 minutes. Remove them from the oil and drain them on a paper towel-lined sheet tray. Cool them to room temperature before proceeding. (Alternately, you can hold them overnight in the refrigerator; just bring to room temp before the second frying.)

6. Just before serving, heat the oil to 325-350 degrees, and add the blanched fries in batches. Cook them until they are golden brown, about 3 to 5 minutes, then remove, season and serve immediately. "And you need to eat them with mayonnaise," says Vandaele. "That's the Belgian way, the real way."

Spice 'em up

Once you've mastered the french fry technique, you may want to branch out, flavorwise. Take inspiration from the cute little book "French Fries," by Zac Williams. You'll find dozens of seasoning ideas from Parmesan to mustard-salt. Try the garlic fries: Saute 2 minced cloves garlic in a little olive oil. Stir in 1 teaspoon chopped fresh rosemary and 2 teaspoons chopped fresh parsley. Sprinkle over hot fries.

Photo 1

Photo 2

IT'S VITAL
THAT THE
FIRST FRYING
IS DONE AT
A LOWER
TEMPERATURE
THAN THE
SECOND.

OLD-SCHOOL TOOL: FOOD MILL USES OLD-FASHIONED TECHNOLOGY TO PRODUCE SMOOTH-AS-SILK PUREES AND SAUCES

I'm pretty much an old-school kind of guy. That's one of the reasons I'm so fond of cooking, I guess. With the exception of the so-called molecular gastronomists, who create dishes with such unusual tools as ink-jet printers or bowls of liquid nitrogen, cooking is totally old school. It's ovens, knives ... what school is older than that?

Let's look at another old tool from the old school, one that's still popular in professional kitchens but which largely has fallen out of favor at home: the food mill.

A food mill is simply a deep round strainer with a crank handle that turns a curved blade, forcing food through holes in the bottom. Most food mills have removable plates with differently sized holes, allowing you to create purees of different smoothness. There are many good brands of food mills on the market. Make sure to get one with multiple discs (or plates) for more versatility (photo 1).

WHY YOU NEED TO LEARN IT

Perfectly smooth food is not just for the young and the toothless. Well-made purees add an element of refinement, creating dishes that virtually kiss your tongue. If that sounds appealing, you need a food mill.

Food mills function similarly to food processors, blenders or stick blenders, but the results are very different. The sharp blades on those latter tools do a great job of pureeing, but they also pulverize seeds, stems and leaves and they don't strain your product. This can leave it with a gritty mouthfeel as well as a bitter flavor. The food mill is designed to strain all the nasty bits out, leaving you with nothing but the pureed flesh.

It's the perfect tool for sauces like tomato and apple, and it works wonders with beans. It's absolutely essential for mashed potatoes.

PUTTING YOUR SKILLS TO WORK
Roasted garlic hummus
(pg. 163)

▶

Photo 1

OLD-SCHOOL TOOL *(continued)*

STEPS TO FOLLOW

Food mills are easy to find and extremely easy to use. All you have to do is dump whatever food you're pureeing into the mill and turn the crank in the direction of the raised blade (generally, this is clockwise, but don't hold me to that). Every so often you should reverse directions. This will scrape up the residue off the floor of the mill so that when you go back to the original direction it will get absolutely all of the usable bits.

Here are a few great uses for a food mill:

Potatoes: Simmer potatoes until cooked through, then drain thoroughly. Pass them immediately through the food mill and, while they're still hot, add your butter, cream or whatever other flavoring ingredients you're using. Fold the potatoes together gently, and you'll be delighted by their texture. Use this same approach for other starches, such as sweet potatoes, parsnips or celery root.

Legumes: Cook dried beans all the way through, then drain and place immediately in the food mill (do you see a pattern emerging here?). The food mill traps the tough outer skin, leaving you with a smooth puree that you can turn into a side dish, a spread for canapes or a dip for crackers. You can also use canned products (see accompanying recipe).

Fruits and berries: Hard fruit, like apples, should be cooked first, then roughly chopped or quartered before placing in the food mill. Softer fruit, such as ripe peaches (minus the pits) or bananas, can be put in uncooked. Berries can be cooked, fresh, or even frozen (and thawed). Use fruit purees as a base for sauces, desserts, smoothies or preserves.

ROASTED GARLIC HUMMUS

1. Heat oven to 350 degrees. Cut the head of garlic in half through its equator; set the halves cut-side-up on a large piece of foil. Drizzle 1 tablespoon of the olive oil over the halves; fold the foil over the top. Roast in the oven until the cloves are soft and golden brown, 30-45 minutes.

2. Place the chickpeas and tahini in the food mill. Squeeze the two halves of the garlic heads, allowing the cloves to fall into the food mill. (Don't worry if any of the papery skin gets in; the food mill will strain it out.) Process it all through the finest plate.

3. Stir in the lemon juice, cumin and salt. If the hummus seems too thick, stir in some of the chickpea liquid to thin. Spoon the hummus into a serving bowl; drizzle remaining 2 tablespoons of the olive oil over the top. Sprinkle with chopped parsley. Lay quartered cherry tomatoes around the edges.

Note: Tahini is a sesame-seed paste that is sold in specialty and Middle Eastern markets and some larger supermarkets.

NUTRITION INFORMATION PER SERVING: 157 calories, 53% of calories from fat, 9 g fat, 1 g saturated fat, 0 mg cholesterol, 15 g carbohydrates, 4 g protein, 308 mg sodium, 3 g fiber

PREP TIME: 10 MINUTES

COOK TIME: 30 MINUTES

YIELD: 8 SERVINGS

1 whole head garlic

3 tablespoons extra-virgin olive oil

1 can (15 ounces) chickpeas, drained, liquid reserved

2 tablespoons tahini, see note

Juice of ½ lemon

½ teaspoon ground cumin

½ teaspoon salt

2 tablespoons chopped parsley

1 cup cherry tomatoes, quartered

STICKING WITH IT: THOUGH SKEWERS ARE A FAMILIAR TOOL, THESE TIPS WILL HELP YOU PERFECT YOUR RESULTS

Most of us know it as shish kebab, a dish of Turkish origin. Still, nearly every culture has some trick for sticking food into fire without burning their hands. French brochettes, South African sosoties, Nepalese sekuwas, Argentinean pinchos. It's all food-on-a-stick, and it's all delicious.

WHY YOU NEED TO LEARN IT

Obviously, we're well beyond needing to plead a case for the smoky goodness of grilled food. One thing that makes skewering so attractive to the cook, however, is its compatibility with advance preparation. All the chopping, mixing, soaking and impaling can be done hours before cooking. When dinner approaches, remove the skewers from any marinade and lay them on the grill or under the broiler. Because everything is in bite-sized pieces, cooking takes only minutes.

PUTTING YOUR SKILLS TO WORK

Chicken satay with peanut sauce (pg. 166)

STEPS TO FOLLOW

On the one hand, instructions for shish kebab and its cousins are simple: Put some food on a stick and grill it. Hence, we'll dispense with our typical routine of 1-2-3 directions in favor of several thoughts and suggestions designed to give you a better-looking, better-tasting product.

The food

Just about anything can be skewered and grilled: meat, fish, vegetables, fruit, even cheese. Two considerations, however, are the shapes of your cuts and the varied cooking times for different ingredients. While multicolored skewers holding several ingredients are admittedly quite festive, I've had my fill of kebabs with perfectly cooked meat next to nearly raw onions and desiccated mushrooms.

Knife cuts: Make sure your pieces are cut in similar shapes and sizes. Then skewer them to expose the maximum surface to the heat. Cut pieces of zucchini or yellow squash on a bias and somewhat thick, and skewer the pieces lengthwise. For pieces of bell pepper, poke the skewer through opposite ends so they lay down flat.

Dedicated skewers: Skewer ingredients separately, or group them together by cooking time. Onions and peppers on one skewer, tomatoes and mushrooms on another, whole shrimp, strips of chicken breast or chunks of beef tenderloin on a third (photo 1).

The skewers

Materials: Metal skewers are easy to use, easy to clean and fairly indestructible. Single-use bamboo skewers, available at most chain grocers, suggest Asia or the tropics. Be sure to soak bamboo for at least half an hour before using to prevent it from burning on the grill. Other natural skewers add an elegant touch along with subtle flavor notes. Rosemary sprigs, lemon grass and slivers of sugar cane are very cool. Chefs in Basque country whittle skewers from licorice root. Remember that any flammable material may succumb to conflagration. When this happens, don't despair: Remove the cooked food from the charred stick and rethread onto a fresh skewer.

Double up: One thing I've always found infuriating is the way food rotates randomly every time I lift the skewer, preventing it from cooking uniformly. An easy solution is to use two skewers. Thread everything onto one skewer, just to one side of the center point. Lay that skewer on your cutting board and push the second skewer up through the food just on the opposite side of center (photo 2). The food stays put, the skewers flip easily on the grill, and it's an interesting plate presentation.

A few final notes

- Remember, skewers cook very quickly. Place them directly over glowing coals and it shouldn't take more than a minute or two per side.

- Also, the speedy cooking demands cuts of meat that are low in connective tissue (which requires long, slow cooking in liquid to break down). Steak cuts—tenderloins, strips, etc.—are terrific.

- Finally, you don't need to load up the entire skewer. Appetizers or hors d'oeuvres can have just one or two elements, but be sure to include a delicious dipping sauce or two.

- Above all, remember what you like and don't like about what you do, then build on that knowledge next time around.

Photo 1

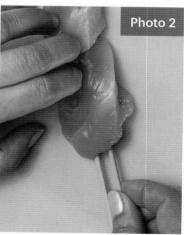
Photo 2

CHICKEN SATAY WITH PEANUT SAUCE

Satay originated in Indonesia, though it's mostly known from its appearances in Thai restaurants.

PREP TIME: 35 MINUTES

CHILLING TIME: 1 HOUR

COOK TIME: 7 MINUTES

YIELD: 8 APPETIZER SERVINGS OR
4 ENTREE SERVINGS

4 boneless, skinless chicken breast halves

2 cloves garlic, minced

1 piece (1 inch-long) ginger root, minced

¼ cup soy sauce

2 tablespoons Thai fish sauce

2 tablespoons peanut butter

1 tablespoon plus 1½ teaspoons brown sugar

1 tablespoon curry powder, optional

Juice of 1 lime

Peanut sauce:

1 cup creamy peanut butter

2 cloves garlic, 1 crushed, 1 minced

½ cup coconut milk

¼ cup fish sauce

¼ cup soy sauce

2 tablespoons minced cilantro, plus 2
   tablespoons more, chopped,
   for garnish, optional

1 tablespoon brown sugar

¼ to ½ teaspoon ground red pepper, optional

Juice of 2 limes

1. Place breasts between two sheets of plastic wrap; pound to about ¼-inch thick. Cut breasts lengthwise into 1-inch-wide strips; set aside. Mix the garlic, ginger, soy sauce, peanut butter, brown sugar, curry powder and lime juice in a large bowl; add chicken strips. Cover; refrigerate up to 1 hour.

2. Meanwhile, soak bamboo skewers in water 30 minutes. For peanut sauce, whisk peanut butter, garlic, coconut milk, fish sauce, soy sauce, cilantro, brown sugar, red pepper and lime juice until smooth in a medium bowl, adding more coconut milk if needed for desired consistency.

3. Prepare a grill or grill pan. Remove chicken from marinade; thread onto skewers. Grill, turning once, until just done, about 3 minutes per side. Transfer to platter or plates. Sprinkle with cilantro; serve with peanut sauce.

NUTRITION INFORMATION PER SERVING
(with 1 tablespoon sauce): 151 calories, 42% of calories from fat, 7g fat, 2.5g saturated fat, 36mg cholesterol, 4g carbohydrates, 16g protein, 804mg sodium, 0.5g fiber

GRILLING WIZARDRY APPLIES TO VEGGIES TOO: THESE TIPS HELP BRING OUT FLAVOR AND PRESERVE TEXTURE

One needn't go on about the pleasures of cooking out of doors. Volumes have been written already, and if you're not one to succumb to the allure of the grill, then you may as well return to your home planet. The rest of us earthlings, we're going to talk about grilled vegetables.

STEPS TO FOLLOW

Occasionally, it makes sense here at Prep School, rather than laying out a 1-2-3 tutorial on what to do and when, simply to offer a few helpful suggestions. This is one such Prep School, primarily because there are so many, many vegetables that if we were to address each one adequately ("Lay the green beans on the grill—crosswise, of course, to keep them from falling through the cracks ..."), we would never get out of here.

Before we begin, remember that all we're doing is applying heat to vegetables. Go forth boldly, and don't be distracted by fears of under- or overcooking. After all, it's only dinner, and even should you screw up mightily, your eggplant scorched into charcoal, you will live to grill again.

Now, on to the suggestions.

Consider the plank

To start, consider that those things that cry out for a grill—steaks, burgers, chops—are generally thin and flattish with a large surface area. These traits ensure an even and appropriate cooking over the speedy high heat of the grill.

Vegetables, then, likewise ought to be cut to maximize their surface area. Larger items—eggplant, fennel, zucchini, yellow squash—can be sliced into ½-inch-thick planks lengthwise or on an elegant diagonal (photo 1, next page). If they're too thin, they may burn up or become unpleasantly limp. If they're too thick, the outside may burn before the inside is even warmed.

WHY YOU NEED TO LEARN IT

It only makes sense that if you're grilling your meat, you may as well throw on your vegetables. Keep the kitchen cool, you know.

Practicality aside, though, there's the whole aesthetic. Just the addition of the adjective "grilled" lends a bit of smoky sophistication to whatever it's attached: grilled asparagus and gruyere omelet; grilled onion compote; BL and grilled T; I could go on ...

Those secondary applications notwithstanding, there's something about a rustic platter of room-temp grilled vegetables—zucchini, yellow squash, eggplant, peppers, all dressed in a supple vinaigrette—that makes me very happy.

GRILLING WIZARDRY APPLIES TO VEGGIES TOO *(continued)*

Beautiful big red onions, too, can be sliced into ½-inch-thick circles. Just run a skewer through the slices from end to end to keep them from coming apart on the grill (photo 2).

Smaller vegetables such as cherry tomatoes or button mushrooms can be skewered together rather than sliced. (If you're using wooden skewers, soak them in water for half an hour before grilling to keep them from incinerating.)

Forget the marinade

Marination is a topic of some debate. Not everyone likes the idea. I'm a recent convert to the no-marinade camp. Unlike meat, with its tough connective tissue and bundles of muscle fibers, vegetables don't need an acid to make them palatable. (Indeed, some chefs feel that an acidic marinade can turn grilled vegetables mushy.) As for the flavor a marinade provides, just add it after grilling.

In any case, be sure to brush or toss your vegetables with oil just before grilling to keep them from sticking.

Go for al dente

Unlike, say, chicken drumsticks, most vegetables are perfectly delicious raw (eggplant being one notable exception). When grilling, then, we can err on the side of timidity and go for an al dente doneness, where the vegetable still has some texture, some bite. When cut into ½-inch planks, pretty much by the time they've got some nice grill marks on both sides (photo 3), they'll be warmed through and perfectly done.

Done in a jiffy

The nature of meat demands that we allow it to rest several minutes after cooking so that it can reabsorb the juices into its tissues. Vegetables cook quickly, generally. Thus, when the meat comes off the vegetables go on. As soon as they're done, the meat is rested and ready to eat.

Photo 1

Photo 2

Photo 3

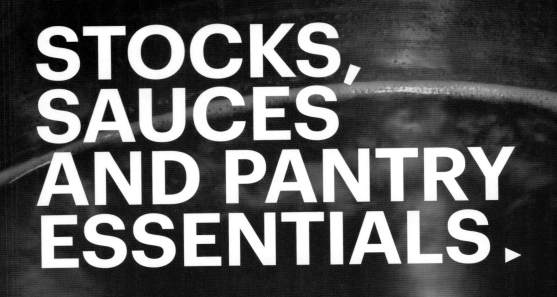

STOCKS, SAUCES AND PANTRY ESSENTIALS ▸

STOCKING UP: IT TAKES LOTS OF TIME, YES, BUT THEN YOUR FREEZER WILL BE FULL OF DELICIOUS HOMEMADE BROTH

Pick a day to make some brown stock. I swear, you'll be glad you did. Stock is simply a flavorful liquid comprised of bones, aromatic vegetables, herbs, water and usually a little acid.

Along with flavor, the bones contribute collagen, a connective tissue that holds muscles together and attaches muscles to bones. All of us have it, and young animals have more than old animals.

Collagen turns to gelatin and water when it's cooked slowly in liquid, and that gelatin gives stock its body. It's why your leftover turkey soup turns to gelatin, and it's why sauces made from stock rather than canned broths (which have no gelatin) have such a great mouthfeel.

Let's make brown veal stock. Because stock takes up so much space, we're also showing you how to reduce it to "glace."

WHY YOU NEED TO LEARN IT

Keep cubes of glace in your freezer. Whenever you're making a braise, stew, soup, sauce or anything that would benefit from a blast of flavor, add a cube. The results are remarkable.

STEPS TO FOLLOW

Unlike white stocks, the ingredients in brown stocks are roasted before simmering in water. Roasting gives brown stock its color along with a depth of flavor not present in white stock.

Typically, white stock is made from chicken and brown stock from veal, but you can make brown chicken stock or white veal stock if you like.

For a general stock formula, consider the following: Whatever weight of bones you start with, use twice that amount of water. Remember that a pound of water is a pint, so for every pound of bones you'll need a quart of water. Ten pounds of bones will need 2½ gallons of water.

You'll also need mirepoix, a 2:1:1 ratio of onions, carrots and celery, roughly chopped. For 10 pounds of bones, figure 2 pounds of mirepoix: 1 pound of onions and ½ pound each of carrots and celery.

Note: Any butcher can get veal bones for you if you give him a couple days' notice.

Photo 1

1. Roast your veal bones in a 450-degree oven about 45 minutes, until they're a nice, dark brown.

2. When the bones are about done, take a generous scoop of tomato paste and smear it across the top so that it, too, roasts a bit (photo 1). The tomato adds color along with acid that helps break down the collagen.

STOCKING UP *(continued)*

3. Place the roasted bones in the stockpot. Discard any fat and deglaze the roasting pan: add 1 or 2 cups of wine or water and set the pan on your stove top over a high flame. Scrape up any browned bits stuck to the bottom of the pan. Add the liquid and bits to the stockpot (photo 2).

4. Add COLD water, 1 quart for every pound of bones.

5. Crank the heat under the pot. Impurities—proteins—will dissolve in the cold water. As the mixture heats, these impurities will coagulate and form a scum at the top of the stock. Skim it off.

6. While the water heats, roast your mirepoix in a single layer on a sheet tray or roasting pan in the hot oven until lightly browned, about 5 minutes.

7. When the water boils, add your roasted mirepoix and a sizable bouquet garni: a bunch of parsley, a tablespoon of dried thyme and 3 to 5 bay leaves. You can tie it all in cheesecloth or just toss it in.

8. Once you've added everything, the liquid should come nearly all the way to the top. If it doesn't, top it off with more water, return it to the boil, then reduce to a simmer.

9. Simmer it a long time: 8 to 12 hours or overnight.

10. When the stock is finished, strain it through a chinois (fine-mesh strainer) or a colander lined with cheesecloth into a clean container.

11a. Cool it in an ice bath before covering and refrigerating or freezing. It will last about a week in the refrigerator, and several months in the freezer.

11b. Or, for glace, degrease the strained stock, then return it to the cleaned stockpot. Reduce it to one-tenth its original volume. It will be somewhat syrupy.

12. Pour glace into a casserole and cool. When it solidifies, cut it into 2-inch squares and freeze. Alternately, pour the glace into ice cube trays (photo 3) and pop them out into freezer bags when they harden.

Photo 2

Photo 3

TAKING STOCK: THAT TURKEY CARCASS HAS LIFE LEFT IN IT AS A SOURCE FOR SOUPS, SAUCES

This year, instead of just tossing a turkey carcass wholesale into a pot to make "turkey soup," let's back up a little, and first turn it into versatile, delicious stock.

WHY YOU NEED TO LEARN IT

Without good stock, you cannot have good soups and sauces. Besides, what else are you going to do with that sad, sad skeleton? Donate it to a college of veterinary medicine?

STEPS TO FOLLOW

We've covered stocks before. Nonetheless, here's a quick refresher: Stock is nothing more than a flavorful liquid made by simmering aromatic vegetables, herbs and, most often, bones in water to extract their flavor. Here's how to do it:

1. As soon after the feast as practical, pull all the meat, skin, fat and assorted nasty bits from the carcass. Save the meat and carcass, and be sure to use the wing tips, neck bones and any other assorted pieces of bone or cartilage. It's all good. Toss the skin and fat.

2. Break or chop the carcass into smaller pieces—not teeny pieces, just small enough for them to fit comfortably in the stockpot. You don't want any big pieces sticking up because they need to be submerged completely in water. Put the pieces in the stock pot and add cold water until it's an inch above the bones.

3. Set the uncovered pot over high heat. As it comes up to temperature, impurities will solidify and float to the top and form a foamy scum. Skim this scum while the stock heats, before it boils. (If the scum is left on and the stock boils, the impurities can break up and dissolve back in, giving you a cloudy stock.)

4. While the stock heats, prepare your mirepoix: a mix of two parts onion to one part carrot and one part celery, roughly chopped into large dice. "How much mirepoix?" you ask. Generally, the weight of the mirepoix should be about 20 to 30 percent of the weight of the bones. So, figure that your bones will account for roughly half of the purchased weight of the bird. Thus, if you buy a 16-pound turkey, figure you've got about eight pounds of bones; 25 percent of that would be two pounds, which means

Photo 1

you'd want one pound of chopped onion and half a pound each of chopped carrot and celery. (If that's confusing, read it over a couple more times.) These amounts do NOT need to be exact, so don't stress out.

5. Once the skimmed stock comes to a boil, add the mirepoix and a sachet (modest and inexact amounts of parsley, thyme and bay leaf, traditionally all wrapped in cheesecloth, but you can just toss it all in; it's getting strained out later anyway). Reduce the heat and simmer the stock for two or three hours (photo 1).

6. When your stock is done, use tongs to remove the bones, then pour the stock through a fine strainer into a storage container. If your strainer is not that fine (or worse, non-existent), line a colander with cheesecloth. You can now use the stock immediately to make soup, a sauce or use as a braising liquid.

7. If you want to store it for later use: Place the container of stock in an ice bath to cool it as quickly as possible. When the stock is cool, cover it and put in the refrigerator or freezer.

LEARNING CURVES: HOW TO BUILD FLAVOR IN A PERFECT PUREED SOUP

If you've made mashed potatoes, then you can make delicious pureed soups. The main difference between the two? Consistency.

Though we add a few more ingredients to give our soups a little depth, it is all about taking something solid and making it liquid. Potatoes, sweet potatoes, carrots, legumes, parsnips—anything with a lot of natural starch can be turned into a wonderful lunch or a luscious first course.

WHY YOU NEED TO LEARN IT

Making great food is not so much about following recipes as it is understanding steps in a process. Pureed soups offer an easy introduction to this important concept. Get a feel for what each of the following steps accomplishes. Then, follow whatever recipe you're using or strike out on your own.

When the soup is finished, see how it turned out. If it's too thick, try thinning it with more liquid. If it's too thin, try reducing it by evaporating some of the liquid over medium heat.

Whatever the result, remember that things aren't usually perfect the first time, and the more soups you make, the better they'll be.

PUTTING YOUR SKILLS TO WORK

Parsnip and apple soup (pg. 180)

STEPS TO FOLLOW

Note that we don't give exact amounts. Also, there's a number of "if/then" points. It's all meant to teach you to pay attention to how different actions or ingredients affect the outcome of a dish. In other words, stop thinking in terms of right vs. wrong; instead, think of cause and effect.

1. Lay down a layer of flavor: Cut some bacon into what the French call lardons (½-inch-wide strips) and fry until crispy. Remove and reserve the crisped bacon and pour out all but a couple tablespoons of the fat.

2. Add more flavor: Saute a couple cups of medium dice aromatics (onion, leeks, celery, maybe some carrots or garlic) in the bacon fat. For a soup that's lighter in color and flavor, cook the aromatics over medium-low heat until limp and translucent (the aromatics, not you). This is called "sweating." If you're looking for a darker soup with a deeper flavor, saute the aromatics over medium-high heat until they're caramelized to a golden brown.

3. Make the soup: Crank the heat and add a couple quarts of liquid—typically stock or broth, but plain water will work too. Heat it to a boil, then add about two pounds of your main ingredient, cut into medium dice. (If you're using dried beans, start with a pound and soak them overnight before making soup.) This is going to lower the temperature of the liquid. Leave the heat on high, and when the liquid heats to a boil

Photo 1

again, turn it down and let it simmer for as long as it takes for the main ingredient to get tender. This could be 30 minutes for potatoes and more than an hour for beans. Keep testing the vegetables to see if they are tender.

4. When all the vegetables are tender, puree the soup using an immersion blender (photo 1) or a bar blender or food processor. You may need to do this in batches.

5. Give it one more blast of flavor: Spices, fresh herbs, sauteed fruits, wine, brown sugar. These all add nuance to a soup. Think about what flavors complement your main ingredient and add a little at a time, tasting as you go. Give the soup one more quick hit with the blender, then season with salt and pepper or a little lemon juice for brightness. For a mellower soup, add a touch of cream. Garnish with the reserved bacon and serve.

PARSNIP AND APPLE SOUP

PREP TIME: 40 MINUTES

COOK TIME: 35 MINUTES

YIELD: 10 SERVINGS

4 to 6 slices bacon, cut into ½-inch strips

1 each, chopped: medium onion, carrot, rib celery

3 large parsnips, peeled, chopped

2 cans or cartons (32 ounces each) low-sodium chicken broth or 2 quarts chicken stock

2 tablespoons butter

4 apples, peeled, cored, chopped

¼ cup brandy, Cognac or Calvados

¼ cup whipping cream, optional

2 tablespoons brown sugar

½ teaspoon cinnamon

½ teaspoon salt

Freshly ground pepper

Fresh lemon juice, optional

1. Cook bacon, turning occasionally, in a Dutch oven over medium heat until crispy, about 6 minutes; set aside on paper towels. Discard all but 2 tablespoons of the fat.

2. Add onion, carrot and celery to Dutch oven; increase heat to medium-high; cook until golden, about 5 minutes. Add parsnips and broth; increase heat to high. Heat to a boil; reduce heat to a simmer. Cook until vegetables are tender, about 25 minutes.

3. Meanwhile, melt the butter in a skillet over medium-high heat. Add the apples; cook, stirring, until golden brown, about 16 minutes.

4. Stir the apples into the Dutch oven. Puree the soup with an immersion blender, or in batches in a blender or food processor and return to Dutch oven. (Soup should be the consistency of whipping cream. If it's too thick, add more broth; if it's too thin, cook over medium heat to reduce the amount of liquid.)

5. Stir in the brandy, cream, sugar, cinnamon, salt and pepper to taste. Taste and adjust seasoning; add a few drops of lemon juice to brighten the flavor if you like. Garnish with reserved bacon.

NUTRITION INFORMATION PER SERVING: 143 calories, 27% of calories from fat, 5g fat, 2g saturated fat, 9mg cholesterol, 22g carbohydrates, 6g protein, 261mg sodium, 3g fiber

CONFIT: AN INGREDIENT FOR THE AGES

Refrigeration has its downside. Sure, it has saved countless lives by preserving food safely. And it keeps last night's pizza fresh for tomorrow's breakfast.

Still, it has rendered unnecessary some of the great old and tasty techniques for preserving food.

Like confit. Confit, from the French verb "confire," meaning to conserve or preserve, is a dish of goose, duck or pork—we're using duck—that's cooked and stored in its own fat.

STEPS TO FOLLOW

Typically, duck confit is made with the legs, including the thighs. If you're working from whole ducks, use the wings too. The tender breast should really be eaten medium-rare, and thus is most often sauteed just long enough to render the fat under the skin. The tougher legs, though, benefit from a long, slow cooking, becoming fall-apart tender.

There's not much actual work involved in making confit, but it does take a couple of days because the meat needs to be cured in salt. Salt draws out moisture that otherwise would allow little microscopic organisms to thrive and spoil the meat. This, along with the fact that confit is stored in fat—an air-free environment—is what allows it to keep for up to six months.

Unless you cook a lot of duck and render and save the fat, you'll need to buy a tub of duck fat from your local butcher. Figure about 1½ cups of fat per leg, give or take. Some recipes combine duck fat with lard; others use olive oil. It all works, but duck fat is the most traditional.

Curing the legs

The word "cure," according to The Oxford English Dictionary, is a centuries-old slurring of the word "cover," just as "over" becomes "o'er" or "never" becomes "ne'er." Traditionally, meat was preserved by being covered—or cured—in salt.

WHY YOU NEED TO LEARN IT

Confit is delicious. It's easy to make. And, it keeps for ages. Serve it as a main course or crumble it over salad. Put it in cassoulet or pound it with a little duck fat into a spread called rillettes.

CONFIT: AN INGREDIENT FOR THE AGES *(continued)*

1. For four legs, use about 2 tablespoons of kosher salt. Salt the legs directly, or pour a layer of salt in a shallow baking pan, lay the legs on top, then sprinkle on the rest of the salt. You can also add herbs and spices, like crushed garlic and shallot, fresh thyme, bay leaf and ground black pepper (photo 1).

2. Cover the container. Let the legs cure overnight or a couple of days. The longer the cure, the longer confit keeps, but the saltier it becomes.

3. When you're ready to cook the legs, scrape off the salt and pat them dry with a clean towel.

Cooking the legs

Heat the oven to 250 degrees.

4. Melt the duck fat in a saucepan.

5. Place legs skin side up in a baking dish. Pour in the melted duck fat until the legs are submerged (photo 2). Place uncovered in the oven; bake at a slow simmer for 2 to 3 hours. The meat should be cooked through completely, until there's no red in the juices when the leg is pricked.

6. Remove the legs to a glass or earthenware bowl. Strain the fat and pour it over the duck legs until they are submerged by an inch (photo 3).

7. Refrigerate for a couple of days to allow the flavors to mellow. It can be refrigerated for a week if the cure was short, or up to six months if the cure was a couple days.

To eat

8. To prepare the confit, remove the duck legs from the fat and place them on a rack in a baking pan in a hot oven for 20 minutes or so, until the skin gets nice and crispy, then serve. Use the leftover fat to saute potatoes or vegetables, or melt it and combine it with vinegar for a warm duck-fat vinaigrette.

Photo 1

Photo 2

Photo 3

A FRENCH SAUCE BLENDS BITTER WITH THE SWEET

Talk about a full-flavored sauce. A gastrique has it all: sweet sugar is melted into bitter caramel, reduced with tart vinegar and savory stock. Though it has only relatively recently been appearing on menus, the gastrique has its roots in classic French cuisine.

WHY YOU NEED TO LEARN IT

Gastriques are a great accompaniment to game, poultry (especially duck) and pork. Still, they're not that common to home cooks. Once you get a handle on the basic idea, though, there are tons of variations that you can prepare.

PUTTING YOUR SKILLS TO WORK

Simple raspberry gastrique (pg. 186)

STEPS TO FOLLOW

The first step—turning sugar into caramel—can be frightening for the home cook. However, with a little practice and a lot of care, it's a technique easily mastered. Moreover, many home cooks and even professional chefs omit the caramel-making step, opting simply to dissolve the sugar in vinegar before reducing. This makes a perfectly delicious sauce (see accompanying recipe), though it loses the bitter element that the caramel adds.

If you haven't worked with melted sugar before, be cautious. Melted sugar is very hot, and by the time it reaches the caramel stage it's well over 300 degrees. Now that's hot. So be careful.

1. Melt ⅔ cup sugar in a small saucepan. If you want to add a tablespoon or two of water to get it started, go ahead. It will turn the sugar into liquid immediately, but it still won't caramelize until well after all the water has evaporated.

2. Cook until the sugar has caramelized—turned a beautiful, rich brown, the color of ... you know ... caramel. Take it off the heat and whisk in ½ cup red wine vinegar. Remember that the caramel is really, really hot, so do this carefully. Stand back from the pan when you pour in the vinegar in case it spatters.

3. When the vinegar is all whisked in and the mixture is nice and smooth, put it back on the stove on a medium heat and reduce it until it has a nice, syrupy consistency.

This is what some chefs consider to be a true gastrique, and they use it not as a sauce, but as an ingredient, a means of adding complexity to brown or tomato sauces.

In modern kitchens, though, it's also combined with other ingredients to make a sauce in and of itself. For example, you can add an equal amount of rich stock and then reduce that until you get a syrupy glaze. You can also add fruit, fresh, dried or preserved. This sauce is then strained, leaving you with a deep brown, deliciously flavored sauce.

SIMPLE RASPBERRY GASTRIQUE

Use this reduced sauce for chicken, duck or pork.

PREP TIME: 10 MINUTES

COOK TIME: 15 MINUTES

YIELD: 4 SERVINGS

¾ cup red wine vinegar

¼ cup raspberry preserves

1 tablespoon sugar, optional

1/8 teaspoon salt

1. Cook the vinegar in a small saucepan over high heat until it reduces to about ⅓ cup, about 10 minutes. Whisk in the raspberry preserves; cook until mixture is a syrupy glaze, about 5 minutes.

2. Taste the sauce for balance, equally sweet and tart. If the vinegar taste is too pronounced, add a bit of sugar. Pass the sauce through a fine strainer; season with salt. Store, covered, in the refrigerator for up to 2 weeks.

NUTRITION INFORMATION PER SERVING: 58 calories, 0% of calories from fat, 0g fat, 0g saturated fat, 0mg cholesterol, 13g carbohydrates, 0g protein, 76mg sodium, 0g fiber

GHEE WHIZ: MAKING CLARIFIED BUTTER IS A SNAP AND GIVES YOU MORE COOKING FAT

By now, loyal reader, you've come to understand that we here at Prep School enjoy greatly the fatty delectables: butter, cream, bacon and so forth—in short, all those things that make food taste good.

Food is so much more than fuel, after all, and it is our belief that for those who practice severe culinary asceticism, their life spans are not longer. They just seem that way.

Thus we turn to butter and how to clarify it. Incidentally, in Ayurveda, the ancient Indian system of medicine, clarified butter, called "ghee," is considered rather healthful.

WHY YOU NEED TO LEARN IT

Consider the cooking term, smoke point. The smoke point of a fat or oil is the temperature at which it begins to break down and smoke. If you keep heating it beyond its smoke point you'll reach its flash point, when the oil catches fire.

Different oils have different smoke points. Oils with high smoke points, such as peanut oil, are well suited to high temperature cooking like sauteing. Oils with lower smoke points, like sesame oil, aren't as desirable for cooking and therefore are used more as flavoring ingredients.

Butter has three main components: butterfat, milk solids and water. When you toss whole butter into a hot pan, first it melts, then the water boils away (that's the bubbling foam you see), and finally the milk solids start to brown (and then burn). The milk solids burn before the butterfat reaches its smoke point, but by removing those milk solids, the butterfat becomes more versatile and you can use it at higher temperatures.

PUTTING YOUR SKILLS TO WORK

Brandied mushrooms (pg. 190)

GHEE WHIZ *(continued)*

STEPS TO FOLLOW

Though clarified butter, like whole butter, is opaque when refrigerated to a solid form, in its liquid form it's a lovely and translucent golden yellow (photo 1). Look for this translucence when you first make the clarified butter. As soon as you see it, you can remove the butter from the heat. If you keep cooking it, the milk solids at the bottom of the pan will start to brown, darkening the clarified butter while imparting a nutty flavor—not necessarily bad, but not what we're looking for here.

1. Put a pound (or whatever amount you want to make) of unsalted butter in a sturdy, heavy-bottomed saucepan. Set it over a medium low heat.

2. Let the butter melt completely, then wait. As the water evaporates, it will bubble to the surface. At the same time, the milk solids will separate out. Most will sink to the bottom, but some will form a film on top.

3. Keep waiting.

4. When the butter has stopped bubbling and turned beautifully translucent with the milk solids resting on the bottom of the pan, skim off the film on the surface (photo 2).

5. Take this now clarified butter off the heat and allow it to cool for a minute or two. Pour it through a layer of cheesecloth into a heatproof container (photo 3). Cool to room temperature.

6. Don't waste the solids at the bottom of the pan. Spread them on some bread or a muffin. You won't be sorry.

7. When the clarified butter has cooled, cover tightly and store in the refrigerator. It keeps forever. (Indeed, in *A Historical Dictionary of Indian Food*, K.T. Achaya refers to the "rejuvenating properties" of ghees kept up to and over 100 years.)

Photo 1

Photo 2

Photo 3

BRANDIED MUSHROOMS

Sauteed over high heat, mushrooms become firm and golden brown rather than limp and gray. On their own, they make a great side dish. Use them to stuff an omelet or dress up a piece of meat. If you like, add some cream at the end to make a filling for crepes or a delicious topping for polenta.

PREP TIME: 10 MINUTES

COOK TIME: 4 MINUTES

YIELD: 4 SERVINGS

2 tablespoons clarified butter

1 package (8 ounces) button mushrooms, cut into quarters or ⅛-inch slices

1 shallot, minced

2 teaspoons minced fresh thyme or parsley, or 1 teaspoon dried herbs

1 tablespoon brandy

½ teaspoon salt

Freshly ground pepper

¼ cup whipping cream, optional

1. Place a large skillet over high heat; add clarified butter to hot skillet. Cook until butter almost begins to smoke, about 2 minutes; add the mushrooms. Cook until mushrooms just begin to release moisture and sizzle, about 15 seconds; stir. Cook until mushrooms begin to turn golden brown, about 15–30 seconds. Add shallot; cook, tossing, until fragrant, about 30 seconds.

2. Remove skillet from heat; add the brandy. Carefully ignite the brandy with a long match or return the pan to the heat, tipping it slightly toward the flame until the brandy ignites. Shake the pan until the flames go out. Stir in the herbs; season with salt and pepper to taste. Stir in cream; heat just until cream begins to boil.

NUTRITION INFORMATION PER SERVING: 68 calories, 73% of calories from fat, 6g fat, 4g saturated fat, 15mg cholesterol, 2g carbohydrates, 2g protein, 294mg sodium, 1g fiber

WHISKED AWAY: EMULSIONS LEAD WAY TO IRRESISTIBLE—AND EASY TO MAKE—VINAIGRETTES AND SAUCES

I've become exceedingly fond of what the Australians call "warm salads," a cool pile of fresh, dressed greens topped with something "from the barbie." Probably three nights a week I'll toss a steak, some chicken or a piece of fish on the grill or under the broiler, whisk up a quick salad dressing, and dinner's ready in 15 minutes.

STEPS TO FOLLOW

An emulsion is a homogenous mixture of two liquids that do not combine naturally, like water and oil. Whisking breaks one of the liquids into tiny droplets which are then suspended throughout the other liquid to form a uniform product. Vinaigrettes and mayonnaise are among the most common emulsions, a group which also includes butter and homogenized milk.

Because the chemical properties of the two incompatible liquids tend to force them apart (causing your vinaigrette to separate), it helps to use an "emulsifier" to promote and stabilize the product. Without getting into the anxiety-producing science of how they work, suffice it to say that the two most common emulsifiers are egg yolk and dried or prepared mustard.

The key to a successful emulsion is the whisking. After combining the vinegar and mustard (for vinaigrettes) or egg yolk, vinegar and mustard (for mayonnaise), the oil must be whisked in slo-o-o-o-o-wly, just a few drops at a time. Once the emulsion begins to form, the oil can be added more quickly, but never so quickly that it overwhelms the emulsion and causes it to break.

WHY YOU NEED TO LEARN IT

Commercial salad dressings are inferior to what you can make at home. It takes two minutes to put together a delicious vinaigrette, and a more rewarding two minutes you may never spend.

Toss vinaigrettes with green salads, of course, but also with grain and legume salads, salsas and grilled vegetables. Spoon them over chicken and fish or drizzle a few drops onto soups for color and flavor.

PUTTING YOUR SKILLS TO WORK

Warm salad of beef with avocado-mango salsa (pg. 194)

WHISKED AWAY *(continued)*

On the topic of broken emulsions, while mayonnaise needs to be stable to be considered successful, a vinaigrette does not necessarily. In fact, a few drops of a broken vinaigrette, especially one where a dark vinegar sets off a lighter oil, can look very attractive drizzled around the outskirts of your dish.

As with most everything else, there's no one "right" way to make a vinaigrette. Usually, we talk in terms of the ratio of oil to vinegar. Depending on the ingredients and your taste, that ratio is generally between 2 to 1 and 4 to 1.

1. In a medium bowl, whisk together a roughly 3-to-1 ratio of vinegar and Dijon mustard along with some salt (photo 1). The mustard can be left out, but your finished product will not be as homogenous and it will separate much more quickly.

2. Whisk in a few drops of oil. Extra-virgin olive oil gives a great flavor, but any oil or combination of oils will do. You may prefer a milder oil, particularly if you'll be adding other flavoring ingredients such as herbs or chipotle. As the emulsion comes together, you'll see it thicken and cloud up.

3. Whisk in the remaining oil (2 to 4 times the amount of vinegar) in a slow and steady stream.

4. Taste for seasoning and add any additional flavoring ingredients.

5. Broken vinaigrettes can be rewhisked. If it fails to emulsify adequately, you can either not worry about it or you can try whisking a few drops into a bit of Dijon, then a few drops more until the emulsion reforms. Continue whisking as you add the remainder in a steady stream.

Photo 1

WARM SALAD OF BEEF WITH AVOCADO-MANGO SALSA

The Australians refer to cooked meat on top of greens as a "warm salad."

PREP TIME: 25 MINUTES

COOK TIME: 7 MINUTES

SERVES: 2 AS AN ENTREE,
4 AS AN APPETIZER

1 rib-eye, New York strip or sirloin steak, about 8 ounces

⅛ teaspoon coarse salt

Freshly ground pepper

Vinaigrette and greens:

1 tablespoon sherry vinegar or other vinegar

1 teaspoon Dijon mustard

¼ teaspoon coarse salt

3 tablespoons extra-virgin olive oil

1 teaspoon honey

8 ounces mesclun mix or other fresh salad greens

Avocado-mango salsa:

2 cloves garlic, minced

1 avocado, peeled, cut into medium dice

1 mango, peeled, cut into medium dice

¼ red onion, cut into small dice

2 tablespoons extra-virgin olive oil

1 tablespoon minced cilantro

½ teaspoon coarse salt

½ teaspoon ground cumin

¼ teaspoon freshly ground pepper

¼ teaspoon dried oregano

Juice of 1 lime

Hot red pepper sauce

1. Season steak with the salt and pepper to taste. Grill, saute or broil to medium-rare, about 3½ minutes per side. Remove from heat; let rest 10 minutes.

2. Meanwhile for the vinaigrette, whisk the vinegar, mustard and salt in a small bowl. Whisk in a few drops of oil to form an emulsion. Continue whisking while adding remaining oil in a slow, steady stream; whisk in honey. Toss greens with vinaigrette.

3. Combine salsa ingredients in a medium bowl; set aside. Divide dressed greens among plates; mound salsa in center. Slice steak on the diagonal into thin strips; fan out across top of salsa.

NUTRITION INFORMATION PER SERVING: 792 calories, 69% of calories from fat, 63g fat, 12g saturated fat, 102mg cholesterol, 37g carbohydrates, 27g protein, 1,165mg sodium,g fiber

IMMERSED IN EMULSIONS: BEURRE BLANC SAUCE IS EASY TO MAKE—AND HERE'S A TRICK TO KEEP IT FROM SEPARATING

OK, show of hands: Who out there only uses margarine and never butter? I ask because beurre blanc really ought to be made with whole butter. Sure, you can do it with margarine. It's just that any satisfaction you get from making it will be overshadowed by the rumbling thunder of 10,000 dead chefs rolling over in their graves.

WHY YOU NEED TO LEARN IT

A little butter never hurt anyone. And besides, this sauce is surprisingly easy to make, and it's silky and delicious. Serve it with fresh seafood, and your friends will love you even more than they do already.

Beurre blanc (which translates from French simply as "white butter") is, along with other sauces like hollandaise, mayonnaise and vinaigrettes, what we call an emulsified sauce.

An emulsion is a homogenous mixture of two liquids that, under normal circumstances, wouldn't combine, like oil and water. To make an emulsion, one of the liquids is broken up into Carl Sagan-like billions and billions of tiny droplets that are completely surrounded by the other liquid. If the emulsion is stable, meaning that it won't break, we call it a permanent emulsion. Mayonnaise is an example of this. If it's unstable, it's called a temporary emulsion. A simple oil-and-vinegar vinaigrette is temporary.

Beurre blanc is temporary, but it's more stable than a vinaigrette, particularly if we take a somewhat cheaty step which we'll get to later.

Butter is mostly fat (about 80 percent), but because it also contains water, it, too, is an emulsion. The idea behind a beurre blanc is to take a small amount of liquid in the form of the reduction of an acid (most often white wine or vinegar or some combination of both) and whisk butter into it over low heat. The challenge that discourages many cooks even from trying a beurre blanc is creating and keeping the emulsion rather than simply allowing the butter to melt. If the butter melts instead of emulsifying, you end up with a greasy pool of liquid butterfat. And no one wants that.

STEPS TO FOLLOW

The method given below will produce about a cup of sauce, enough for eight 1-ounce-size servings.

1. Finely chop 1 shallot and add it to a heavy-bottomed saucepan along with about 3 to 4 ounces each of white wine and white wine vinegar (photo 1). Heat this mixture to a boil and let it reduce until there are only about 2 tablespoons of liquid left. (Try to avoid letting the shallots brown; it won't hurt the sauce, really, but it will give it an off color).

2. Take the pan off the heat and let the liquid cool a little bit. Remember, we don't want the butter to melt, and if the pan is still very hot, it's a little risky.

3. When the pan has cooled for 30 to 60 seconds, place it over medium-low heat and whisk in about half a pound (2 sticks) of cold, whole butter that you've cut into 1-inch cubes (photo 2).

The key to success with this sauce is the whisking. As soon as you add the butter, whisk away as though the fate of Western civilization depended on it. Don't let the butter pieces sit anywhere long enough to melt; that's the death of this sauce. You can add all the butter at once, or you can toss in a few cubes at a time. Just keep whisking.

Photo 1

Photo 2

THE KEY TO SUCCESS WITH THIS SAUCE IS THE WHISKING.

IMMERSED IN EMULSIONS *(continued)*

4. When your sauce is done, when all your butter is added, strain it through a chinois or fine mesh sieve. This step isn't necessary, but it gives the sauce a wonderfully smooth mouthfeel.

5. Hold your finished sauce for up to a couple hours over low heat (or safer yet, in a bain-marie or double boiler). It shouldn't be kept any hotter than about 125 degrees, and don't let it cool because it will turn back into butter.

A few more ideas

To decrease the chances that your sauce will break, add a couple tablespoons of whipping cream to the reduced liquid before adding the butter. This is sometimes referred to as sauce nantais and is the cheaty step mentioned above.

Substitute other acids such as grapefruit juice or lemon juice for the white wine and vinegar. Then up the flavor by adding the zest of those fruits' peels or even segments of the fruit itself.

Add herbs or roasted garlic or anything else you can think of: fruit puree or chutney or whole-grain mustard or horseradish. Add these after the butter is incorporated, then bring the sauce up to temperature and strain it or not, as you wish.

THE WONDER OF HOMEMADE VINEGAR: SIMPLE PROCESS HAS SWEET REWARDS

Remember in the New Testament when Jesus was on the cross and someone gave him a vinegar-soaked sponge to drink from? When I first heard this story back at Holy Trinity Catholic Grammar School, I was horrified. Vinegar, to my 6-year-old mind, was just about the worst substance on earth.

Fortunately, in the ensuing decades I have discovered what a wonder vinegar is. Here, we'll talk about making our own from red wine.

STEPS TO FOLLOW

Vinegar can be made from many things: wine, beer, fruit juice. It's an ancient process, the natural result of bacteria converting alcohol into acetic acid. While you can make red wine vinegar simply by leaving an open bottle of red wine out for a few weeks, you'll have a better product if you use what's called a "mother."

The mother is the gelatinous mass of bacteria called *Mycoderma aceti* that converts the alcohol to acid. It forms on the top of developing vinegar and ultimately sinks to the bottom. You may have seen one in an older bottle of vinegar in your cupboard.

Good quality mothers can be purchased online or from shops that sell beer- and wine-making supplies. Or, if you have a friend who makes vinegar, ask for a piece of the mother. You can also look for organic vinegar with the mother inside (such as the Bragg brand at Whole Foods Markets.)

Now let's talk about the vessel. You can use a wide-mouth glass jar; just wrap a towel or tape some paper around it to keep out the light. (I specify "wide mouth" because the bacteria that convert the alcohol need a plentiful oxygen supply.) But an earthenware crock with a spigot on the bottom is even better, because you can drain the vinegar without disturbing the mother on top. Ask the place where you get your mother about these.

Other than that, all you'll need is wine. Anything you like drinking will make a vinegar that's probably better than any you've bought.

WHY YOU NEED TO LEARN IT

Though there are excellent commercial balsamic and sherry vinegars, really good quality red wine vinegars are a bit harder to find. Making your own, using wine you enjoy drinking, can result in a more robust, complex product that's also mellower than the often highly acidic commercial varieties.

THE WONDER OF HOMEMADE VINEGAR *(continued)*

1. Thoroughly wash your vessel, then turn it over on a clean surface to drip dry. You don't want any other bacteria lurking inside.

2. Add a bit of store-bought red wine vinegar and swirl it around the inside of the vessel to kill any lingering beasties.

3. Add the mother and enough red wine to come about half- to three-quarters of the way up the vessel. You want lots of air moving across the surface.

4. Cover the top with cheesecloth, then secure it so it doesn't blow off.

5. Set the vessel in a warm place where it won't be disturbed, such as the top of your fridge, and let it stay there for about two to three months. Check it after a few weeks to make sure a fresh mother has started to form on the surface.

6. After a couple of months, smell the vinegar and sample a little to see if it's acidic enough for your taste. If not, let it go another week or four. It will continue to get more acidic until all the alcohol is converted. When it's done, drain the vinegar into a clean container and give the mother to a friend or use it to start a fresh batch.

DIY flavored vinegars

If this seems like too much trouble, you might want to use commercial vinegar to create your own flavored vinegars. Fill a clean glass jar halfway with a selection of fresh herbs. Fill the jar all the way with vinegar. White distilled vinegar is cheap and works fine, but you can also use wine or cider vinegar. Cover the vessel and keep it out of the sunlight, shaking it a little every day. Start tasting after a week. If the flavor's not there yet, let it sit for as long as it takes, up to several weeks. When the flavor is right, strain out the herbs and bottle the vinegar in a fresh, clean jar.

HOMEMADE MAYONNAISE WHISKS UP IN A JIFFY—AND IS WORTH THE EFFORT

The first time I made mayonnaise, many years ago, my not-yet wife came and stood at my side and watched, silently, while I whisked oil slowly and deliberately, drop by drop, into a beaten egg yolk. "You know," she said, after a while, "they sell big jars of that stuff down at the grocery store."

WHY YOU NEED TO LEARN IT

OK, maybe you don't need to learn this, like you need to learn how to—oh, I don't know—make toast. But, come on. It's a sauce, like any other, so after a lifetime of factory-made bottled equivalents, why not try the real thing? It's as simultaneously similar to and different from a jar of Hellmann's as your homemade tomato sauce is to a jar of Ragu.

There's nothing wrong with the bottled stuff, in truth; it's just not your own.

PUTTING YOUR SKILLS TO WORK

Garlic potato salad (pg. 204)

STEPS TO FOLLOW

Mayonnaise, like a vinaigrette, is an emulsion—droplets of one liquid dispersed and suspended in another, incompatible liquid. In this case, oil is dispersed into water in the form of vinegar or lemon juice and egg yolk.

There are a couple keys to any emulsion: First, the ingredients, including the egg yolk, should be at room temperature. Emulsions that are too cold will have a harder time forming, and heated emulsions can break.

Second, the oil must be added very slowly at first. The whisking breaks it into literally billions of drops that are then suspended in the water, according to Harold McGee in "On Food and Cooking." This suspension is the emulsion, and as it grows, it thickens and strengthens. As it strengthens, you can begin to add the oil more quickly.

The following steps will give you about 2 to 2½ cups of mayo.

1. Whisk together two egg yolks, 1 teaspoon prepared mustard (or ½ teaspoon dried mustard), and 2 tablespoons total vinegar, lemon juice or a combination of both, ½ teaspoon of salt and a pinch of white pepper (photo 1). If you're concerned about salmonella, use pasteurized eggs.

2. Continue whisking while you add a few drops of oil. Extra-virgin olive oil is very traditional, but it gives rather a strong flavor. More neutral oils like canola, vegetable or peanut are less intrusive. Remember, there's no right or wrong to this: It's just that different tasting oils and vinegars will give different tasting results. Continue whisking until the oil is absorbed into the yolk mixture, then repeat.

3. As the emulsion grows, add the oil more quickly, but don't flood it. Stay in control and watch that the oil is absorbed continuously and completely.

4. Keep adding oil until your mayonnaise is the consistency of, you know, mayonnaise (photo 2). One rule of thumb (which McGee disputes, but is handy nonetheless) is that each large egg yolk will hold about 1 cup oil.

5. When the oil is all added and the mayo is the right consistency, taste it for seasoning. You may need more salt or a few more drops of lemon juice. If it's too thick, add warm water, lemon juice or vinegar, a teaspoon at a time, to thin it.

6. Mayonnaise traditionally is served at room temperature. It will keep for a few days in the refrigerator, but push a piece of plastic wrap onto its surface to keep out air. When you remove the mayo from the refrigerator, let it come to room temperature before whisking or it may break. If it does break ...

7. To fix a broken mayonnaise, whisk another egg yolk into a clean bowl. Add a small amount of the broken mayo and whisk it to reform the emulsion. As the emulsion strengthens, add the rest of the broken mayo in a slow, steady stream.

Note: Mayonnaise also can be made in a blender. Using whole eggs rather than just the yolks, pulse all the ingredients except the oil to combine, then let the blender run while adding the oil in a steady stream.

GARLIC POTATO SALAD

Anoint this potato salad with the goodness of your newly mastered homemade mayonnaise.

PREP TIME: 30 MINUTES

COOK TIME: 15 MINUTES

CHILLING TIME: 2 HOURS

YIELD: 10 SERVINGS

3 pounds red potatoes

1 teaspoon salt

2 pasteurized egg yolks

2 to 4 cloves garlic, crushed

1 tablespoon cider vinegar

1 tablespoon lemon juice

1 teaspoon Dijon mustard

½ teaspoon white pepper, optional

1½ to 2 cups vegetable oil

Hot red pepper sauce, optional

3 ribs celery, thinly sliced

1 small red onion, diced

1. Cover potatoes with water in a large saucepan; add ½ teaspoon of the salt. Heat to a boil over high heat. Reduce heat to low; cook until potatoes are fork-tender, 15 to 25 minutes, depending on size of potatoes.

2. Meanwhile, whisk egg yolks, garlic, vinegar, lemon juice, mustard, remaining ½ teaspoon of the salt and white pepper in a small bowl. Whisk in a few drops of oil until incorporated; add another few drops, whisking. Add remaining oil as the emulsification strengthens. Adjust seasoning with more salt, a few drops of red pepper sauce and more lemon juice, if desired.

3. Drain potatoes; cool. Cut into ¾-inch dice. Combine potatoes, celery, onion and mayonnaise in a large bowl; mix lightly. Cover with plastic wrap. Refrigerate at least 2 hours.

NUTRITION INFORMATION PER SERVING: 415 calories, 71% of calories from fat, 33g fat, 5g saturated fat, 41mg cholesterol, 28g carbohydrates, 3g protein, 269mg sodium, 3g fiber

ROUX THE DAY: VERSATILE BASE LENDS ITSELF TO MYRIAD SAUCES AND SOUPS

It's a given that pretty much everything is improved by the addition of a sauce. It's why we put ketchup on burgers and hot sauce on eggs. Good sauces cling to food, which means they must have body. There are many ways to achieve this, including the classic roux.

WHY YOU NEED TO LEARN IT

In truth, roux thickened sauces went out of fashion with the advent of "nouvelle cuisine" back in the '70s. Still, fashion requires neither usefulness nor inherent quality (remember leisure suits?), and knowing how to make and use roux allows you to create magnificent sauces for meat, fish, poultry and vegetables.

PUTTING YOUR SKILLS TO WORK

Veloute (pg. 209)
White wine cream sauce (pg. 209)

STEPS TO FOLLOW

Roux is nothing more than equal parts by weight of fat—in the form of butter, oil or animal fats—and flour. Flour is mostly starch, and starch is composed of tiny granules that swell when dissolved in water (or stock or milk, etc.). When the water is heated, the granules swell even more, and chains of molecules form webs that trap the water, thickening the liquid. This process is called gelatinization.

What you don't want to do is add straight flour to a hot liquid. The flour clumps and the starch on the outside of the clumps gelatinize, preventing the granules on the inside from dissolving. This gives us the dreaded lumpy sauce. In a roux, the individual granules are coated with fat, which allows them to dissolve without clumping.

Other ways to incorporate flour include the slurry, in which flour is dissolved in cold water and then poured slowly into hot liquid, and beurre manier, an uncooked paste of flour and whole butter which is whisked into a hot liquid.

What sets roux apart from the slurry and beurre manier is the fact that it's cooked. In French cuisine, roux is cooked to one of three stages: white, blond and brown. (New Orleans cuisine has even more shadings, including red and black.) The longer the cooking period, the darker the roux.

Cooking the roux has two main benefits. First, it gets rid of the raw, starchy flavor of the flour. Second (and this is with darker roux), it adds color to a dish. Thus, white and blond roux are used for light colored sauces and brown roux is used for darker sauces.

One further result of cooking is that ultimately it reduces the thickening power. It can take up to three times the amount of

Photo 1

Photo 2

Photo 3

dark brown roux as white roux to thicken the same amount of liquid. In general, 1 ounce of white or blond roux will thicken 1 cup of liquid.

And now, directions for what will give you about 1 cup of roux:

1. Set a small, heavy saucepan (don't use aluminum or your roux may turn gray) over a medium heat. When it's hot, add 1 stick (8 tablespoons) butter.

2. When the butter stops foaming, whisk in ½ cup. Don't worry if your measurements are not exact. Err on the side of too much flour and you'll be fine. You want the mixture to be moist and somewhat solid, not runny.

3. Continue whisking until the roux is done. For a white roux, this will be only a few minutes (photo 1). Blond roux takes more like 5 to 10 minutes (photo 2), and brown roux can take up to 20 minutes (photo 3). For brown roux, constant whisking is not necessary, but do take care not to let it burn.

Incorporating roux into a sauce can be troublesome, but with practice you'll be able to do it without any lumps. In general, whisk cool (not icy cold) liquid into hot (not too hot or the fat will spatter) roux or whisk room temperature roux into hot liquid. Bring the sauce to a simmer; let it go for about 20 minutes to cook out the starchy taste.

THE LONGER THE COOKING PERIOD, THE DARKER THE ROUX.

VELOUTE

This is one of the classic five "mother sauces" of French cuisine. It's simply a white stock—chicken, fish or veal—that is thickened with roux.

1. Heat the stock to a simmer in a heavy sauce pan. Whisk in the roux until it is completely dissolved.

2. Simmer until the sauce coats the back of a spoon, 15-20 minutes. Season with salt and white pepper to taste. Strain through a fine strainer.

NUTRITION INFORMATION PER TABLESPOON: 10 calories, 69% of calories from fat, 1g fat, 0.5g saturated fat, 2mg cholesterol, 0.4g carbohydrates, 0g protein, 67mg sodium, 0g fiber

PREP TIME: 2 MINUTES
COOK TIME: 15-20 MINUTES
YIELD: 2 CUPS

1 pint chicken or fish stock or broth

¼ cup roux

¼ teaspoon salt

White pepper to taste

WHITE WINE CREAM SAUCE

Use the veloute sauce to make this, a great combo with fish or chicken. For herbs, try fresh thyme, tarragon, chives or parsley.

1. Heat wine in a small sauce pan over medium-high heat to a boil; cook until wine is reduced by half, 2 minutes.

2. Add the veloute; heat to a simmer. Cook 2 minutes. Add the cream and fresh herbs. Remove from heat. Whisk in the cold butter. Season with salt, pepper to taste and a few drops of lemon juice. Pass the sauce through a fine strainer.

NUTRITION INFORMATION PER TABLESPOON: 20 calories, 90% of calories from fat, 2g fat, 1g saturated fat, 5mg cholesterol, 0g carbohydrates, 0g protein, 104mg sodium, 0g fiber

PREP TIME: 10 MINUTES
COOK TIME: 5 MINUTES
YIELD: 1 CUP

2 tablespoons white wine

1 cup veloute, see recipe

1 tablespoon warmed whipping cream

1 tablespoon minced fresh herbs or ½ teaspoon dried herbs

1 tablespoon cold butter

¼ teaspoon salt

White pepper, fresh lemon juice

A TREASURE-TROVE OF FLAVORS CAN BE FOUND IN PAN SAUCES

I've got nothing against steak sauce. Worcestershire, A.1., Heinz 57. I grew up on them.

But when you saute meat in a pan, you can make use of that pan and its meaty residue to create a unique, sophisticated homemade sauce that can beat A.1. with its fresh flavor.

Behold: the underutilized pan sauce.

WHY YOU NEED TO LEARN IT

This method provides an endless array of delicious and nearly effortless sauces that will add new layers of sophistication to your dinners. And it can be done in the time it takes for the meat to rest after cooking. Your dining companions will be amazed. Envious, even. Besides, everything needs a little sauce, right?

PUTTING YOUR SKILLS TO WORK

Mushroom pan sauce (pg. 213)

STEPS TO FOLLOW

For right now, let's assume you've just sauteed a couple of pork chops. Sure, you could do a steak or a chicken breast or a salmon fillet or even a fat slice of breaded eggplant—the method is the same for everything.

You've browned the chops in a small amount of hot fat and cooked them to a medium to medium-well doneness. Now you've removed the chops and set them on a plate to rest five minutes. There, in the bottom of the pan, is a mixture of the original oil, rendered pork fat and little brown bits of solidified pork juice, called fond in French. It's the fond that really makes a great pan sauce.

1. If there's a lot of fat left in the pan, pour out all but a couple of tablespoons. Put the pan back on medium-high heat, and toss in some minced aromatics, like garlic, shallot, onion, etc. Mushrooms would be a nice touch too (photo 1). Saute just for a minute or so—less for garlic, more for larger and heartier vegetables.

2. Deglaze the pan. This means pouring in an ounce or two of liquid (photo 2). Wine, brandy, juice, balsamic vinegar—even water, though that won't contribute any flavor, of course. If it flames, shake the pan until the alcohol burns off completely and the flames go out, and then use a wooden spoon to scrape up the fond as the liquid reduces to next to nothing—what's called au sec, or "until dry."

3. This part is optional: If you want a further flavoring ingredient, now's the time to stir in a teaspoon or two of that. Dijon mustard is great, and so are chutneys, preserves, any condiment-y kind of thing.

Photo 1

Photo 2

SAUTE JUST FOR A MINUTE OR SO—LESS FOR GARLIC, MORE FOR LARGER AND HEARTIER VEGETABLES.

▶

A TREASURE-TROVE OF FLAVORS CAN BE FOUND IN PAN SAUCES *(continued)*

4. Add your main liquid. Canned chicken or beef broth would be perfect in most cases. Tomato sauce or canned or fresh tomatoes also are great. Heat it to a boil.

5. If you're using tomatoes, you can probably skip this next step. Otherwise, when the sauce boils, let it reduce a little, then add a small amount of a thickening agent, like a slurry (cornstarch mixed with cold water) or beurre manie (whole butter mashed to a paste with an equal amount of flour). Heat the mixture to a boil and reduce the heat to a simmer.

6. Taste for seasoning and add your final flavoring ingredients: fresh minced or dried herbs, a splash of booze, a little horseradish, whatever you want. If you're going to add a tablespoon or two of cream, do it here. Regardless, whisk in a couple tablespoons of cold whole butter at the end. This is called "mounting with butter" and it adds richness, sheen and body to the final sauce.

7. Plate your chops and pour the sauce over. For a silky smooth sauce, pour it through a fine sieve or chinois.

MUSHROOM PAN SAUCE

After you saute a piece of meat or fish, don't clean out the pan. Instead, dump out all the oil except for a couple tablespoons, and proceed with this recipe.

1. Place the pan with drippings over medium-high heat. Add the mushrooms; cook, stirring, until just browned, about 1 minute. Add the garlic; cook, stirring, 30 seconds. Add the white wine. Raise the heat to high; cook wine until reduced to au sec (almost dry), about 5 minutes.

2. Whisk in the broth, mustard, and fresh herbs; heat to a boil.

3. Lower heat to a simmer; cook 1 minute. If sauce is too thin, mix cornstarch and water in a small bowl; add a little of the mixture to the sauce. Cook until thickened, adding more cornstarch mixture if needed.

4. Turn off the heat; whisk the cold butter into the sauce until incorporated and smooth. Season with salt and pepper to taste.

NUTRITION INFORMATION PER SERVING: 78 calories, 69% of calories from fat, 6g fat, 4g saturated fat, 15mg cholesterol, 4g carbohydrates, 2g protein, 408mg sodium, 1g fiber

PREP TIME: 5 MINUTES

COOK TIME: 4 MINUTES

YIELD: 4 SERVINGS

½ pound button mush-rooms, sliced

2 cloves garlic, minced

¼ cup white wine

½ cup chicken broth

1 teaspoon Dijon mustard

1 tablespoon minced fresh herbs or ½ teaspoon dried herbs

1 tablespoon cornstarch

1 tablespoon cold water

2 tablespoons cold butter

½ teaspoon salt

Freshly ground pepper

FOLLOW THESE SIMPLE STEPS AND YOU'LL GET THE PERFECT SAUCE … AND THE REST IS GRAVY

French chefs talk about the five "mother sauces" from which all other sauces emerge. In America, we tend to keep it simple: We've got barbecue sauce, spaghetti sauce, and gravy. Here, we're going with gravy.

WHY YOU NEED TO LEARN IT

Apart from ascetic mendicants hellbent on using their own suffering as a form of ritual purification, no one should lead a gravy-free life. Seriously, do you really want to eat dry mashed potatoes?

PUTTING YOUR SKILLS TO WORK

Chicken breasts with herbed mushroom gravy (pg. 218)

STEPS TO FOLLOW

Before we get to the play by play, I want to lay down exactly what we mean by "gravy." To me, gravy is a thickened liquid that is used to moisten, flavor and garnish meat and starch dishes. Many of my Italian friends call red tomato sauce "gravy," but I'm not going to include that, simply because it's tomato-based rather than stock- or broth-based.

Gravy has three basic components: the liquid, the thickener and the flavoring elements. While pretty much any liquid can be used, meat stock or broth are most common. Homemade stock is best, but seriously, how many of us have that floating around our kitchens? The next best thing is a good-quality, low-sodium canned broth (low-sodium not because it's more healthful, but rather because you want to have full control over the seasoning of your gravy).

Gravy usually contains a starch thickener, such as flour, cornstarch, potato starch or arrowroot. To prevent clumping, they should be stirred into a small amount of liquid before adding. Alternately, flour can be mixed with an equal amount of butter, called a beurre manie when it's raw, or a roux when it's cooked.

Flavoring components can be just about anything: fortified wines like madeira, marsala, sherry or port; spirits, mustard, herbs, spices, mushrooms, etc.

The best gravies often include some juice and flavorful browned bits from the cooking of the meat. In fact, we'll start at the moment the meat is finished cooking.

Photo 1

1. Whether it's a roast in the oven or some chops in a skillet, remove the finished meat to a plate and skim the fat from the pan, leaving the juice and whatever brown bits are stuck to the bottom.

2. Deglaze the pan. This entails setting the pan over medium-high heat and adding a few ounces of liquid—stock, juice or wine—just enough to cover the bottom of the pan. While the liquid simmers and evaporates, scrape up the brown bits with a spatula or wooden spoon to dissolve them into the liquid (photo 1).

FOLLOW THESE SIMPLE STEPS AND YOU'LL GET THE PERFECT SAUCE *(continued)*

3. Add your main liquid to the pan and heat to a simmer (photo 2). Because you're going to reduce the liquid to concentrate the flavors, you want to start with about one and half times the amount of liquid that you want to end up with. For example, for 2 cups of gravy, start with 3 cups of broth.

4. While the liquid simmers, stir in your thickener (photo 3). If you're using flour (in a roux, beurre manie or slurry), let it simmer at least 15 minutes to get rid of the starchy flavor. The other thickeners are ready as soon as they return to the boil.

5. Add whatever flavoring ingredients you want.

6. Strain your gravy through a fine sieve or chinois (photo 4).

7. For added richness, whisk in some cold butter or heavy cream

8. Taste for seasoning and add salt if necessary. If your gravy feels heavy on your tongue, add a few drops of fresh lemon juice to brighten it.

Photo 2

Photo 3

Photo 4

START WITH ABOUT ONE AND HALF TIMES THE AMOUNT OF LIQUID THAT YOU WANT TO END UP WITH.

CHICKEN BREASTS WITH HERBED MUSHROOM GRAVY

PREP TIME: 10 MINUTES

COOK TIME: 30 MINUTES

YIELD: 4 SERVINGS

4 boneless, skinless chicken breast halves

¾ teaspoon salt

Freshly ground pepper

½ cup flour

¼ cup vegetable oil

½ pound button mushrooms, sliced

1 ounce brandy or cognac

1 tablespoon Dijon mustard

¼ cup white wine

2 cups low-sodium chicken broth

½ teaspoon dried herbs, such as thyme or tarragon

3 tablespoons beurre manie (equal parts flour and butter mashed into a paste)

¼ cup heavy cream

Juice from half a lemon

1. Season the chicken breasts with ½ teaspoon of the salt and pepper to taste; dredge in flour. Heat a skillet over medium-high heat; when hot, add 2 tablespoons of the oil. Add the chicken to the skillet; cook until brown on one side, 4-5 minutes. Turn chicken over; cook until brown on the other side, 4-5 minutes.

2. Meanwhile, heat another skillet over high heat; when the pan is very hot, add the remaining 2 tablespoons of the oil. Add the mushrooms; allow them to sit to get some color, about 2 minutes. When they've browned a little bit, saute by flipping them in the pan or stirring with a spatula cooked through, about 3 minutes. Off flame, add the brandy; flame it with a stick lighter or by tilting it toward the flame. When the flames die out, season the mushrooms with the remaining ¼ teaspoon of the salt and pepper to taste. Remove from heat; set aside.

3. When the chicken breasts are nicely browned and have reached an interior temperature of 165 degrees, remove to a warm plate; allow to rest 10 minutes.

4. Meanwhile, for the gravy, skim any leftover fat from the skillet (the one in which the chicken was cooked). Return the skillet to medium-high heat. Whisk in the mustard; deglaze with the white wine.

5. Add the broth and dried herbs; raise heat to high. When the liquid starts to boil, reduce the heat; whisk in the beurre manie. Reduce heat to a simmer; cook until the raw starchy taste is gone, about 15 minutes. If it's too thick, thin with a little more broth.

6. Pass the gravy through a fine sieve or chinois; return it to the sauce pan over medium-low heat. Add the cream; taste for seasoning. If it seems heavy, squeeze in a few drops of lemon juice. Add the chicken breasts and mushrooms to the pan to reheat; serve.

NUTRITION INFORMATION: PER SERVING: 453 calories, 54% of calories from fat, 27g fat, 9g saturated fat, 105mg cholesterol, 19g carbohydrates, 33g protein, 575mg sodium, 1g fiber

DAIRY, EGGS AND BREAKFAST DISHES ▸

EGG POACHING SECRET: LEAVE IT ALONE

One can only guess as to the reticence of home cooks when it comes to cracking fresh eggs into hot water. I think that because the process can become so messy so quickly, with errant tendrils of lacy albumen—the protein in the white—tumbling gracelessly through clouded liquid, we assume immediately that something has gone awry.

Or maybe the egg itself was done perfectly, but drops of poaching liquid adhering to its surface so soaked the toast upon which it rested as to make the entire dish unpalatable.

So many pitfalls. And yet, when they are overcome, a poached egg is a wonderful, wonderful thing.

WHY YOU NEED TO LEARN IT

Poached eggs, with their compact shape and dry exterior, hold their molten yolks like a golden drippy prize, virtually demanding imaginative presentations. Spend a couple bucks on a couple dozen eggs you have no intention of eating, and practice your poaching. You will not regret it.

PUTTING YOUR SKILLS TO WORK

Warm white bean salad with poached egg (pg. 223)

STEPS TO FOLLOW

Delicate proteins, such as eggs or salmon fillets, toughen in too high a heat. Moreover, the increased jostling of higher temperature liquids can damage fragile items. So, while boiling occurs at 212 degrees, and simmering is between 180 and 205, poaching liquid is kept between 160 and 180.

We want three things in a poached egg: a warm, liquid yolk, a fully cooked white and a neat, oval appearance. It's this latter that trips us up most often, and it's because of the white.

An egg white has two parts, the thin white and the thick white (photo 1). The thick white surrounds the yolk, while the watery thin white spreads out and away.

It's the thick white that gives the poached egg its lovely shape, and the thin white that cooks quickly and floats off, mucking up the water. This is why the freshest eggs work best: as an egg ages, the thick white turns into thin white.

1. Heat about three inches of water to a boil in a saucepan, then turn down the heat. (Different chefs prefer more or less liquid. I like enough to keep the egg from sticking to the bottom, while not so much that it floats about aimlessly.) The surface should be relatively calm, with just a few bubbles attached to the sides of the pan and none rising from the center bottom.

Some people add a teaspoon of salt or an acid such as vinegar or lemon juice to the liquid. Both quicken the coagulation of the

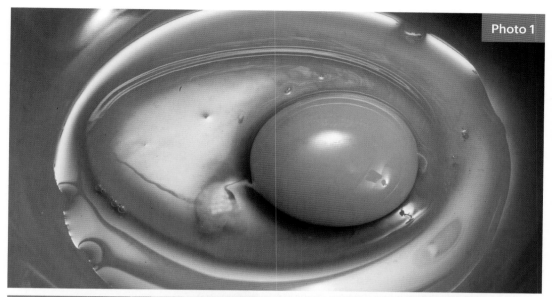

Photo 1

Photo 2

protein. While this contributes to a nicer shape, it can affect the flavor. I'm happy enough with un-adulterated water, but I would encourage you to experiment.

2. Crack an egg into the poaching liquid, or if you've never done this before, crack the egg into a bowl, then slide the egg into the pot (photo 2).

▶

EGG POACHING SECRET *(continued)*

3. Just wait (photo 3). Don't poke the egg. Don't swirl the water, regardless of what you've heard. For one thing, it's unnecessary. For another, if you're doing more than one egg, the roiling vortex will collide them into a big, poachy mess. (With practice, you can cook up to four eggs at once: Crack the eggs into the water, one at a time, leaving enough space between eggs to keep them from running together.)

4. After about 3 minutes, lift the egg gently from the liquid with a slotted spoon. The white should be firm, not jiggly, while the yolk should remain liquid. Press with your finger on the white near the yolk to make sure it's firm.

5. Blot the liquid from the top of the egg very carefully with a clean towel. Set the bowl of the slotted spoon on the towel to get it dry as possible (photo 4), then serve.

Note: Eggs can be poached hours or a day in advance. Dip them in ice water to stop the cooking, and drain. Refrigerate in a covered container. At serving time, repoach the eggs just long enough to warm through, about 1 minute.

Photo 3

Photo 4

DON'T POKE THE EGG. DON'T SWIRL THE WATER.

WARM WHITE BEAN SALAD WITH POACHED EGG

1. Whisk mustard into the vinegar in a small bowl; set aside. Cook bacon, turning occasionally, in a medium skillet over medium heat until crisp, about 5 minutes. Drain on paper towels; set aside. Pour off all but ¼ cup of the fat; whisk mustard mixture into fat in skillet over medium heat.

2. Stir in the bell peppers, onion and garlic. Cook, stirring, 30 seconds; turn off the heat. Stir in beans, parsley, salt and pepper to taste; set aside. Divide lettuce equally among 6 salad plates; top each plate equally with bean mixture. Set aside.

3. Heat a Dutch oven or deep skillet with 3 inches of water to a boil over high heat; reduce heat to low, waiting for simmering to just end. Crack the eggs into the water, one at a time, leaving enough space between eggs to keep them from running together. Poach until the whites are fully cooked but the yolks are warm and still liquid, about 3 minutes.

4. Remove eggs separately with a slotted spoon; blot each dry with a clean towel. Place one egg on top of each salad. Sprinkle with cracked pepper.

NUTRITION INFORMATION PER SERVING: 307 calories, 24% of calories from fat, 8g fat, 3g saturated fat, 218mg cholesterol, 38g carbohydrates, 21g protein, 479mg sodium, 9g fiber

PREP TIME: 25 MINUTES

COOK TIME: 20 MINUTES

YIELD: 6 SERVINGS

2½ teaspoons coarse mustard

2 tablespoons red wine vinegar

6 slices bacon, cut into ½-inch wide pieces

1 each, diced: green and red bell pepper

1 small red onion, diced

4 cloves garlic, creamed

2 cans (15½ ounces each) white beans such as navy or cannellini, drained

2 tablespoons minced fresh parsley

½ teaspoon salt

Fresh coarsely ground pepper

1 bag (10 ounces) mixed salad greens

6 eggs

THE ELEGANT EGG: FRENCH APPROACH TO OMELETS CREATES LOVELY PRESENTATION AND GREAT FLAVOR

Now that the good ol' anti-everything-French days are but a dim memory, let's talk about omelets. We can divide them into two camps: French and American.

American omelets—by far the most familiar, given our present location—are shaped like half-moons, often browned on the outside and thoroughly cooked inside. They're nearly always stuffed with something delicious.

Also, because we like to do things our own way, American omelets generally are not seasoned: Salt and pepper are added at the table.

French omelets are somewhat different. Instead of semicircular, they're football shaped: folded like a letter and plated seam-side down. Exhibiting a pure yellow exterior with possibly a hint of browning, the interior—rather than being cooked solid—is moist and fluffy. Also, salt and pepper are added before cooking, thus ensuring that every bite will be perfectly seasoned. Fluffy and moist, French omelets certainly can be stuffed, but they are beautiful plain too.

WHY YOU NEED TO LEARN IT

In terms of quick and elegant eats, nothing surpasses an omelet. Once you get good at the technique, you won't believe how fast you can make an absolutely wonderful lunch. In the time it takes to toast some nice bread, your omelet's done and lunch is ready.

STEPS TO FOLLOW

You'll have the best results with an 8- or 9-inch non-stick saute pan. You'll also need a fork and a warm plate onto which you can transfer the omelet as soon as it's done. Try to keep the metal fork from scratching the surface of the non-stick surface.

We'll be making two-egg omelets. Large, multi-egg omelets grow quickly unwieldy. Even if you're cooking for several people, the two-egg jobs cook so quickly—less than half a minute—that it's just as well to do everyone's individually.

As with all things, don't expect perfection the first or even second or third time you try: Buy a dozen eggs just to practice, and don't feel guilty about tossing some out.

1. Crack two eggs into a bowl. Whisk them into a homogenous yellow mixture. (Some people prefer less whisking, to give the finished product a two-tone appearance—generally yellow with streaks of white marbled across the top.)

2. Season the beaten eggs with salt and pepper. Many chefs advocate white pepper for omelets because it's invisible in the final product. Regular pepper will show up as small black spots dotting the surface of your otherwise pristine yellow omelet. Though I prefer the flavor of black pepper to white pepper, I agree that the small black dots make for a less palatable appearance

3. Set your non-stick pan over a flame that's on the high side of medium-high. We want the pan to be very hot so the liquid egg coagulates immediately upon touching the surface.

4. When the pan is hot, add a bit of fat. I prefer clarified butter for its taste and higher smoke point. Whole butter will work, though you'll probably end up with a somewhat browner final product. Oil is fine too: I recommend something light with a higher smoke point such as peanut or canola oil.

5. When the fat is hot, add the eggs. In about five seconds, there will be a thin layer of solid egg on the bottom of the pan, covered by the rest of the still liquid egg. Now it begins:

Using the flat side of the fork (photo 1), begin stirring up that solid layer. At the same time—and here's where it gets tricky, like patting your head and rubbing your stomach—move the pan with speedy, confident vigor forward and back across the burner. These continuous combined motions cause more and more liquid to touch the pan bottom and coagulate. As it coagulates, it's moved out of the way by the stirring and the shaking, making room for more liquid. You'll notice the coagulated eggs mounting a bit in the center of the pan, exactly what you want for a nice, fluffy omelet.

Photo 1

THE ELEGANT EGG *(continued)*

6. In about 30 seconds, all the liquid will be gone. The eggs will be moist and curdy on the top but solid and dry on the bottom. Take the pan off the flame. If the eggs are still a bit gooey, don't worry. Carryover cooking will complete the job once the omelet is folded.

7. Here's the hardest part: Tilt the pan to a 45-degree angle and use your fork to fold down the top third of the omelet (photo 2). Next, loosen the bottom edge with your fork and begin sliding the omelet out of the pan and onto the plate. When the unfolded portion makes it onto the plate (photo 3), flip the remaining folded part over on top, pushing it slightly to position the seam underneath.

In theory, what you'll end up with is a fluffy, seamless, oval-shaped omelet with a smooth yellow top (photo 4). Good luck.

OVER EASY, OVER AND OVER! YOU HAVE TO BREAK A FEW (DOZEN) EGGS TO MASTER THE TECHNIQUE

The perfect over-easy egg has a fully cooked white with no bubbles, no browning and no lacing. The yolk is a warm and golden liquid with no trace of the light yellow opacity that indicates coagulation has occurred.

Having said that, I know we all have our own definition of "perfect." After all, if anything is true in this life, it is this: There's no accounting for taste. You may like a brown, lacy white that's more shawl than egg. You may prefer your eggs over medium. Or over hard, heaven help us.

Regardless of how you define perfection, the path to its achievement—the technique—is the same. And it involves flipping the egg, one handed, in the pan. How cool will that be?

STEPS TO FOLLOW

It goes against many of our grains to throw out perfectly good food. But we're going to do just that. You see, this technique is difficult; you'll need to practice to get the hang of it.

Seriously, be prepared to destroy some eggs. If you're worried about ruining food, you won't relax enough to allow your muscles to learn and memorize the motions. By allowing yourself to destroy a dozen or two eggs, any concerns about the fate of an individual egg are subsumed by the growing realization that, as you practice, you're getting better and better.

Now, I know you want two eggs, but let's practice with just one first, OK?

For one egg, use a small (7-inch) non-stick skillet. Heat it over a medium-low flame and add a bit of fat—clarified butter, whole butter, oil.

1. Crack the egg directly into the hot fat. Or, if that makes you nervous, crack it into a small bowl and pour it gently into the pan. If your egg bubbles or gives off that "shhhhhhh"—that classic breakfast sizzling sound—your heat's too high. Turn it down.

2. Wait. With the heat low, it will take a few moments for the egg white to coagulate on the bottom. Resist the urge to poke at it or shake the pan.

WHY YOU NEED TO LEARN IT

What percentage of the eggs you've eaten have been cooked perfectly? Mm-hmm. And how happy would you be to create perfect eggs, always? Mm-hmm. And how satisfying is it to have your spouse or a friend say, "This egg ... it's ... it's ... perfect."

OVER EASY, OVER AND OVER! *(continued)*

3. Once your white has firmed up on the bottom and appears to have some good structure, give the pan a gentle shake to make sure the egg is moving freely. Remember: gentle; don't be splattering the remaining liquid white all over everything.

4. When the white has coagulated fully on the bottom but still has a bit of liquid on the top, it's time to flip. Don't panic. Just practice steps 5 and 6 several times.

5. With the pan brushing the top of the burner, move it firmly about six inches straight ahead and stop suddenly WITHOUT PULLING BACK ON THE PAN. After the pan stops moving, notice how the momentum of the egg carries it toward and partially up the sloped front of the pan (photo 1).

6. Pull the pan back quickly to where you started and stop suddenly. Notice again how the momentum of the egg carries it back across the flat surface after the pan has stopped.

7. Practice the forward and backward moves several times until the pan begins to feel more natural in your hand. Remember, we're not flipping now, we're just getting the feel of the egg as it moves in the pan.

8. Now, put steps 5 and 6 together without stopping in between: Move the pan forward, then pull back immediately while giving a very slight upward flick of your wrist. By pulling backward as the egg travels forward, you'll send the leading edge of the egg up the sloped side of the pan. By adding that very slight wrist flick, you'll flip the egg gently over onto its back (photo 2), like a roller coaster going through a loop. Ready? Now.

9. OK, not bad. Now look, regardless of how it turned out for you, whether you did it perfectly or the yolk broke or the egg is now on your shirt, keep practicing with the same egg, over and over again until it has been cooked right to death. (Well, not if the egg is on your shirt; in that case, just peel it off, toss it out and start with a fresh one.)

10. When you've flipped the first egg a dozen times or so, thank it for its tireless sacrifice. Discard it. Grab another egg and start again.

SHIRRED PLEASURE: EASY-TO-MAKE EGG DISH PERFECT FOR BRUNCH

In the dustier corners of culinary arcana lie shirred (aka "baked") eggs, so off the beaten path that the origin of the word "shirred" is a mystery. We do know shirred eggs are wonderful. Baked in a small dish, the just-set whites and warm, liquid yolk smother small bits of bacon or ham or vegetables or any wonderful thing.

WHY YOU NEED TO LEARN IT

Shirred eggs are an excellent brunch dish because they're easy to prepare for a lot of guests. Plus, with the host of ingredients available to put inside, the dish is extremely versatile and can be as simple or elaborate as you like.

STEPS TO FOLLOW

First, a little background: The French have a similar preparation called "en cocotte," in which eggs are placed in a small dish (la cocotte) and baked inside a water bath.

Although shirred eggs also are baked in small dishes called ramekins, most recipes call for them to be baked directly in the oven, not inside a water bath.

We recommend the water bath. We're still going to call them shirred, because we're speaking English, but here's why we we're not going to put them into the oven straight:

Eggs are largely composed of protein, and that means the best way to cook them is gently. Without going too far into the science, protein-rich items like eggs or meat have strands of protein that tighten with heat (the scientific term is "coagulate") and begin to squeeze the water out of whatever you're cooking. That's why overcooked eggs can seem rubbery, and overcooked chicken breasts tough and dry.

But ramekins surrounded by simmering water can never get hotter than the temperature of that water (about 185 degrees), even inside a 350 degree oven. Ramekins exposed to nothing but the heated air of that oven, though, will continue to get hotter and hotter, and that heat will transfer to the eggs, increasing the risk of overcooking. Baking your eggs in a water bath exposes them to a much gentler heat, decreasing the risk of overcooking.

One last note: Ramekins come in all shapes and sizes. The rule of thumb is the same as with any cooking vessel: It should be just large enough to hold all the ingredients comfortably.

Here is the method for one serving in one ramekin. As you increase the number of ramekins, the cooking time may increase as well.

1. Grease a 6- to 8-ounce ramekin with butter, oil or nonstick cooking spray.

2. Add precooked flavoring ingredients. (Raw ingredients won't be cooked by the time the eggs are done.) Crumbled bacon, slices of ham or sausage, smoked fish, vegetables—such as sauteed mushrooms, asparagus tips or even leftover ratatouille—and shredded cheese. Anything you can imagine putting inside an omelet will work at the bottom of a ramekin.

3. Add your egg(s) (photo 1). Two per serving seem reasonable, but one or three will work too. (Just remember the rule that all ingredients fit comfortably into the ramekin.)

SHIRRED PLEASURE *(continued)*

4. Top with a little butter, grated cheese or cream. (Interestingly, the oldest known reference to shirred eggs, in the Century Dictionary and Cyclopedia published in the late 19th century, defines "shirr" as "to poach (eggs) in cream instead of water.") You may also do this after the eggs have set to keep the dairy ingredients on top.

5. Set the filled ramekin inside a larger, straight-sided dish (such as a casserole dish), then add very hot or simmering water until it comes up to the level of the egg mixture (photo 2). Be careful not to pour water directly into the ramekin. Place the dish with the ramekin in the center of a 350-degree oven and bake until the whites are set and the yolks are warm and liquid. Depending on how many eggs you're using, what other ingredients you have in there, how well your oven works, etc., the time can vary greatly. After 6 minutes, check every minute or so until the eggs are done. Remove from oven, rest for a minute, then serve in the ramekin (pictured on page 219).

Photo 2

EGG + MILK + BREAD—SIMPLE EQUATION ADDS UP TO A FOOLPROOF DISH: FRENCH TOAST

God bless the French. Their fries are divine. Their Champagne's to die for. And don't get me started on their kisses. But best of all, is their toast. French toast. Is there anything cheerier?

STEPS TO FOLLOW

This is one of those foods with a bazillion variations. You shouldn't worry too much, then, about recipes or exact amounts.

One of the many nice things about French toast is that it's simple to figure out how much to make. Generally, I don't like to eat more than a couple pieces at a time, with the syrup and all, and one egg combined with an ounce of milk will make enough batter for those two pieces. This is an approximation, of course, and it depends on how thick your bread is, how soaked you like it to be, and so on.

Right now, we're going to make just enough for ourselves. If you're having company and want to make more, just do the math.

Another great thing about French toast is that it freezes very well, so you may well want to make a bunch more anyway. Then, later in the week, you can put them straight from the freezer into the toaster or microwave.

One last note about the bread: Feel free to experiment with different kinds. My tastes are simple, but many people like whole-grain breads or challah or brioche or some other fantastic artisanal loaf. Again, try different types—they'll all be good, I reckon, just different.

1. Crack an egg into a wide, shallow bowl, then whisk it. Whisk it good. If your batter's not perfectly homogenous, your French toast will end up with streaks of cooked egg white on the surface. While this isn't bad, really, for some reason that visible coagulate on my otherwise golden brown French toast gives me the heebie-jeebies. But that's just me.

WHY YOU NEED TO LEARN IT

French toast is one of the happiest things you can put in your mouth. It tastes great. It's easy to make. And, it's even pretty good for you, in a carbs and protein kind of way.

EGG + MILK + BREAD *(continued)*

2. Whisk in about half as much milk as you have egg, more or less. Since the average large egg weighs 2 ounces, and since milk's volume is roughly equal to its weight, this means you want about 1 ounce of milk (or 1/8 cup or 2 tablespoons) for every egg. I use 2-percent milk, just because that's what we drink at my house. You can use whole milk or skim milk, of course. Some of my friends even use heavy cream, if you can imagine that.

3. Finally, whisk in whatever flavoring you like. My favorites are vanilla and cinnamon. For one egg I usually use just a few drops of vanilla extract—maybe 1/8 teaspoon—and even less cinnamon (a pinch is fine). One thing to keep in mind with cinnamon is that it doesn't dissolve like sugar or salt. This means that you have to whisk it pretty well in order to distribute it throughout the batter (photo 1).

4. Dunk your bread into the batter and flip it to cover both sides (photo 2). Now, this here's an area of much discussion. Personally, I'm pretty much of an "in and out" kind of guy as far as French toast batter goes. Some people, though, like to drop the bread into the batter and then take the dog out for a walk. Then, when they finally remove the bread it's got the texture of a seat cushion on the Edmund Fitzgerald. As with the visible streaks of egg white, I find that particular characteristic somewhat off-putting. You do what you like, of course.

5. If you've got a well-seasoned cast-iron griddle or a non-stick pan, you can cook your French toast without any fat. I, on the other hand, like to cook it in butter (photo 3). This gives it a great flavor, and then at the table I'll just use maple syrup. Or sour cream. Or powdered sugar. Or fresh berries. Or apples or bananas sauteed in butter. Or some combination of all of the above. With French toast, you really can't go wrong.

Photo 1

Photo 2

Photo 3

WITH CREPES, DINNER OPTIONS ENDLESS

If my kids had to choose between pancakes and air, we may as well move to the moon.

Me, I can take them or leave them, but, when it comes to their French cousin, I'm a sucker. Here, my friends, is the crepe.

WHY YOU NEED TO LEARN IT

Aside from being a wonderful, warm, sweet snack when they're spread with butter and sprinkled with sugar, the real beauty of crepes is that, like pizza dough, they're blank canvases waiting to be turned into something extraordinary: Warm some delicious leftovers or give a quick saute to fresh ingredients and it'll be great in a crepe.

PUTTING YOUR SKILLS TO WORK

Basic crepes (pg. 240)

STEPS TO FOLLOW

Crepes are found across France, of course, but they originated in Brittany, the Celtic region on the northwest coast. It seems as though every road or country lane in Brittany is marked by handmade signs pointing to creperies.

Like American pancakes, crepes are pretty simple: flour moistened with eggs, milk and/or water and enriched with a little butter (photo 1).

The ratios vary from recipe to recipe, but in general the consistency of the batter should be close to that of heavy cream.

In Brittany, sweet crepes are made with regular wheat flour whereas savory crepes often are made at least partially with buckwheat flour and are referred to as "galettes." As distant from Brittany as we are, we won't be making that distinction; our basic batter using wheat flour will serve equally well for sweet and savory crepes.

If you're making sweet crepes, feel free to add a couple tablespoons of sugar.

Conspicuous by their absence in crepe batter are leaveners like baking powder or soda, since, unlike fluffy American pancakes, crepes need to be wafer thin.

After combining the ingredients (photo 2), it's best to rest the batter for an hour.

This allows the starch granules in the flour to become fully hydrated while letting any bubbles or foam dissipate. Bubbles in the batter can interrupt the crepe's smooth surface and, because the crepes are so thin, make them more likely to tear.

WITH CREPES, DINNER OPTIONS ENDLESS *(continued)*

Breton crepes also are much larger and thinner than most of us are used to seeing. For our typically smaller crepes, we suggest using a good, nonstick skillet, 8- or 9-inches in diameter. Set it over a medium high flame and when it's good and hot, brush it with clarified (or melted) butter. Another technique is to wrap a chunk of butter in a clean towel and rub it over the surface of the pan.

The idea is to keep the crepes from getting greasy.

After pouring the batter into the pan, tilt the pan to coat the entire bottom (photo 3). Add only enough batter to cover it in the thinnest possible layer, about 2 to 4 tablespoons. (Expect the first couple of crepes to be less than perfect as you tweak the heat or the amount of batter.)

Cook the first side for about a minute, until it's lightly browned. Flip it and cook another 30 to 60 seconds (photo 4).

Remove the crepe to a plate and make the remaining batter. Use them right away or freeze them in stacks. They freeze really well.

Photo 3

Photo 4

BASIC CREPES

PREP TIME: 20 MINUTES

COOK TIME: 2 HOURS

YIELD: 8 CREPES

1½ cups flour

Pinch of salt

---

3 eggs

---

2 cups milk (or 1 cup
  each: milk, water)

½ stick (4 tablespoons)
  melted butter, plus
  more for the skillet

---

1. Combine flour and salt in a bowl; make a well. Whisk eggs in a separate bowl; add milk and melted butter.

2. Whisk egg mixture into flour mixture until just combined. (Or blend ingredients in a blender until smooth.) Batter should be consistency of heavy cream. If it's too thick, thin with additional milk or water. Rest batter in refrigerator, 1 hour.

3. Heat an 8-inch nonstick skillet over medium heat. When hot, brush with melted butter. Pour in just enough batter to coat bottom of pan, about ¼ cup. Cook until light brown on 1 side, about 1 minute. Flip with a spatula or your fingers; cook on other side, 20-30 seconds. Remove to a plate; repeat with remaining batter.

NUTRITION INFORMATION PER SERVING: 260 calories, 16g fat, 9g saturated fat, 45mg cholesterol, 15g carbohydrates, 14g protein, 416mg sodium, 2g fiber

Fillings

- Saute spinach or mushrooms in butter or oil until tender. Sprinkle with flour; stir 1 minute. Add enough chicken broth to achieve a creamy consistency. Heat to a boil; reduce heat. Cook 1 minute; add a little cream. Add fresh herbs if you like, or a splash of white wine.

- Do the same as above, only with chicken, shrimp or salmon, instead of spinach and mushrooms. If you're using fish, substitute clam juice for chicken broth.

- Saute diced or sliced fruit—apples, pears or bananas—in butter until brown, then sprinkle with brown sugar and cinnamon. Flame with brandy, if you like, then add a little cream, bring to a boil and reduce to thick consistency.

- Use leftovers, like stews or curries. Just make sure everything's nice and moist. If it looks too gloppy, just add a little stock when you heat it up. Then just lay it down the center of each crepe and roll up.

WHIPPING UP HOMEMADE RICOTTA GETS YOU BRAGGING RIGHTS AND A FRESH, PURE RESULT

Let's explore two of the three mysteries embedded in the nursery rhyme, "Little Miss Muffet," namely, what exactly are these "curds and whey" about which we've heard so much? Well, there's no better way to illustrate and understand what they are than by making our own fresh ricotta cheese. As for the third mystery ("What is a tuffet?"), we'll just have to leave that for another day.

WHY YOU NEED TO LEARN IT

First off, let's not dismiss bragging rights. I mean, can you imagine the reaction at your next dinner party when the bruschetta you pass is spread with your own, homemade ricotta?

On the less self-aggrandizing side, however, knowing how to make ricotta means you have an understanding of how proteins work, and particularly how they respond to heat and acid.

And finally, our cheese will contain nothing more than milk, salt and acid in the form of vinegar or lemon juice. Compare that to the pharmacopia you often will find polluting the ingredients list of store-bought ricotta, and you may never go back.

STEPS TO FOLLOW

As is our wont, before we get to the 1-2-3's, let's talk about what's going on with our ingredients. And because we're making cheese, we need to talk about milk.

Like many things, milk is best when it's fresh, and the best way to keep it fresh is to keep it cold. Old milk, or milk that's been left out of the fridge for too long, can turn "sour" and curdle. Here's what that means:

Milk is made up mostly of water with a little bit of milk fat and some proteins. The proteins in milk—and there are a bunch of different ones—fall into two basic types: curds and whey.

Proteins are long strands of amino acids that are wadded up and suspended in water. When they are exposed to heat or acid, those strands unravel and bond to each other.

In a nutshell, then, when acid is added to milk, the curd proteins clump together into a mass, leaving behind the whey proteins still suspended in the liquid. This is precisely why we say that the milk "curdles."

This can happen naturally as the milk ages and bacteria that live in the milk have a chance to multiply and feed on the sugars in milk, converting them to acid which causes curdling. It's also why milk that's left out turns sour more quickly, because

Photo 1

bacteria thrive at warmer temperatures. In the case of ricotta, we cause the curdling intentionally simply by heating the milk and adding acid.

Traditionally, ricotta is made from the whey that's left over from other cheese, such as provolone. In fact, the name "ricotta" means "recooked" in Italian, and is a reference to this second use. It takes a lot of whey to make a little bit of ricotta (4 gallons of whey yield about 1 pound of cheese) and you probably don't have a big bucket of whey. Thus, we're going to do it the easy way and use whole milk. This will give us a nice, rich ricotta with a better yield (just 1 gallon of milk yields close to 2 pounds of cheese).

We'll start with half a gallon of milk to end up with about a pound of cheese. (Note: For an even richer ricotta, add some heavy cream—1 to 4 ounces—to the milk.) The only other ingredients are salt and white vinegar. (You can use lemon juice instead, or other types of vinegar, though these ingredients will impart their flavors to the end product.)

WHIPPING UP HOMEMADE RICOTTA GETS YOU BRAGGING RIGHTS AND A FRESH, PURE RESULT *(continued)*

1. Combine half a gallon of milk, 3 tablespoons white vinegar and ½ teaspoon salt, and heat it to about 185 degrees. You can do this in a heavy-bottom saucepan on the stove top or in a glass or ceramic bowl in the microwave. If you do it stove top, stir frequently to prevent it from scorching on the bottom. As it heats, you'll start to the see the chemical reaction of the curd proteins clumping together (photo 1, previous page). Once it comes to temperature, take it off the heat and let it sit for about 10 minutes to make sure that it curdles completely (photo 2).

2. Line a colander with five or six layers of cheesecloth. Set the colander over a bowl to save the whey. (Use it in place of milk for pancakes or muffins or anything that uses milk.) Ladle or pour the curds gently into the cheesecloth (photo 3) and let it drain from 5 to 30 minutes. If you drain it quickly, you'll have a creamier cheese; if you drain it a long time, it will be drier and coarser. Pick up the bundle and gently squeeze out remaining whey, if you like (photo 4).

3. Use the cheese while still warm on bruschetta (photo 5) or pasta, or seal it in an airtight container and refrigerate it. It'll keep for several days, but it's best to use it within two days.

Photo 2

Photo 3

Photo 4

Photo 5

ANATOMY OF A SMOOTHIE: LEARNING TO MASTER THIS DRINK CAN LEAD TO FURTHER IMPROVISATION IN THE KITCHEN

One of the easiest things to do with juicy produce is to turn it into a healthy, delicious drink that takes just minutes to make. Here, we explore the ultimate blender drink: the smoothie.

STEPS TO TAKE

1. Put some fruit, yogurt and crushed ice in a blender.

2. Turn the blender on.

3. Turn the blender off.

4. Drink the smoothie.

See what I mean? Easy. I think I even saw a chimp make one once on Animal Planet.

But listen: It's precisely because the method is so easy that we need to have an understanding of our ingredients. Until we know what each ingredient contributes to the whole, we won't know how much of each to add.

Thus, instead of talking about the individual steps, we'll talk about the ingredient categories found in smoothies and their functions.

Primary ingredients

I'm giving general proportions. And remember, they're very general. Add more or less of whatever you want to improve your smoothie.

Fruit: Fruit adds flavor and texture, and will account for probably half to two-thirds of the total volume. Different fruits have different amounts of liquid, fiber and overall flavor, all of which can vary depending on the ripeness or variety of the fruit. Also, naturally juicy fruits like berries will thin the smoothie, while bulkier fruits like bananas can make them thicker.

WHY YOU NEED TO LEARN IT

Smoothies are a great way to internalize the idea that real cooking is not about following recipes. Real cooking requires knowledge of methods of preparation coupled with an understanding of ingredients. If you know how ingredients work and you know how to put them together, you can create dozens—if not hundreds—of delicious variations of any given idea.

Enjoy smoothies on their own merits, of course. But at the same time, as you make your first dozen and come to understand how they're all pretty much the same, begin to believe that you can achieve the same comfort level with soups, sauces, sautes and stews.

ANATOMY OF A SMOOTHIE *(continued)*

Frozen fruit works just as well as fresh, and because everything's getting ground up, this is the perfect way to use up fruit that's a little past its prime.

Dairy: This adds the creaminess that gives the smoothie its name. The most common dairy addition is yogurt because of its association with healthful diets. However, you can use milk or ice cream—or soy or rice-milk products.

Figure that roughly a quarter of the total volume will be dairy. The more dairy you add, the richer and smoother your product will be. However, it will also dilute the fruit flavor and, if you're the type that thinks about such things, increase the calorie count.

Ice: Ice adds cold liquid, thinning and chilling the smoothie and making it drinkable. Some ice crystals will also get suspended in the mix, adding some interesting textural notes.

Crushed ice works best. If you don't have a crushed ice feature on your fridge, just put ice cubes in a plastic bag and whack them with a hammer or cast-iron skillet. Figure about a quarter of the total volume—or an amount roughly equal to the amount of dairy—will be crushed ice.

Additional ingredients

Fruit juice: Not all smoothies use juice. Juice adds flavor and also thins out the final product. Therefore, smoothies with juice tend to use less ice than smoothies that use fruit alone.

Crunchy bits: You can turn your smoothie into an all-in-one breakfast by adding a couple handfuls of your favorite cereal. Granola would be in keeping with the spirit of the smoothie, but I suppose you could use Cap'n Crunch if you were so inclined. Cereal adds a nice textural contrast as well as other nutrients, though admittedly, it's not my cup of tea. Call me crazy, but I don't like to have to chew my drinks.

Dietary supplements: Here's where you can imitate the big smoothie chains. Throw in some whey powder for a protein blast or gingko biloba for whatever that is supposed to do. You can even get nutty and grind up a vitamin pill.

Whatever you do, remember, you're in control and you can change the flavor and texture of the smoothie simply by changing the proportion of ingredients.

The steps are easy, but success depends on nailing the proportions of fruit, dairy and ice.

RICE, PASTA, VEGETABLES AND FRUITS

AS SIMPLE AS STIR, STIR, STIR: LEARN RISOTTO BASICS, THEN DIVE INTO A GAZILLION VARIATIONS OF CLASSIC DISH

Risotto seems very much a grown-up dish, maybe because I never had it until I was one myself. Creamy and luxurious, risotto flows across the plate, and each sensuous bite makes your mouth fairly glow. While in most other rice preparations the individual grains are either wholly separate or stuck together in a glutinous mass, the grains of rice in risotto are enrobed in velvet.

WHY YOU NEED TO LEARN IT

Risotto is extremely satisfying as a simple lunch or a separate course in an elegant dinner. Once you master the method, you can change out the ingredients for—literally—gazillions of variations. Barley, Israeli couscous, farro, quinoa—pretty much any grain will work. As for flavoring ingredients, there's nothing you cannot try.

PUTTING YOUR SKILLS TO WORK

Israeli couscous risotto (pg. 253)

STEPS TO FOLLOW

Learn the method with traditional arborio rice (other authentic varieties to look for are carnaroli and vialone nano). Once a specialty item, this short-grained Italian variety now is available in nearly every major chain grocer. Use one cup of arborio to start. That will make enough for four small servings.

1. Heat a pot of stock or broth to a simmer. Plan on 2 to 3 cups of liquid for every cup of dry rice.

2. While the stock is heating, cut half an onion into small dice. (If the onion pieces are too big, I think it gets a little weird texturally. But that's just me.)

3. Heat a saucepan over a medium flame, then add a little fat—oil, butter, bacon drippings, etc. Sweat (slowly cook) the onion until it's soft and translucent or, if you prefer, saute it over higher heat until it's browned. Caramelized onion will give the risotto a darker flavor and color.

4. Over medium heat, add a clove or two of minced garlic and stir it until fragrant, about 30 seconds.

5. Stir your arborio into the fat (photo 1). After a minute or so it will take on a pearly sheen.

6. Deglaze the pan: Add an ounce or two of liquid—white wine is common for risotto—and use it to loosen any flavorful browned bits that may be stuck to the bottom of the pan (photo 2). Stir until the wine has nearly disappeared. This is called "reducing 'au sec' (until dry).''

Photo 1

Photo 2

AS SIMPLE AS STIR, STIR, STIR *(continued)*

7. Ladle in 2 to 4 ounces of simmering stock. Keep stirring, just enough to keep the rice from sticking to the pan. The stock will disappear gradually, absorbed into the rice or evaporated. (That gentle stirring, by the way, is what gives the dish its signature creaminess: As the grains bump into each other, their starch is rubbed off and incorporated into the liquid.)

8. When the first addition of stock is gone, add another ladleful and continue stirring.

9. Continue adding more stock as the previous addition is absorbed, until the rice is done. The individual grains will be cooked "al dente," tender with just a touch of firmness. They will retain their shape, but they'll be lounging in a creamy goo. The consistency will be thicker than a thick soup but thinner than pudding. (The best idea is, before you make this at home, order a plate at a nice Italian restaurant.)

10. When the rice is done and the consistency is correct, stir in one final ladle of stock. This will make the risotto too thin, but in the time it takes you to serve it, the starch from the rice will have firmed up enough to bring it back to the correct consistency.

11. We can now make any number of additions to the risotto: Whole butter and/or cream may be stirred in for richness. For flavor, Parmesan cheese is very common (photo 3). Also, delicate or precooked ingredients such as blanched and shocked asparagus or sauteed mushrooms may be added here.

Note: Sturdier ingredients—ground beef, sausage—may be added raw after the onions, sauteed until browned and then cooked along with the rice. Other items such as raw shrimp or whole clams should be added during the last few minutes. When the rice is finished they'll be perfectly cooked.

12. Season with salt and serve immediately.

Photo 3

GENTLE STIRRING GIVES THE DISH ITS SIGNATURE CREAMINESS.

ISRAELI COUSCOUS RISOTTO

1. Heat the chicken broth in a medium saucepan to a boil; lower heat to a simmer. Meanwhile, cook the bacon in a large skillet over medium heat until crispy. Remove from skillet; set aside.

2. Pour off all but 2 tablespoons of the bacon fat; return skillet to medium-high heat. When the fat is almost smoking, add the onion; cook until lightly browned, about 3 minutes. Add garlic; cook another 30 seconds.

3. Add the couscous; stir to coat with the fat. Cook until the couscous begins to turn a light brown, about 2 minutes.

4. Deglaze the pan by adding the wine and scraping up any browned bits from the bottom with a wooden spoon. When the wine has reduced completely, add ½ cup of the hot broth. Keep stirring enough to keep the couscous from sticking or burning. When the broth has nearly disappeared, add another ½ cup, stirring until the liquid reduces. Repeat until the couscous is cooked to an al dente texture, about 15 minutes.

5. If there's no more liquid in the risotto, stir in another small ladleful; remove from heat. Add the butter, Parmesan cheese and cream, stirring until the butter and cheese melt. The risotto should have a loose, almost pourable consistency. Add the salt and pepper to taste. Garnish with parsley and reserved bacon.

Note: Israeli couscous, a toasted pasta resembling tiny pebbles, is available in the ethnic section of supermarkets, in boxes specifically marked as Israeli couscous.

NUTRITION INFORMATION PER SERVING: 266 calories, 29% of calories from fat, 8g fat, 5g saturated fat, 22mg cholesterol, 36g carbohydrates, 10g protein, 620mg sodium, 2g fiber

PREP TIME: 10 MINUTES

COOK TIME: 20 MINUTES

YIELD: 8 FIRST COURSE SERVINGS

2 cans (14½ ounces each) chicken broth

4 slices bacon, diced

1 onion, diced

2 cloves garlic, minced

2 cups Israeli couscous, see note

¼ cup white wine

3 tablespoons butter

¼ cup grated Parmesan cheese

2 tablespoons to ¼ cup heavy cream, optional

½ teaspoon salt

Freshly ground pepper

Finely chopped parsley

FILLING YOU IN ON STUFFED PASTA: MASHED POTATOES HELP REVEAL THE SECRETS

Stuffed pasta takes advantage of that problem leftover: mashed potatoes. In my never-ending quest for solutions, I've encountered many winners: potato pancakes, potato croquettes, potato soup, potato smoothies (OK, that last one I just made up ...) and, now, potato ravioli.

Think of leftover mashed potatoes as the Rosetta Stone of ravioli, the ingredient that will forever unlock the mystery of how to stuff pasta.

WHY YOU NEED TO LEARN IT

If you understand why mashed potatoes work as a filling for pasta, you can transfer that knowledge to other ingredients, and you may just find yourself cranking out countless varieties of delicious stuffed pastas.

PUTTING YOUR SKILLS TO WORK

Potato, ricotta and bacon ravioli with tomato sauce (pg. 256)

STEPS TO FOLLOW

We're using the term ravioli simply because it's probably the most recognizable form of stuffed pasta. Don't forget, though, the idea of wrapping pasta or some other simple dough around something delicious is found the world over. There's a reason for this international popularity: Ravioli (or whatever) is easy to make and completely delicious.

Still, the fact that the possibilities are endless may make the entire concept somewhat daunting for the less confident cook.

And that's where mashed potatoes come in. Think of all the ways you've enjoyed them, all the wonderful things they've been mashed with. Because they're delicious on their own, they'll also be delicious wrapped in pasta.

The real ravioli lesson, then? Think "leftovers" and try the filling pasta with some other delicious food, like sauteed spinach or pureed winter squash or beef stew or shredded chicken.

Here are a few things to consider when using leftovers for ravioli:

- Any stuffing should be mashed or finely chopped.
- Stuffings should be somewhat dry, so as not to make the pasta soggy or prevent it from sealing properly.
- Don't overstuff. There should just be a dollop in the center of your pasta.
- Make sure your stuffing ingredients are already cooked and seasoned.

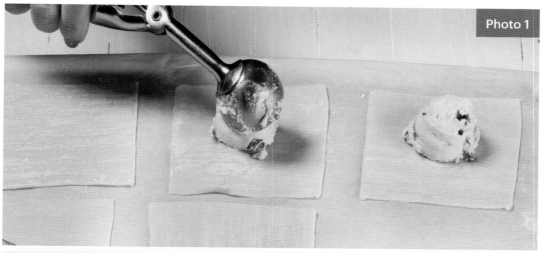

A word about the pasta: If you love your pasta machine, you know you can have dough ready in about 15 minutes. Otherwise, you can check your local specialty shop for sheets of fresh pasta. Or go to the Asian section of your supermarket and get some wonton wrappers. They're essentially just square sheets of eggless pasta dough, and they make great ravioli.

If you're new at this, here's what you do: Lay eight wonton wrappers on a floured board and cover the rest with a damp cloth. Place a rounded tablespoon of filling in the center of each wonton (photo 1), then wet your finger and trace a circle around the filling (photo 2). Lay another sheet on top of the first and press down around the filling to glue the pieces together. (Trim them down if you feel they're too big.)

To cook, drop them in boiling water for 3 to 5 minutes, until tender and hot, then serve with a simple sauce.

POTATO, RICOTTA AND BACON RAVIOLI WITH TOMATO SAUCE

PREP TIME: 40 MINUTES

COOK TIME: 10 MINUTES

YIELD: 8 SERVINGS

1 pound mashed potatoes, see note

1 cup ricotta cheese

1 egg

¼ cup grated Parmesan cheese

½ pound bacon, cooked, crumbled

¼ cup chopped fresh basil

1¼ teaspoons salt

Freshly ground pepper

64 wonton wrappers (or as needed)

Flour, as needed

1 can (25 ounces) plum tomatoes, drained, liquid reserved

2 tablespoons olive oil

1 large clove garlic, minced

1. Combine potatoes, ricotta, egg, half the Parmesan, half the bacon and half the basil in a bowl. Season with ¾ teaspoon salt and pepper to taste.

2. Lay 8 wonton wrappers on a floured work surface. Cover remaining wrappers with a damp towel. Place a rounded tablespoon of potato/ricotta filling in center of each wrapper. Dip your finger in water; trace a circle around filling (or use a pastry brush). Top each with another wrapper; press down to seal top to bottom. Place ravioli on a lightly floured baking sheet; cover with a damp cloth. Repeat until all filling is used.

3. Puree tomatoes in a food processor. Heat a medium skillet over high heat, and when hot, add olive oil and garlic; cook, 30 seconds. Add pureed tomatoes; simmer to reduce, 5 minutes. Season with ½ teaspoon salt and pepper to taste.

4. Cook ravioli in batches in a large pot of salted boiling water, until tender, 3-5 minutes; plate 4 ravioli per serving. Top with sauce; sprinkle with remaining Parmesan, bacon and basil.

Note: If the potatoes are stiff, heat them in a pan with a little milk or stock.

NUTRITION INFORMATION PER SERVING: 424 calories, 16g fat, 6g saturated fat, 67mg cholesterol, 51g carbohydrates, 17g protein, 1,360mg sodium, 3g fiber

More stuffings

- Acorn squash, roasted and mashed with butter and brown sugar or maple syrup. Sauce: Browned butter with fresh sage and walnuts.

- Crumbled sausage, sauteed with diced onion and pepper, bound with breadcrumbs and eggs or mashed potatoes. Sauce: Cream sauce (like Alfredo).

- Small dice of portabello mushroom sauteed in butter with minced shallot, blanched and minced spinach and ricotta cheese. Sauce: Tomato sauce.

- Fresh green peas, sauteed with bacon and garlic, pureed and thickened with ricotta. Sauce: Light tomato sauce.

THE SKINNY ON FRESH HERBS: SLICING TECHNIQUE TAKES PRACTICE, BUT WILL GIVE DISHES AN ELEGANT FINISH

Here's yet another reason why summer rules: fresh herbs. A simple but surefire pleasure, fresh herbs will make your food, and therefore your life, better. We'll cut them into the thin strips known as chiffonade.

WHY YOU NEED TO LEARN IT

What recipe doesn't call for fluffy piles of filament-thin green herbs? OK, lots of them. But plenty do: stuffings and sauces, salads and vinaigrettes. So many dishes can benefit from the addition of a few fresh herbs, even if it's only as a simple but arresting garnish.

The ability to turn uneven leaves into neat little strips is a challenge to acquire, but once you start practicing, you'll never want to stop.

PUTTING YOUR SKILLS TO WORK

Herb-tomato vinaigrette (pg. 260)
Fresh herb oil (pg. 261)

STEPS TO FOLLOW

1. Separate the herb leaves from their stems. Wash in cold water and dry in a towel or salad spinner (photo 1).

2. Grab a handful and mash them into as tight a ball as you can in your guide hand (the one that's not your knife hand). Put the ball on the cutting board and anchor the back of the ball with your thumb, ring finger and pinky while holding down the front of the ball with your index and middle fingers. The ball will try to unfold and expand. Don't let it.

3. Keeping your index and middle fingers curved down and back, position your knife so that the blade is flat against their middle joints (photo 2). (This, as you'll recall, loyal readers, is the proper way of using the fingers of your guide hand to guide your knife as you cut.)

4. Start by cocking the blade, pulling it up and back so that the edge is positioned just over the outermost edge of the ball of herbs. You're going to cut thin slices by moving the knife blade down and forward across the herbs, then very slightly moving the fingers on your guide hand back to expose just the tiniest amount more of the ball.

5. Now, to get really, really thin slices, we're going to practice cutting nothing; then we're going to practice cutting next to nothing. Start by not moving your guide fingers after the first cut. Keep slicing with your knife, even though you won't be cutting anything. After you've made several cuts moving your guide fingers back not at all, move them back almost not at all and make another cut. How thin are your strips now? Can you make them even thinner?

Photo 1

Photo 2

MOVE
THE KNIFE
BLADE
DOWN AND
FORWARD
ACROSS
THE HERBS.

A final note

Dedicated Prep Schoolers will know we have been doing our share of blanching and shocking of late, plunging items into boiling water for a few short seconds before removing them to an ice water bath.

Up to now, we've used this technique for the purpose of removing pesky fruit and vegetable skins.

Try it with herbs to make beautiful and delicious herb oils. Blanch the whole leaves for just as long as it takes to turn their natural green hue vibrant and sharp—seconds is all we're talking. Then, shock them in ice water, dry, and put them in a blender with your oil of choice.

HERB-TOMATO VINAIGRETTE

Of course you can use this on fresh green salads, but don't stop there. Spoon it over grilled chicken or fish, or toss it with chilled pasta for a quick and delicious lunch. Lower a spoonful into the center of a fresh summer soup like minestrone or chilled potato, then let your guests swirl it in.

PREP TIME: 10 MINUTES

YIELD: 1½ CUPS

2 tablespoons red wine vinegar

1 tablespoon Dijon mustard

3 tablespoons extra-virgin olive oil

3 tablespoons canola oil

1 cup diced fresh tomatoes or tomato concasse

Small handful of mixed fresh herbs, cut into chiffonade

½ teaspoon salt

Freshly ground pepper

1. Whisk together the vinegar and mustard in a medium bowl until smooth. Drizzle in the olive oil very slowly, whisking constantly, to form an emulsion. Add the canola oil in a stream, whisking constantly. Stir in the tomatoes and the herbs until well blended; season with salt and pepper to taste.

NUTRITION INFORMATION PER TABLESPOON: 33 calories, 92% of calories from fat, 3g fat, 0.3g saturated fat, 0mg cholesterol, 0.6g carbohydrates, 0.1g protein, 70mg sodium, 0.2g fiber

FRESH HERB OIL

This oil is lovely to have on hand in a squirt bottle. It adds a blast of flavor at the end of a dish, and the rich green color lends a distinctive visual element to the plate. Top off your favorite summer soups, drizzle over slices of tomato and fresh mozzarella, or decorate grilled or broiled fish and meats.

1. Heat a large saucepan of salted water to a boil. Have a bowl of ice water ready. Add herbs; cook just until they turn a vibrant green, about 10 seconds. Drain; plunge them into ice water. Drain herbs; pat dry with a towel.

2. Place the herbs and oil in a blender; blend at high speed. Season with salt. Pour the oil through a fine sieve into a bowl. Transfer oil to a squeeze bottle. Oil can be stored in the refrigerator for 1 week.

NUTRITION INFORMATION PER TABLESPOON: 125 calories, 99% of calories from fat, 14g fat, 1g saturated fat, 0mg cholesterol, 0.2g carbohydrates, 0.1g protein, 145mg sodium, 0.2g fiber

PREP TIME: 15 MINUTES

COOK TIME: 5 MINUTES

YIELD: ½ CUP

1 bunch fresh herb of choice

½ cup canola oil

½ teaspoon salt

ROLLING WITH PEPPERS FOR A CLEAN, EFFICIENT CUT

Everyone has his or her own way of cutting up a bell pepper, but this one is really fun. After cutting off the ends, we're going to roll the pepper with the knife edge inside, removing the core and the ribs as we go. Do this in front of your friends and their appreciation will be palpable.

WHY YOU NEED TO LEARN IT

The ribs have very little flavor and a somewhat unpleasant, mushy texture, and their bland, off-white color distracts from the bright green vibrancy of the pepper's meat and skin. Plus, with the ribs out, the pepper will be easy to cut into shapes.

PUTTING YOUR SKILLS TO WORK

Sausage and peppers (pg. 265)

STEPS TO FOLLOW

1. Cut off both ends of the pepper and set them aside. Remove just enough to see inside.

2. Lay the pepper with one of the cut ends toward you. Rest your guide hand on top of the pepper and hold your knife with the blade parallel to the board. Angling your knife blade slightly downward, slice into the pepper just above where it rests on the cutting board (photo 1).

3. Making sure that the edge of the knife is riding along the top of the pepper wall, parallel to the board, begin cutting with a forward and back motion. As you cut, think of a tank tread and use your guide hand to roll out the pepper in the same direction as the knife (photo 2). As the pepper flattens, keep the knife blade parallel to the board. The goal is to remove the core and ribs without removing any (or much) of the green flesh. When it is all rolled out, the core will come out in one piece, and you'll end up with one long rectangular piece of pepper (photo 3).

The first few times you try this you'll probably need to go back over the pepper to remove any pieces of rib you may have missed. With practice, however, you'll be able to get the core and the ribs in one quick, smooth motion.

Photo 1

Photo 2

Photo 3

ROLLING WITH PEPPERS FOR A CLEAN, EFFICIENT CUT *(continued)*

Making the cuts

1. Cut the pepper in half to make it easier to work with. Always keep the skin side down so that you're cutting through the meat side.

2. For batonnets, lay one pepper half skin-side down and cut it into ¼-inch slices (photo 4). As you improve your skills, you can double your speed by laying one half on top of the other.

3. For small dice, grab several batonnets and turn them at a 90-degree angle to your knife. Grip the batonnets between your thumb and your ring finger and pinky and anchor them with your middle and index fingers on top. Remember to keep the knife blade flush against the middle section of your index and middle fingers, then cut the batonnets at ¼-inch intervals (photo 5).

4. Don't forget about the two ends that you have reserved. Because they're round and thick and uneven, they're harder to cut into perfect pieces. You might just want to eat them there at your cutting board while they're crisp and raw and delicious and no one's watching. If you want to use them, just cut them into slices (and then dice, if you want) as well as you can and don't worry about what they look like.

Photo 4

Photo 5

SAUSAGE AND PEPPERS

The spices in the sausage flavor the sauce as it cooks, making this dish an easy addition to your permanent repertoire. You also can try this with andouille sausage. Serve the mixture over pasta or polenta with grated Parmesan, or make a grinder (sub sandwich) with crusty Italian bread and a couple slices of provolone.

1. Heat the oil in a large skillet over medium-high heat; add the onion. Cook, stirring, until it just begins to turn brown, about 4 minutes. Add the green pepper; cook until it begins to soften, 1 minute. Add the garlic; cook until fragrant, 30 seconds.

2. Add the sausage and tomatoes; heat to a boil. Reduce heat to a simmer; cook, stirring occasionally, until the sausages are cooked through and the sauce thickens, about 30 minutes. Season with salt.

NUTRITION INFORMATION PER SERVING: 277 calories, 67% of calories from fat, 20g fat, 6g saturated fat, 33mg cholesterol, 10g carbohydrates, 12g protein, 1,180mg sodium, 2g fiber

PREP TIME: 30 MINUTES

COOK TIME: 35 MINUTES

YIELD: 6 SERVINGS

2 tablespoons olive oil

½ red onion, finely chopped

1 large green pepper, cored, seeded, ribbed, cut into ¼-inch strips

2 to 4 cloves garlic, minced

1½ pounds hot Italian sausage, cut into 3-inch lengths

1 can (28 ounces) plum tomatoes, finely chopped

½ teaspoon salt

MINCING OR CREAMING CONTROLS THE BITE OF GARLIC

Ignore the peevish wags who warn against garlic's linger. Such chat reeks—more than garlic itself—of tired provincialism. Garlic is wonderful, and it is very, very good for you. Eat it every day, and I guarantee you will never, ever be bothered by vampires.

WHY YOU NEED TO LEARN IT

As wonderful as garlic is, few of us like it in chunks. Mince it small, and it's perfect when added at the end of a saute.

If you want it raw, or if you're using it for a smooth-textured item, cream it. Creaming turns your minced garlic into a velvety paste that disappears into soups and melts into vinaigrettes.

PUTTING YOUR SKILLS TO WORK

Garlicky balsamic tomato relish (pg. 269)

STEPS TO FOLLOW

Mincing

1. Set an unpeeled garlic clove on your cutting board. Place the flat side of your chef's knife directly on top. Place your guide hand on the blade and press straight down, just enough to break the skin with an audible crack. Peel away the skin and trim off the hard root end.

2. Place the flat end of the knife back on the garlic and with a mighty rap of your hand, smash the garlic into small particles. Set this aside and repeat with as many cloves as you need.

3. Gather the garlic into a mound with your guide hand. Hold the index and middle fingers on the front top of the pile, exposing just a little bit to your knife. With the blade flush against those fingers, cut across that little bit (photo 1). Move your fingers back and repeat until you've cut up the whole pile.

4. Rotate the pile 90 degrees. Make another series of cuts, again keeping the knife blade flush against your guide fingers.

5. Gather the pile again. This time, anchor the tip of the blade with the palm of your guide hand, keeping your digits arched up and away from the blade. Bring the blade up and down like a paper cutter, fanning it left and right across the garlic (photo 2). Do this until the garlic is finely minced.

Creaming

1. Pile your minced garlic in the center of the board and sprinkle with kosher salt. The salt helps grind down the garlic, making your job remarkably more easy.

Photo 1

Photo 2

BRING THE BLADE UP AND DOWN LIKE A PAPER CUTTER.

2. Hold the spine parallel to the cutting board with the edge of the knife facing up and away from you at a 45 degree angle.

3. Wrap the four fingers of your knife hand around the handle, with the side of your index finger touching the heel. Extend your thumb, as if you were hitchhiking, and place it on the knife blade. Now let go with your guide hand.

4. Place the index and middle fingers of your guide hand on the side of the blade, close to the tip of the knife. Lower the knife to the board, spine down, between you and the pile of minced garlic. Keep the blade angled up and away.

▶

MINCING OR CREAMING CONTROLS THE BITE OF GARLIC *(continueD)*

5. Push the spine up to the garlic pile. Imagine that it is hinged to the cutting board, and using those two guide fingers, fold the blade down over the garlic.

6. Pull the knife back toward you while your two guide fingers press the edge into the garlic, smashing it into the board (photo 3).

7. When you've gotten a nice garlic smear, flip the edge back up to a 45 degree angle.

8. Repeat this process: Move the spine forward, pushing the garlic into another heap. Fold the blade over the garlic and press the edge down with your two guide fingers as you draw it back toward you. It's the edge, not the side of the blade, that's doing the work. Each time you do this, you'll smush the garlic a little more until it becomes a smooth paste.

A note to remember

This process, from whole clove to garlic mush, can take several long minutes. Be patient and work slowly. Remember that this technique, like so many others, is all about muscle memory. The more you do it, the easier and more natural it will become.

Photo 3

GARLICKY BALSAMIC TOMATO RELISH

Spread this on bruschetta or spoon it over fresh greens for a simple salad. Use as a garnish for grilled chicken and fish, or add it to a bowl of your favorite soup along with a dollop of sour cream or creme fraiche.

1. Combine all ingredients in a small bowl; set aside at room temperature to blend flavors, about 30 minutes.

NUTRITION INFORMATION PER SERVING: 70 calories, 86% of calories from fat, 7g fat, 1g saturated fat, 0mg cholesterol, 2g carbohydrates, 0.3g protein, 150mg sodium, 0.4g fiber

PREP TIME: 15 MINUTES

STANDING TIME: 30 MINUTES

YIELD: ABOUT ½ CUP

2 tomatoes, peeled, seeded, diced

2 -4 cloves garlic, creamed

¼ cup extra-virgin olive oil

2 tablespoons thinly sliced fresh herbs such as basil

2 tablespoons balsamic vinegar

½ teaspoon salt

Freshly ground pepper

Chopped pitted kalamata olives, drained capers, diced avocado, lemon zest, minced anchovy fillets, optional

GETTING TO THE ROOT OF THE MATTER WITH PARSNIPS

Parsnips are similar to carrots in shape and, therefore, approach, and the two go together quite well. Here, we'll break down the parsnip.

WHY YOU NEED TO LEARN IT

All root vegetables, including parsnips and carrots, take particularly well to the cooking methods that attract us during the colder months. Roasts, soups, stews and braises all benefit from their inclusion.

In the fall, you'll see many more root vegetables in markets. Take advantage of the season and start working with these wonderfully earthy, healthful foods.

PUTTING YOUR SKILLS TO WORK

Roasted parsnips and carrots with fresh herbs (pg. 272)

STEPS TO FOLLOW

Note: There are a lot of peelers out there. Twin-bladed swivel peelers are easy to use and follow a vegetable's uneven form. Choose one with a large, comfortable handle.

Parsnips tend to be more conical than carrots, with thinner tips and wider tops. Try to find nice fat ones, evenly shaped with a gentler taper; they'll reduce waste and make for easier prep.

To peel

1. Trim off both ends of the parsnip.

2. With your guide hand, hold the parsnip by the fatter, stem end at a 45-degree angle, the thin tip resting on your cutting board. Starting about two-thirds of the way toward the stem end, run the peeler down the side (photo 1). Rotate the parsnip and repeat until the entire bottom is peeled.

3. Flip the parsnip and hold it by the tip end, again at a 45-degree angle. Finish peeling using the same technique as above.

To cut

4. Cut the parsnip in half. Steady one half with the tips of your guide fingers (arched down and back), and shave off a thin slice to create a flat surface.

5. Lay the parsnip on the flat side, steady it with your guide fingers, and shave off another side. Repeat this action twice more to give yourself a four-sided box (photo 2). From here, you can cut the parsnip into planks, batons or dice.

6. For large dice, cut the parsnip box in half lengthwise. Lay the halves together and cut them in half lengthwise to get four thick sticks called batons (photo 3).

7. Grip the back of the pile of batons between the thumb, ring finger and pinkie of your guide hand. Place the tips of your index and middle fingers on top of the pile toward the front. Keep the middle section of these two fingers vertical, with the tips curled slightly back. Place the flat side of the blade flush against the two vertical fingers, exposing about ¾-inch of the batons. Slice through the pile to get large dice.

8. Keeping the parsnips gripped with your thumb, ring finger and pinkie, draw your index and middle finger backward to expose another ¾-inch. Make this cut and repeat until you have a nice pile of large dice (photo 4).

ROASTED PARSNIPS AND CARROTS WITH FRESH HERBS

PREP TIME: 20 MINUTES

COOK TIME: 20 MINUTES

YIELD: 8 SERVINGS

1 tablespoon olive oil

1 tablespoon melted butter

1 pound carrots, peeled, cut in large dice

1 pound parsnips, peeled, cut in large dice

1 to 2 tablespoons minced fresh herbs such as rosemary, oregano, thyme, chives, or any combination

½ teaspoon salt

Freshly ground pepper

1. Heat oven to 425 degrees. Combine the oil and melted butter in a large bowl; add carrots and parsnips. Toss to coat.

2. Transfer parsnips and carrots in a single layer on a baking sheet lined with parchment and sprayed with vegetable spray. Bake until tender and starting to brown, about 20 minutes.

3. Return vegetables to the bowl; toss with herbs, salt and pepper to taste.

NUTRITION INFORMATION PER SERVING: 82 calories, 35% of calories from fat, 3g fat, 1g saturated fat, 4mg cholesterol, 13g carbohydrates, 1g protein, 191mg sodium, 4g fiber

WHIP POTATOES INTO SHAPE: SECRETS ON AVOIDING A GLUEY, STIFF OR LUMPY FLAVORLESS MESS

Though mashing and whipping are different techniques, when applied to potatoes, the terms are pretty much interchangeable.

Nomenclature aside, potatoes as a rule are bland. They scream, in their lackluster way, for butter, cream and salt. Should this heroic trio give your diet pause, then tonight, and tomorrow night if it makes you feel better, skip dessert.

STEPS FOR COOKING

What makes whipped potatoes creamy is moisture. Given that water has no flavor, however, we want as little moisture in the form of water as possible. Thus, we recommend russet potatoes, which have the lowest moisture content. White and yellow potatoes work well, too, but avoid red, purple or other high-moisture potatoes.

Start by boiling or baking.

If baking, prick holes in unpeeled potatoes to prevent them from exploding. Bake in a 425-degree oven until done, when a toothpick or dull knife penetrates easily.

For boiling, potatoes can be left whole or peeled and cut into large chunks. Peeled and cut potatoes cook more quickly, but stripped of their protective skin and with an increased surface area, they're more prone to waterlogging.

Start potatoes in cold water to encourage even cooking. Turn the flame to high and when the water boils, reduce the heat and simmer until done.

Drain potatoes immediately and return them to the pan over low heat for several minutes to evaporate more moisture. Shake the pan to keep the potatoes from sticking. Alternately, spread the potatoes on a sheet tray and place in a hot oven 3 to 4 minutes.

WHY YOU NEED TO LEARN IT

Just because whipped potatoes are easy to do doesn't mean they're easy to do well. Too often, it's the gravy that gets the accolades. And why not, if the potatoes are lumpy or stiff, gluey, cold or simply flavorless? Whipped potatoes, as all things, ought to be delicious.

PUTTING YOUR SKILLS TO WORK

Creamy, creamy mashed potatoes (pg. 276)

WHIP POTATOES INTO SHAPE *(continued)*

STEPS FOR WHIPPING

As always, we control the process. Here, we're adding butter and cream until the potatoes reach the desired consistency. Don't worry about amounts; instead, follow the progress as you add more and more.

1. Pass the hot potatoes through a ricer or food mill (photo 1). This "potato puree" is the basis for many wonderful preparations. If you prefer a lumpier (I mean, more "rustic") final result, use a potato masher instead.

2. Add room temperature (not melted) butter (photo 2) and hot liquid: cream or milk, even stock. Just remember, the richness of your ingredients is passed to your final product. Figure about ¼ cup each butter and liquid for every pound of potatoes. To be safe, start with half that amount, and be prepared to add more. Then add any other flavoring or seasoning ingredients (see below).

3. Mix until smooth with a spatula. If you're using a stand mixer, use a paddle attachment if you have one and avoid overmixing, as that breaks down the starch, making your potatoes gummy.

STEPS TO FLAVORING

1. Be sure to add enough salt: about a teaspoon of kosher salt or ⅔ teaspoon table salt per pound. Most people skimp on salt out of health concerns. Seriously, though, the fury you'll feel over underseasoned potatoes will raise your blood pressure far more than the salt you're trying to avoid.

2. Black pepper, while delicious, creates suspicious black specks in your otherwise pristine product. You may want to use white pepper, or just skip it altogether.

3. Potatoes take very well to other flavors: roasted garlic, avocado, minced rosemary, horseradish, chipotle chilies, wasabi—the list is endless. The amount is your call. One caveat: Make sure any added vegetable is cooked properly. You don't want your silky mash marred by the harsh crunch of a piece of, say, raw onion.

Note: Keep potatoes warm in a bain-marie. This is a bowl resting on a saucepan with a few inches of simmering water. The steam heats the bowl gently, warming its contents. Cover the bowl with plastic.

Photo 1

Photo 2

CREAMY, CREAMY MASHED POTATOES

PREP TIME: 12 MINUTES

COOK TIME: 23 MINUTES

YIELD: 6 SERVINGS

2 pounds russet potatoes, peeled, cut into large chunks

¾ cup whipping cream, half-and-half or chicken broth

5 tablespoons unsalted butter, softened at room temperature

2 teaspoons coarse salt, see note

1. Place the potatoes in a saucepan of cold, unsalted water; heat to a boil over high heat. Reduce heat to a simmer. Simmer until fork-tender, about 20 minutes. Drain potatoes; return to the dry saucepan. Heat over very low heat to dry the potatoes, shaking the pan to keep them from sticking, about 3 minutes.

2. Meanwhile, heat the cream in a small saucepan over medium heat almost to a boil.

3. Press hot potatoes through a ricer or food mill into a large bowl; add the butter, kosher salt and half of the cream to potato puree. Combine with a rubber spatula until smooth. Add extra cream, if necessary, to achieve desired consistency. (Remember, potatoes will stiffen up as they cool.)

Note: Coarse salt, with its larger flake, occupies more volume than table salt. Thus, if you're using table salt, reduce the amount by a third—in the case of this recipe, use 1⅓ teaspoons of table salt.

NUTRITION INFORMATION PER SERVING: 308 calories, 59% of calories from fat, 21g fat, 13g saturated fat, 66mg cholesterol, 29g carbohydrates, 3g protein, 795mg sodium, 3g fiber

WE'RE READY: BRING ON THE TOMATOES! CONCASSE IS SPRINGBOARD FOR USING SEASON'S BOUNTY

"Only two things that money can't buy
That's true love & homegrown tomatoes"
—Guy Clark from "Homegrown Tomatoes"

In a few weeks, if we're lucky, we'll be sick of tomatoes. For now, though, when they're falling off the vine, filled with sun, it's in many ways the best time of year.

Personally, I go for tomato sandwiches: one fat slice, cut from the center like a chateaubriand, pressed between two slices of really good white bread slathered with too much mayonnaise and just enough kosher salt and pepper from the mill.

Just to get crazy, though, let's take a few apart, removing the skin and seeds, then dice them into large cubes for cold raw dishes or the freshest sauce you'll ever taste.

WHY YOU NEED TO LEARN IT

Concasse (kawn-ka-SAY) is the standard, basic preparation for a fresh tomato. Embrace it, and a hundred delicious ideas—one for every tomato in your back yard—will unfold in your head.

Furthermore, blanching and shocking—the method by which we'll remove the skin—is one of the great multipurpose kitchen techniques.

Now, that's cooking.

PUTTING YOUR SKILLS TO WORK

Spaghetti alla puttanesca
(pg. 280)

STEPS TO FOLLOW

1. Heat a pot of water to a boil.

2. Core the stem end of the tomato with a knife (photo 1), then make an "X" through the skin on the bottom.

3. Plunge the tomato into the boiling water 10 to 20 seconds, then remove it immediately to an ice bath. This stops the cooking and prevents the flesh from getting mushy.

4. That "X" you cut will now turn into four little flaps that you can grab and use to pull off the skin in four easy pieces (photo 2).

5. To remove the seeds and gooey interior, cut the tomato in half along its equator. Grab the halves one at a time, cut side down, and squeeze them gently over a bowl (photo 3). Use a finger to pull out any stubborn seeds or gooey bits. (This sounds a lot worse than it is. After all, it's just a tomato.)

6. Put the halves on a cutting board and, recalling your excellent Prep School-informed knife technique, chop them into large or small dice (photo 4), depending on your whims and the request of your recipe.

SPAGHETTI ALLA PUTTANESCA

The name of this wonderful, sensuous sauce comes from the Italian word for "prostitute." Given its air of permissiveness, feel free to play with the amounts of the various ingredients. Serve this to close companions with a simple green salad and big red wine, then watch them sweat.

PREP TIME: 30 MINUTES

COOK TIME: 12 MINUTES

YIELD: 6 SERVINGS

1 pound spaghetti

¼ cup olive oil

5 cloves garlic, minced

10 anchovies, minced

3 tablespoons minced Italian parsley

6 medium tomatoes, peeled, seeded, halved, finely chopped, see note

½–1½ teaspoons hot red pepper flakes

½ cup pitted kalamata olives, coarsely chopped

3 tablespoons capers, drained

½ teaspoon salt

Freshly ground black pepper

1. Heat a stockpot of salted water to a boil; cook spaghetti according to package directions.

2. Meanwhile, heat the oil in a large skillet over medium heat; add the garlic and anchovies. Cook, stirring, until garlic becomes fragrant, about 1 minute. Stir in the tomatoes, parsley and red pepper flakes.

3. Heat to a boil over medium-high heat. Reduce heat to a simmer; cook until mixture begins to thicken, about 8 minutes. Add the olives and capers; cook until ingredients are heated through, about 2 minutes. Season with salt and pepper to taste; drain pasta. Toss with sauce.

Note: to peel the tomatoes, score a shallow "X" in the bottom of the tomatoes. Immerse them in boiling water about 30 seconds; transfer with a slotted spoon or wire skimmer to ice water to cool. Peel off the skin starting at the "X."

NUTRITION INFORMATION PER SERVING: 394 calories, 28% of calories from fat, 12g fat, 2g saturated fat, 6mg cholesterol, 59g carbohydrates, 12g protein, 673mg sodium, 5g fiber

HOW TO MAKE THE MOST OF AUTUMN'S APPLE HARVEST

Autumn brings apples from nearby orchards. Think pies, tarts, sauces, chutneys, relishes, stuffings ... the possibilities are as endless as the types of apples.
The Michigan Apple Committee reports that its state alone grows dozens of varieties, while worldwide there are more than 2,000.

That's a lot of yummy pie, so let's learn how to make the most of the apples you bring home, starting with coring and moving on to slicing and dicing.

STEPS TO FOLLOW

To core an apple

1. Set the apple on its side and slice a thin piece off the top and bottom.

2. Hold the apple vertically in your guide hand. Grip a swivel peeler, using the fingers of your knife hand and resting your thumb on the bottom of the apple for leverage. Draw the peeler down to remove a thin slice of peel. Rotate the apple and repeat until completely peeled.

3. Set the apple right side up on the board. Place your chef's knife on top, about half an inch from the center—the approximate radius of the core—and flush against the middle section of the index and middle fingers of your guide hand. Cut straight down (photo 1, next page).

4. Rotate the apple 180 degrees and make a second cut parallel to the first on the other side of the center.

5. Rotate the apple 90 degrees and make a third cut. Rotate it another 180 degrees and make a fourth and final cut. You'll be left with a rectangular box containing the core. You'll have a little waste, but it's minimal. The speed with which you can make these cuts more than compensates for any small amount of loss. Besides, now you've got something to nibble on.

WHY YOU NEED TO LEARN IT

Good food preparation balances time against the desire to limit waste. Many pros use a paring knife to peel apples, but you can lose some apple along with the peel. Most home cooks prefer peelers. We'll compromise with a peeler but use it as we would a paring knife.

PUTTING YOUR SKILLS TO WORK

Apple cream sauce (pg. 284)

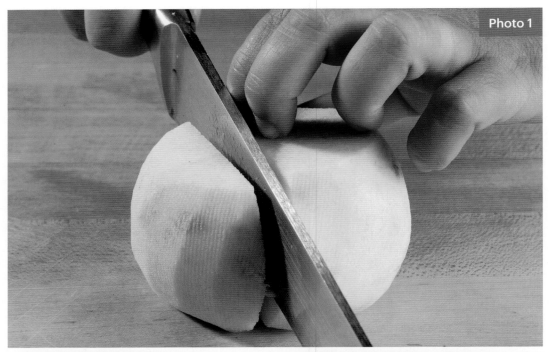

Photo 1

Photo 2

HOW TO MAKE THE MOST OF AUTUMN'S APPLE HARVEST *(continued)*

To cut slices

1. Place an apple piece on the board, cut side down. Hold it in back with your thumb, ring finger and pinky. Rest your index and middle fingers toward the front, their tips curled down and in. Place your blade flush against the vertical, middle section of these two fingers and cut straight down (photo 2). The apple's structure makes a chopping motion easier than a slicing motion.

2. Keeping your index and middle fingers flush against the blade, pull them backward across the apple as you cut. Curving your fingertips inward will prevent them from getting cut.

To dice

1. Place a piece of apple on the board, cut side down. Steady it with the fingers of your guide hand and make a horizontal slice carefully through the middle of the apple (photo 3).

2. Reassemble the two pieces and secure them with your guide hand, as in the instructions for cutting slices. Cut thick slices, keeping your blade flush against your guide fingers as they move backward across the surface of the apple.

3. To dice, rotate the apple slice 90 degrees and make another series of cuts of similar size to form cubes (photo 4).

Photo 3

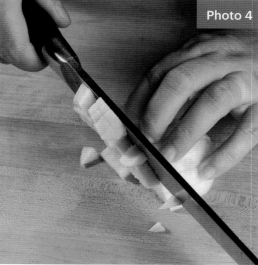

Photo 4

APPLE CREAM SAUCE

This is a versatile sauce that can be nudged into very different directions with a few simple tweaks. Use it as is over meats. To turn it into a dessert sauce, omit the shallots and sweeten it at the end with brown sugar, maple syrup or honey. Cinnamon would be good, too, or any warm spices such as cumin, coriander, nutmeg or curry powder.

PREP TIME: 15 MINUTES

COOK TIME: 8 MINUTES

YIELD: 6 SERVINGS

2 tablespoons butter

2 to 3 Granny Smith or other crisp, juicy apples peeled, diced

1 tablespoon minced or creamed shallot

2 tablespoons Cognac or apple brandy

1 carton (½ pint) whipping cream

¼ teaspoon salt

1. Melt butter in a large skillet over medium-high heat; add the apples. Cook, tossing, until cooked through and slightly browned, about 5 minutes. Add the shallot; cook, tossing, until the shallot is fragrant, 30 seconds.

2. Remove the pan from the heat; add the brandy. Carefully ignite the alcohol with a long match or kitchen lighter; shake the pan until the flame goes out. Add the cream; cook over medium-high heat, stirring, until reduced and thickened slightly, about 1 minute. Stir in the salt.

NUTRITION INFORMATION PER SERVING: 192 calories, 84% of calories from fat, 18g fat, 11g saturated fat, 64mg cholesterol, 7g carbohydrates, 1g protein, 139mg sodium, 1g fiber

HOLIDAY MEALS ▶

7 STEPS TO A SUCCESSFUL HOLIDAY MEAL

Every year, a brand new crop of home cooks gets introduced to the "joys" of cooking Thanksgiving dinner. To those turkey tyros, and to those whose efforts last year were somewhat less than fulfilling, here are a few suggestions.

WHY YOU NEED TO LEARN IT

I can't predict the future, of course, but I'm betting that this Thanksgiving won't be the last time you cook for a big party. If you're a novice, or even if you just have the confidence of a novice, think of next week as one more step along your path to learning, one more opportunity to practice your skills. And you can be thankful for that.

STEPS TO FOLLOW

There's a lot of conflicting advice out there. Without seeming presumptuous, at the very least take No. 1 and No. 7 to heart. The rest of it, well, it works for me.

1. Remember, it's just one meal, so don't panic. Even if dinner is somehow ruined, order some pizza and enjoy the company of your companions. Friday is another day.

2. Choose a nice bird: sustainably raised and minimally processed, fresh—not frozen, and no plastic pop-up thermometer jammed into its poor little hide. Naturally raised birds are better for everybody, and even if they cost a little more, you'll more than make up for it in good karma.

3. Plan a few relatively simple sides, but make them very, very delicious. One day of indulgence will not kill you.

Mash your potatoes with real butter and cream and please, use enough salt.

Blanch and shock a bunch of green beans a couple days before. When the bird comes out of the oven you can heat the beans in butter while it rests.

Make sure you skim the fat from the juices before making the gravy, then pass that gravy through a fine mesh strainer a couple times. Then whisk in some cold, whole butter and season it. And make sure it's hot.

No canned cranberries (unless they're a personal favorite). Fresh cranberry sauce is the easiest thing in the world. Follow the directions on the bag.

As for stuffing, there are a billion tasty recipes out there. Just remember to cook and serve it separately from the turkey.

4. I like to brine my birds the night before. Line a large container with a plastic garbage bag and set your turkey inside, breast side down. Add your brine solution: 1 cup each of salt and sugar dissolved in 2 gallons of cold water. (Heat up a couple cups of the water to dissolve the sugar and salt, then mix that into the remaining cold water.)

Seal the bag and put the container in the refrigerator overnight. Or, if it's chilly outside (40 degrees or lower), set the container on the back porch covered by an upturned garbage bin to protect it from critters. The next day, drain and toss the brine solution, then dry off your bird inside and out with paper towels.

5. I like to rub something fat and tasty under the skin. Like butter. It bastes the bird while it cooks and helps crisp up the skin. Combine softened butter with anything you think would add some nice flavor: herbs, spices, mustard, citrus, chilies, minced garlic, etc.

After your bird has been brined and dried, wedge your hand up under the skin and move it around gently, separating skin from flesh. Take care not to tear the skin.

Rub the buttery goo under the skin. Be generous, and use one hand to push it in and the other hand to flatten it from the outside. Distribute it as evenly as possible.

6. Roast your bird according to our handy chart. Make sure you let the turkey rest for at least 15 minutes to allow the juices to become reabsorbed. Roasting squeezes the moisture from the cells; if you cut into meat as soon as it is cooked, the juices will spill onto your cutting board.

7. Reread Step #1.

THAWING TIMES

You can thaw the holiday bird in the refrigerator if you have time, or speed things up by submerging it in cold water that you change every 30 minutes, according to the USDA. Do not thaw the turkey on the counter at room temperature. If thawing in the refrigerator, place the turkey on a tray or pan to contain any juices that may drip.

In the refrigerator
(about 24 hours per 4 pounds)

WEIGHT	TIME
8 to 12 pounds	2 to 3 days
12 to 16 pounds	3 to 4 days
16 to 20 pounds	4 to 5 days
20 to 24 pounds	5 to 6 days

In cold water
(about 30 minutes per pound)

WEIGHT	TIME
8 to 12 pounds	4 to 6 hours
12 to 16 pounds	6 to 8 hours
16 to 20 pounds	8 to 10 hours
20 to 24 pounds	10 to 12 hours

7 STEPS TO A SUCCESSFUL HOLIDAY MEAL *(continued)*

ROASTING TIMES

Because today's standard turkey is younger and more tender than in the past, it cooks more quickly. Use these up-to-date USDA recommended times instead of those found in older cookbooks and references. Cook at 325 degrees. A whole turkey is safe when cooked to a minimum internal temperature of 165 degrees as measured with a food thermometer. Check the internal temperature in the innermost part of the thigh and wing and the thickest part of the breast. If cooking stuffing inside the bird, make sure the center of the stuffing reaches 165 degrees.

RAW WEIGHT	UNSTUFFED	STUFFED
8 to 12 pounds	2¾ to 3 hours	3 to 3½ hours
12 to 14 pounds	3 to 3¾ hours	3½ to 4 hours
14 to 18 pounds	3¾ to 4¼ hours	4 to 4¼ hours
18 to 20 pounds	4¼ to 4½ hours	4¼ to 4¾ hours
20 to 24 pounds	4½ to 5 hours	4¾ to 5¼ hours

HOW TO CARVE A TURKEY: TAKE THE BIRD APART IN THE PRIVACY OF THE KITCHEN WITH THESE DETAILED STEPS

Unless you're that rare bird who cooks a whole turkey more than twice a year, you may feel a bit unsteady when it comes to the task of holiday carving.

STEPS TO FOLLOW

The most nerve-racking way to carve is at the table, removing the meat directly from the carcass slice by slice. If you can do this already, you don't need to read any further. A better way, if you can get away with it, is in the privacy of your kitchen, away from the watchful wide eyes of your guests. (Best done on a large cutting board with grooves to collect the juices.)

Before cooking the bird, examine its structure: Pull on the legs and wings. Notice how the skin fits like a shirt: If you were to cut through it, you'd see where the limbs join the carcass. Feel all the joints to understand how they work; you'll be cutting through them later.

The leg/thigh

1. After resting the cooked bird for at least 15 minutes, lay it on its back with the legs facing you.

2. Using an electric or very sharp carving knife, cut through the skin between the leg/thigh and the carcass. Pull back on the leg to expose the joint. Cut through the joint and remove the leg/thigh (photo 1, next page).

3. Next, cut straight down through the knee joint to separate the leg and thigh. Lay the thigh skin side down and cut out the bone.

4. Hold the drumstick vertically and cut straight down against the bone to remove the meat.

5. Repeat steps 2 through 5 to remove the other leg.

6. Cut the dark meat into serving pieces and place on a platter.

WHY YOU NEED TO LEARN IT

You're going to all that trouble to make a beautiful dinner. Don't let it end up looking like a crime scene.

▶

Photo 1

HOW TO CARVE A TURKEY *(continued)*

The breast/wing

7. Make a shallow incision along the entire length of the breast bone (photo 2).

8. Using the tip of your knife, cut and scrape down one side of the rib cage, pulling gently on the breast to free it.

Photo 2

HOW TO CARVE A TURKEY *(continued)*

9. Follow the bone down until you reach the wing joint. Cut through this joint to keep the wing attached to the breast.

10. Continue cutting down along the carcass until the breast comes free.

11. Lay the breast skin side up on the cutting board with the wing toward your guide hand. Steady the wing with your guide hand and make a slanting cut to remove the wing (photo 3).

12. Place your guide fingers on the cut surface and make another biased cut to get an even slice. Slice the entire breast in this fashion (photo 4).

13. Repeat steps 9 to 13 to remove and slice the other breast.

Photo 3

Photo 4

SIMPLE STEPS FOR MATZO BALLS THAT FLOAT

It's one of the highlights of Passover and one of Earth's mighty delights: the matzo ball.

WHY YOU NEED TO LEARN IT

Full disclosure: This Irish Catholic writer is as goyish as they come, so, why matzo balls? Why not something more suited to my heritage, like potatoes? Or beer?

Regardless of your heritage, it never hurts to have some traditional dishes under your belt from a variety of traditions. And quite frankly, a bowl of matzo ball soup, at any time of year, makes me happy.

PUTTING YOUR SKILLS TO WORK

Matzo ball soup (pg. 296)

There are probably as many matzo ball recipes as there are grandmothers, and true aficionados tend to divide them into two camps: floaters and sinkers. Matzo balls are commonly found in a bowl of beautifully seasoned chicken broth, and depending on how they're made, they may contain enough air bubbles to cause them to float in that broth. Conversely, they may be so dense that they sink to the bottom of the bowl.

Let's talk about what goes into matzo balls, then, and what ingredients are likely to make them float or sink.

The main ingredient in matzo balls is matzo meal, which is simply ground matzo bread, itself made from flour and water. Available in most supermarkets, matzo meal comes in fine to coarse grinds, not unlike bread crumbs. To make matzo balls, you also need fat. Rendered chicken fat, called schmaltz, is traditional, but you could substitute oil or butter (though butter conflicts with kosher dietary restrictions prohibiting combining meat with dairy). Fat gives matzo balls a smooth texture, a silky mouthfeel and also adds tenderness and flavor, especially schmaltz.

There are a couple ways to get schmaltz: If you're making your own chicken broth (which we heartily recommend), chill it after it's done, and the fat will rise to the top and solidify. Scoop it off and melt it over low heat. Alternately, any time you work with chicken, trim away the extra fat before cooking and render it in a small skillet over low heat. Or, cut chicken skin into small pieces and render the fat. The browned bits, called "gribenes," can be used to garnish other dishes or flavor the matzo balls.

Eggs bind everything together because of the albumen in the whites. Some floater fans whip the whites separately before folding them into the dough to make a lighter product.

Liquid is also needed. This is most often water or chicken stock. For an airier product, substitute soda water or seltzer, and the

Photo 1

Photo 2

gas bubbles will lighten the dough. Another way to get bubbles into the dough is with a chemical leavener, such as baking powder.

Generally, you'll need 3 to 4 eggs per cup of matzo meal, along with a 1 to 2 ounces of fat and, if needed, a couple ounces of liquid. One teaspoon of salt should be enough.

STEPS TO FOLLOW

1. If you're using whole eggs, beat them in a metal bowl with liquid and melted fat. If you're whipping whites separately, start with only the yolks, liquid and fat.

2. Gently fold in the dry ingredients. If you've whipped the whites to soft peaks, fold them in carefully to avoid losing air.

3. Rest dough in the refrigerator overnight to fully hydrate the matzo meal.

4. Wet your hands and roll pieces of dough into the desired size (photo 1).

5. Simmer the balls in salted water or stock until cooked through, about 30 to 45 minutes, depending on their size (photo 2).

6. Serve matzo balls in flavorful chicken stock, and freeze any leftovers in the stock.

MATZO BALL SOUP

A friend, Jennifer Diamond, shared her grandmother Muriel Diamond's soup recipe with me. This version is adapted from that recipe. For best flavor and matzo ball texture, make this the day before serving.

PREP TIME: 30 MINUTES

CHILL: OVERNIGHT

COOK TIME: 2 HOURS

YIELD: 8 SERVINGS

3 pounds chicken thighs or 1 whole cut up chicken

1 tablespoon kosher salt

2 large sweet onions, cut into large dice

6 each, cut into bite sized pieces: carrots, celery ribs

3 to 6 cloves garlic, peeled, minced

2 bay leaves

½ cup parsley, chopped

2 eggs, beaten

½ cup matzo meal

2 tablespoons chicken fat skimmed from soup

½ teaspoon coarse salt

Freshly ground pepper

⅓ pound thin egg noodles, cooked in water

1. Place chicken in a stock pot with salted water to cover. Heat to a boil; reduce to a simmer. Cook until chicken is tender, 45-60 minutes. Remove chicken from stock; reserve. Add vegetables, bay leaves and parsley to stock; simmer until vegetables are almost soft, 30 minutes. Cool slightly.

2. Meanwhile, make matzo balls. Combine eggs, matzo meal, chicken fat and salt in a bowl. Work into a dough. Refrigerate dough and soup, covered, overnight.

3. Remove dough from refrigerator; roll into walnut-size balls. Heat soup to a boil; reduce heat to a simmer. Drop matzo balls into soup; simmer, covered, 30 minutes.

4. Meanwhile, cut chicken into bite-size pieces. Season soup to taste. Place 1 or 2 matzo balls, some of the chicken, vegetables and cooked noodles in a bowl; ladle hot soup over.

NUTRITION INFORMATION: PER SERVING: 280 calories, 25% of calories from fat, 8g fat, 2g saturated fat, 125mg cholesterol, 29g carbohydrates, 23g protein, 297mg sodium, 4g fiber

AFTER A LONG, SLOW COOK, EVEN THE TOUGHEST BIRD (OR MEAT) IS READY TO BE PULLED APART

If you're like me, you're at least as excited about the coming Thanksgiving leftovers as you are about the feast. This year, I'm doing something different: pulled turkey.

WHY YOU NEED TO LEARN IT

You have the leftover bird, and the principles for its preparation are the same as for pulled pork or pulled beef or pulled rhino—whatever you have a hankering for.

PUTTING YOUR SKILLS TO WORK

Basic barbecue sauce (pg. 300)
Creamy sweet and sour coleslaw (pg. 302)

STEPS TO FOLLOW

What makes any pulled meat dish so tantalizing is its tenderness, and to achieve that you have to start with the right type of meat. By the "right type" I'm referring to what part of the animal it came from.

Meat is muscle, and different muscles have different culinary properties. Individual muscles are made up of strands of muscle fiber, and these fibers are bound to one another by connective tissue. More connective tissue holds the individual muscles to each other and to the bones. The more use a given muscle gets, the more connective tissue it has.

Also, the more exercise a muscle gets, the larger its individual muscle fibers become. This means it's more work for the teeth to chomp through them. You may have heard people talking about the "grain" of meat. Muscles with lots of small, individual fibers packed tightly together are said to have a fine grain and are more tender. Muscles with fatter individual fibers are said to be coarse grained.

Finely grained meats are typically found on the backs of hoofed animals and are naturally tender. Those meats, such as steaks, chops and tenderloins, don't require much cooking.

Meat from muscles that get the most use, from the legs and shoulders, need tenderizing. One way is through long, slow cooking that literally dissolves the connective tissue called collagen, making the meat fall-apart tender. And it's these cuts of meat that are perfect for pulling apart, because the cooking has done most of the work for you.

Photo 1

That's exactly what happens with your turkey legs—the roasting makes the meat fall-apart tender. Just use your hands to shred it into strips.

(For pulled pork, I recommend the shoulder, also called the Boston butt. Slow roast it at 250 degrees or braise it in stock, beer or tomato sauce for 4 to 6 hours, until it's falling apart, then let it cool before pulling it apart by hand (photo 1). For beef, go with the chuck roast, and slow roast or braise it until it's falling apart.)

The last step is to combine the pulled turkey (or other meat) with your favorite sauce so that it will be tender and juicy. Some form of barbecue sauce is an obvious choice, but it would be great with a brown gravy or a tomato sauce as well.

Include some crunchy coleslaw, and you got some mighty good eating.

BASIC BARBECUE SAUCE

PREP TIME: 10 MINUTES

COOK TIME: 60 MINUTES

YIELD: ABOUT 2 CUPS

1 medium onion, cut into small dice

2 tablespoons vegetable oil or bacon fat

4 cloves garlic, minced

1 can (10½ ounces) beef stock or bouillon

1 cup ketchup, tomato sauce or canned tomato puree

6 ounces cider or red wine vinegar

2 tablespoons Worcestershire sauce

½ cup brown sugar

2 tablespoons Dijon mustard

1 tablespoon paprika

1 tablespoon chili powder or cumin

½ teaspoon cayenne, optional

½ teaspoon salt

Freshly ground black pepper

1. Cook onions in oil in a large saucepan over medium heat until lightly brown, about 5 minutes. Add garlic; cook until fragrant, about 30 seconds. Add remaining ingredients; simmer until reduced to a thick sauce, 45 to 60 minutes. Serve as is or, for a smoother consistency, puree in a blender and pass through a fine mesh sieve.

NUTRITION INFORMATION PER TABLESPOON: 31 calories, 1g fat, 0g saturated fat, 0mg cholesterol, 5g carbohydrates, 0g protein, 158mg sodium, 0g fiber

CREAMY SWEET AND SOUR COLESLAW

PREP TIME: 20 MINUTES

YIELD: 8 SERVINGS

1 small to medium head red cabbage or ½ large head green cabbage, shredded

1 medium onion, julienned

1 large apple, peeled, julienned

3 tablespoons sugar

¼ cup seasoned rice wine vinegar

½ cup mayonnaise

½ teaspoon salt

Freshly ground pepper

1. Combine cabbage, onion and apple in a large bowl. Whisk sugar into vinegar until (mostly) dissolved in another bowl; combine with mayonnaise. Toss cabbage mixture with half the dressing. Add more dressing as needed; season with salt and pepper to taste.

NUTRITION INFORMATION PER SERVING: 154 calories, 11g fat, 1g saturated fat, 5mg cholesterol, 13g carbohydrates, 1g protein, 240mg sodium, 2g fiber

BAKING AND DESSERTS

WHIPPING UP DESSERT: DISCOVERING MANY LEVELS OF GOODNESS OF FRESHLY WHIPPED CREAM

One key to healthful living is moderation in all things. But a little whipped cream never hurt anyone, so we're going to do it by hand.

WHY YOU NEED TO LEARN IT

Learning to cook is more than just following recipes: It's about understanding ingredients and the processes that change them.

Although I'm not one to pooh-pooh modern conveniences (stand mixers whip cream quickly and painlessly, plus, who can argue with the pleasures of canned whipped cream eaten straight from the nozzle?), there's nothing more satisfying than taking an icy whisk to a bowl of chilled heavy cream.

PUTTING YOUR SKILLS TO WORK

Caramelized pear trifle (pg. 307)

STEPS TO FOLLOW

Whipping incorporates air into cream. Globules of fat surround the air bubbles, giving the cream structure. Because fat is stiffer and stronger at lower temperatures (compare chilled butter to room-temperature butter), cream whips up best when cold. (For an excellent discussion of this and much more, see Harold McGee's "On Food and Cooking: The Science and Lore of the Kitchen.")

Also, don't worry about whether it's "ultra-pasteurized" or not. As long as it's labeled heavy or whipping cream it should whip up just fine.

One note on equipment: Choose a whisk with more wires, because it will add more air more quickly.

1. Chill all tools and ingredients: Place a whisk and metal bowl in the freezer for 10 minutes. Keep cream refrigerated until ready to whip.

2. Remove tools from freezer and pour cream into the cold bowl.

3. Whisk in a "figure 8" design across the bottom of the bowl. As this process takes several minutes, it's likely your muscles will tire. You can ease any discomfort by switching between two grips: The most common grip is similar to holding a tennis racket or ice cream cone. With this grip, your wrist is bent downward (photo 1). With the second grip, keep your wrist straight and grasp the whisk as if you're holding a pen (photo 2).

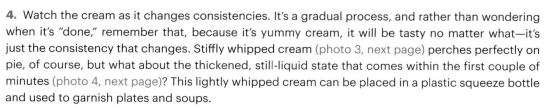

4. Watch the cream as it changes consistencies. It's a gradual process, and rather than wondering when it's "done," remember that, because it's yummy cream, it will be tasty no matter what—it's just the consistency that changes. Stiffly whipped cream (photo 3, next page) perches perfectly on pie, of course, but what about the thickened, still-liquid state that comes within the first couple of minutes (photo 4, next page)? This lightly whipped cream can be placed in a plastic squeeze bottle and used to garnish plates and soups.

5. Add sweeteners and flavoring ingredients when the cream is just short of where you want it. Whisking in confectioners' sugar or a liquid flavoring extract adds extra air and can make your cream stiffer than you intended. Completely overwhipped cream turns ultimately to butter—again, delicious, but probably not what you want.

WHIPPING UP DESSERT *(continued)*

Flavoring ideas

For a subtle savory flavor, you can place several sprigs of fresh herbs in your cream the night before you need it, then strain them out before whipping. In general, however, most professional cooks flavor their cream with high quality extracts. Anise, clove, peppermint, lemon, almond, coffee, chocolate—there is a host of options available at area grocers, spice merchants and cookware shops.

To tint your cream, food coloring works great, though some red dyes can add an off flavor. Try grating a fresh beet onto cheese cloth and wringing out the juice. There'll be next to no beet flavor, and the juice will add a rich pink color to your cream.

CARAMELIZED PEAR TRIFLE

Firm pears work best with this, though they may require just a touch of salt to enhance the flavor. This dish can be made a couple of hours ahead of time and chilled. Eaten immediately, there's a nice temperature contrast between the cold cream and warm pears. For extra decadence and flavor, you can saute the poundcake cubes in butter.

1. Place a whisk and metal mixing bowl in the freezer to chill. Heat 2 tablespoons of the butter over medium-high heat until melted and foam subsides. Add the diced pears; cook, tossing, until lightly browned, about 2 minutes. Add the brown sugar, cinnamon and salt; toss to coat the pears.

2. Remove skillet from heat; add the brandy. Carefully light the brandy with a long match. Gently shake the pan until the flames are extinguished. Swirl in remaining tablespoon of the butter. Set aside.

3. Remove the bowl and whisk from the freezer; add the cream to the bowl. Whisk with a "figure 8" motion until moderately thick but still very pourable. Add the confectioners' sugar and the almond extract, whisking another few seconds to incorporate.

4. Place 2 tablespoons of the whipped cream on the bottom of four large, wide-mouth wine glasses. Add to each a layer of poundcake cubes, 1-2 tablespoons of the caramelized pears and a drizzle of cream. Repeat until the glasses are full, topping off with a layer of cream. Garnish with lemon zest.

NUTRITION INFORMATION PER SERVING: 642 calories, 62% of calories from fat, 45g fat, 27g saturated fat, 210mg cholesterol, 56g carbohydrates, 6g protein, 294mg sodium, 5g fiber

PREP TIME: 40 MINUTES

COOK TIME: 7 MINUTES

YIELD: 6 SERVINGS

3 tablespoons butter

4 pears, peeled, cored, cut into medium dice

1 tablespoon plus 1½ teaspoons brown sugar

¼ teaspoon cinnamon

¼ teaspoon salt, optional

2 tablespoons brandy or pear liqueur

2 containers (½ pint each) whipping cream

2 tablespoons confectioners' sugar

1 teaspoon almond extract

Grated zest from 1 lemon

4 slices poundcake, cut into cubes

CONQUER ALL MUFFINS: ONCE YOU MASTER THE BASIC METHOD, BAKING IS A BREEZE

Something quite unexpected has gotten hold of me over the past couple of years. Somehow, I've developed a sweet tooth. Maybe it's my own creeping age, or, conversely, the youthful enthusiasm of my 4-year-old daughter. Whatever the source, all I know is that for the past several months we've been making muffins about every other weekend at my house. Eating a few and freezing the rest, life has rarely, if ever, been sweeter.

WHY YOU NEED TO LEARN IT

The muffin method is one of the basic mixing methods for quick breads, the category of baked goods that includes, among other things, such lovelies as scones, pancakes, crepes and banana bread. Get this simple method down, and every muffin recipe will pretty much fall into place; all you'll need is the exact ingredient amounts.

Think about muffins for breakfast tomorrow. And because they do freeze really well, muffins can be had any day you want.

PUTTING YOUR SKILLS TO WORK

Chocolate-chip muffins (pg. 310)

STEPS TO FOLLOW

1. Always start by heating your oven: 350 to 400 degrees should do it, but check your recipe.

2. Sift or mix the dry ingredients into a bowl (photo 1). These include flour, bran, cornmeal, wheat germ, those sorts of things, as well as salt, sugar and usually some kind of chemical leavener like baking soda or baking powder. Make sure everything is evenly distributed.

3. Combine all of the liquid ingredients in a separate bowl. If you're using eggs, put them in the bowl first. The more you beat them, the lighter the muffin. Add to this the main liquid component. Typically this is a dairy product like milk or cream, though some recipes will call for something wild, like coffee, tea, even beer and liquor. Flavor extracts can go in now, too, along with any fats like oil or melted butter. Finally, include any mostly liquid ingredients like yogurt, sour cream, honey, molasses, etc.

4. Assemble any other flavoring items: dried or fresh fruit, nuts, chocolate chips, citrus zest, fresh or frozen berries, etc. Remember gravity, though, and its habit of drawing larger pieces of things toward the bottom of muffin tins before the batter sets up in the oven. A very light dusting of flour on these items will help suspend them in the batter (photo 2).

5. Pour the liquid mixture into the dry ingredients all at once, then add other flavoring items. Use a rubber spatula to combine

Photo 1

Photo 2

Photo 3

everything as quickly as possible and make sure to scrape the sides and bottom. Flours ground from wheat (such as all-purpose flour) contain a protein called gluten. When it is combined with liquid and mixed, it toughens up. This is why we knead bread for several good, long minutes, to give it a nice, chewy crust and a sturdy crumb. Those qualities are exactly what we don't want with cakes or muffins, however, which is why we want to take care not to overmix the muffin batter. In fact, with muffins, it's not even necessary to achieve a smooth batter. Instead, mix just long enough to moisten all the dry ingredients (photo 3), and don't worry if there are a few lumps.

CHOCOLATE-CHIP MUFFINS

PREP TIME: 15 MINUTES

COOK TIME: 18 MINUTES

YIELD: 1 DOZEN

1 cup plus 2 teaspoons all-purpose flour

1 cup oat bran or oat flour

½ cup sugar

1 tablespoon baking powder

½ teaspoon kosher salt

3 eggs

½ stick (¼ cup) unsalted butter, melted

1 cup half-and-half

1 cup dark chocolate chips

1. Heat oven to 400 degrees. Sift 1 cup of the all-purpose flour, oat bran, sugar, baking powder and salt together in a medium bowl; set aside.

2. Whisk eggs in a medium bowl until light and airy. Whisk half-and-half and melted butter into eggs; set aside. (Don't worry if some of the butter solidifies when it hits the cold liquid.)

3. Toss the chocolate chips with remaining 2 teaspoons of the flour; set aside. Make a well in center of the dry ingredients. Add liquid all at once; add the chocolate chips. Quickly combine with a rubber spatula, scraping from the bottom of the bowl. Mix only until the dry ingredients are just moist, a few seconds. (Don't worry if there are lumps.)

4. Divide batter evenly among greased muffin tins with a ¼-cup measuring cup; bake until light brown and a tester inserted in the center comes out clean, about 18 minutes.

NUTRITION INFORMATION PER MUFFIN: 236 calories, 42% of calories from fat, 12g fat, 7g saturated fat, 70mg cholesterol, 32g carbohydrates, 5g protein, 229mg sodium, 2g fiber

IN PIE HEAVEN: A PERFECT DOUGH BEGINS WITH UNDERSTANDING THE FAT

If I could take but one dessert with me to eternity, truthfully, it would have to be ice cream. If I could take two, however, the second would be pie, wonderful pie.

Or, pie for breakfast. Seriously, I don't know why more people don't do that. The crust is wheat flour and butter (like toast), the fruit filling's like jam, and the optional ice cream? Well, that's the cream in your coffee.

STEPS TO FOLLOW

The first step in making pie dough is cutting the fat into the dry flour. Each small chunk of fat then becomes coated with flour. Obviously, the more we cut, the smaller the pieces of fat become.

There are two basic types of pie dough, each with the same ingredients. The only difference is the size of the chunks of fat.

"Flaky" dough contains large chunks of fat, about the size of peas or peanuts. When rolled out, these chunks are flattened between layers of dough. As it bakes, the fat melts and its liquid evaporates, separating those layers and causing the crust to flake. This dough is perfect for topping pies. (While it can be used on the bottom, it tends to give a soggier crust because it is fairly absorbent.)

The second type, called "mealy" dough, has its fat cut into rather fine pieces into the flour until the consistency resembles coarse cornmeal. Cutting the fat so finely exposes more of its surface area, meaning more flour is in contact with fat. Flour that is in direct contact with fat loses some of its ability to absorb liquid. Thus, mealy pie dough requires less water to hold it together. Moreover, that decreased absorbency makes it well suited for the bottom crust, especially with juicy fruit pies.

Remember, these two doughs are variations of the same thing. Both will work as upper or lower crusts; it's just that flaky is slightly better suited to upper while mealy is slightly better suited to lower.

WHY YOU NEED TO LEARN IT

Simple pie dough contains flour, salt, a solid fat—butter, vegetable shortening or lard—and cold water. As with many things, the more you understand how it all works, the more likely you are to have success.

When flour is mixed with water, it forms long strands of gluten, a protein that allows cakes, breads and pie crusts to hold their shape. When fat is added to the mix, these strands quite literally are shortened and the finished product is rendered more tender.

PUTTING YOUR SKILLS TO WORK

Peach almond pie (pg. 314)

IN PIE HEAVEN *(continued)*

Making the doughs

1. Sift together 2 cups of all-purpose flour with 1 teaspoon of salt.

2. Cut three-quarters of a stick of cold, unsalted butter into roughly ¾-inch cubes. (DO NOT obsess about the dimensions.) Add the cubes of butter, along with 4 tablespoons of shortening, to the flour. (Why are we using both butter and shortening? Butter gives better flavor but encourages a brittle crust. Vegetable shortening gives a more pliant crust but, because—unlike butter—it does not melt at body temperature, it leaves a discernible film on the inside of the mouth. Butter melts at 86 degrees and leaves your mouth feeling wonderful.)

3. Cut the fat into the flour until you have fairly uniform pea-sized chunks. You can do this with a pastry cutter or two butter knives held parallel (photo 1). Or, you can put the whole mess into a food processor and pulse it four or five times. You also may use your fingers, but you must work very quickly so as not to melt the fat with your body heat.

4. Remove half of the mixture to another bowl and set aside. This will become your flaky dough (photo 2, right).

5. Continue cutting the remaining mixture until it is the consistency of coarse cornmeal. This will become the mealy dough (photo 2, left).

6. To each bowl add about 1 ounce of icy-cold water. (Cold water keeps the fat from melting too soon.) You want just enough to make the dough hold together while still looking dry. Work the doughs into separate balls, then cover and refrigerate for 1 hour or overnight.

7. Roll chilled doughs into circles slightly larger than a pie pan. Place the mealy dough on the bottom, fill the pie, then cover with the flaky dough, crimping the edges together to seal the pie. Make a few slits in the top to allow steam to escape and brush the top with milk, then bake.

Photo 1

Photo 2

PEACH ALMOND PIE

PREP TIME: 30 MINUTES

COOK TIME: 45 MINUTES

YIELD: 8 SERVINGS

7 medium peaches, about 2½ pounds

⅔ cup sugar

Juice of 1 lemon

2 tablespoons plus 1½ teaspoons cornstarch

1 teaspoon almond extract

½ teaspoon ground cinnamon

½ teaspoon salt

1 recipe pie dough, see steps in article

1. Heat oven to 400 degrees. Heat a large pot of water to a boil over high heat; add peaches. Cook 30 seconds; transfer to a large bowl of ice water to stop cooking. Cut each peach in half; remove pits. Cut each crosswise into ½-inch thick slices.

2. Combine peaches, sugar, lemon juice, cornstarch, almond extract, cinnamon and salt in a large bowl. Set aside.

3. Roll out mealy pie dough into a ⅛-inch-thick, 10-inch-diameter circle. Fold dough in half; fold in half again. Place dough carefully inside a 9-inch pie pan; unfold. Press down lightly.

4. Roll out flaky dough to a ⅛-inch thick circle, big enough to cover the pie with a little overhang. Fold in half; fold in half again. Set aside; cover with a towel.

5. Pour peach mixture into pie shell. Lay flaky crust carefully on top; unfold. Crimp edges of pie to seal. Cut several slashes into top crust to allow steam to vent. Bake until top is browned and filling is bubbling, about 45 minutes. Cool on wire rack.

NUTRITION INFORMATION PER SERVING: 370 calories, 37% of calories from fat, 15g fat, 7g saturated fat, 23mg cholesterol, 55g carbohydrates, 4g protein, 438mg sodium, 3g fiber

HERE'S LOOKING AT YOU, COOKIE: HOW TO GIVE HOME-BAKED TREATS A PROFESSIONAL LOOK

I've always been a savory kind of guy—no sweet tooth to speak of, really. As a result, I'm not much of a baker. Even around the holidays, when I should have been making cookies … well, my mother always did such a terrific job that I never bothered. Fortunately, I have a good friend, Melina Kelson-Podolsky, who is a chef/instructor on the baking faculty of Kendall College.

When I realized that Prep School would have to devote some space to holiday baking, I threw myself upon her mercies. On a recent Sunday, our children played and I took notes while she talked and plied me with peanut butter-chocolate chip cookies and hot chocolate. Who says learning is a chore?

WHY YOU NEED TO LEARN IT

Face it. Unless my mother owes you one, you're going to be making some cookies over the next couple of months. Here is a chance to practice some new skills.

STEPS TO FOLLOW

Keep in mind that consistency is a hallmark of professional cookies. Work on your technique and pay attention to how everything feels in your hands. Use your senses to develop muscle memory. And think beautiful.

"It comes down to the extra touches, putting some love into what you're doing," Kelson-Podolsky said.

For perfectly consistent drop cookies, such as your basic chocolate chip, buy a trigger-release portion scoop (like an ice cream scoop, only fancier). The 2-ounce size is pretty standard, said Kelson-Podolsky, though "the petite ones tend to look cuter."

For pressed cookies (also called spritz cookies), many cooks use a cookie press. However, a piping bag works just as well. Practice your technique before you settle in to make the cookies: Use shortening or canned frosting, or whip up a batch of mashed potatoes. Reusing the dough can overwork it, causing small tunnels in the cookies.

If you haven't used a piping bag before, keep in mind these tips:

1. Put the desired tip into the bag. To fill the bag, fold the top third of it down around the outside of the bag; hold the top open with your hand in a `C' shape. Use a spatula to get the dough inside the bag as far as you can, then wipe the spatula against the inside of the bag as you take it out. Fill the bag only halfway (or even just a quarter of the way for stiff cookie doughs), then roll up the top of the bag and twist it tight to force the dough down into the tip. You want to get rid of any air bubbles that can mess up your cookies if they get pressed through the tip.

2. With your strong hand, pinch the top of the bag in the crook between your thumb and index finger, then fold your other fingers down over the bag.

3. Squeeze the dough gently from the top—not the sides—of the bag. At the same time, use your other hand to guide the tip. Keep the tip above the cookie sheet; don't press it down or it will smear the dough. As the dough emerges from the tip, let gravity lay it gently on the cookie sheet (photo 1).

Photo 1

HERE'S LOOKING AT YOU, COOKIE *(continued)*

4. After you pipe a cookie, release the pressure with your strong hand as you twist the tip gently to break off the dough in a nice point.

Melt some candy dipping chocolate. It's also called "summer chocolate" or "coating chocolate." (Wilton and Ghirardelli both have lines of it.) Dip half of your baked cookie into the melted chocolate, then roll it in crushed nuts, sprinkles or grated chocolate (photo 2).

Make royal icing, which is more durable than other frostings: Combine a couple of pasteurized egg whites (to avoid salmonella) with 1 or 2 tablespoons of lemon juice and 3 or 4 cups of confectioners' sugar. Blend in a stand mixer until smooth, and add a couple drops of food coloring if you like. This icing hardens when exposed to the air, so use it quickly or store it in an airtight container.

Save a bundle and make your own colored sugar: Add just a drop or two of food coloring to a couple cups of granulated sugar. Wearing rubber gloves, work the coloring through the sugar until it is evenly distributed. Keep it in an airtight container.

Photo 2

FROSTING A CAKE LIKE A PRO

I'm no baker. I have neither the patience for exactitude that baking requires, nor the sweet tooth that would drive me to practice my skills. Fortunately, when I need baking advice, I have many colleagues in the baking and pastry department at the Cooking and Hospitality Institute of Chicago, where I'm on the culinary faculty.

Recently, I sat down with chef/instructor Marilyn McNabb to talk about frosting a cake like a pro.

STEPS TO FOLLOW

Because decorating a cake can be very messy, it can be a little daunting for beginners. McNabb recommends starting with as clean an area as possible. Have towels available to wipe down errant crumbs and frosting.

Start with a soft frosting. "What you buy in the store is hard and it's more likely to crumble the cake," McNabb said, "so start with buttercream or simple whipped cream."

Also, equipment is important. Many of us try to frost cakes with a butter knife, a spoon or even a plastic spatula. The pros use a cake spatula with its long, thin, flexible metal blade. Cake spatulas can be straight or offset; offset spatulas can be found in kitchenware stores as well as craft stores such as Michael's, JoAnn and Hobby Lobby.

"You want it a little soft but not too flexible because you have to push the frosting around," McNabb said. "And since most cakes are not very tall, get one that's only 6 to 8 inches and you'll have better control."

McNabb offered a bit of advice that I could have used four years ago:

1. Start with a level cake. (Use a serrated knife to evenly and gently slice off the cake's domed top.) Place the layer, cut side up, on a cake stand or board. Place a large spoonful of icing on the layer. Spread the icing to an even thickness about ¼ inch. Don't worry if the top is crumb-y; you are going to place the second layer on top of this. Just clean off the spatula before proceeding to the second layer.

WHY YOU (AND I) NEED TO LEARN THIS

Four years ago I made a cake for my daughter's second birthday party. It looked like a Dali painting. To this day, I have yet to hear the last of it from my friends.

PUTTING YOUR SKILLS TO WORK

Classic buttercream frosting (pg. 323)

FROSTING A CAKE LIKE A PRO *(continued)*

2. Top with the second layer, this time with the cut/crumb side down. Place a big mound of frosting on top of the cake and push it around the top (photo 1), holding your spatula perfectly horizontal to achieve an even thickness of about ¼ inch. Don't let the frosting mound up in the middle.

"Push the frosting, not the cake," advised McNabb, "because that makes crumbs." If the frosting is too crumb-filled, clean off the spatula and add a bit more frosting. (Another tip the pros use: Warm the spatula by putting it in a glass of hot water, then wipe it dry before adding more frosting.) To avoid a crumb-riddled cake, every few strokes wipe your spatula on the side of a second, empty bowl (so you don't re-introduce crumbs into the unused frosting).

3. When the frosting reaches the cake edge, push it over the sides and down. Hold the spatula perfectly perpendicular to the board, and push the frosting around the side of the cake (photo 2). "As you go around the sides, the frosting [should] creep up until it's higher than the top of the cake," McNabb said. "So the last thing [you do] is to take the spatula and smooth out the top again."

4. You can stop here and have a beautiful cake, or you can add a few extra touches that will really impress your friends. Using the back of a spoon, make little waves or indentations, creating attractive peaks in the frosting. "This is how they'd do it back in the '70s," McNabb said, "and it's kind of marshmallow-fluffy.

Press grated chocolate, dried coconut, chopped nuts or even crushed cereal onto the side of the cake (photo 3, next page). Make decorative patterns in the frosting using a pastry comb, also available at kitchen supply stores and craft stores.

"You can also go to a hardware store and buy a spackling tool or a grouting tool, something with teeth," says McNabb, "and run it around the frosting in straight lines, ripples or ribbons. It'll make your cake look very professional."

Photo 1

Photo 2

Photo 3

CLASSIC BUTTERCREAM FROSTING

This frosting, adapted from "Joy of Cooking," will frost an 8- or 9-inch layer cake. It can be refrigerated up to 6 days but will need to be softened before using. To soften, heat in a micro-wave on low (50 percent) power for 15- to 30-second intervals until some of the buttercream begins to melt. Stir with a spatula until the frosting is smooth and spreadable.

1. Combine sugar, water and cream of tartar in a medium sauce-pan over medium heat; heat to a simmer. Cover; cook until sugar dissolves, about 2 minutes. Uncover; wash any sugar crystals from the sides of the pan with a wet pastry brush. Cook, uncov-ered, until syrup registers 238 degrees (soft ball stage) on a can-dy thermometer. Meanwhile, fill a wide deep skillet with 1 inch of water; heat to a simmer over medium heat.

2. Beat the egg yolks with a mixer on high speed in a medium bowl until thick and pale. Beating constantly, pour the hot syrup in a thin steady stream into the eggs at the edge of the bowl. Set the bowl in the skillet of simmering water, whisking constantly until the mixture registers 160 degrees on an instant-read ther-mometer. Remove from the heat. Wash the beaters; beat the hot mixture until it cools to room temperature.

3. Beat in the butter, 1 tablespoon at a time, beating until the but-tercream is smooth and spreadable.

NUTRITION INFORMATION PER TABLESPOON: 71 calories, 76% of calories from fat, 6g fat, 4g saturated fat, 36mg cholesterol, 4g carbohydrates, 0g protein, 2mg sodium, 0g fiber

PREP TIME: 25 MINUTES

COOK TIME: 10-15 MINUTES

YIELD: 3 CUPS

1 cup sugar

½ cup water

¼ teaspoon cream of tartar

5 egg yolks, at room tem-perature

3 sticks (1½ cups) butter, room temperature

IT'S THE LAYERS: SIMPLE GUIDELINES HELP YOUR PUFF PASTRY RISE

OK, you didn't hear this from me (Mr. "You Need to Learn This," Mr. "You Should Really Make Everything From Scratch"). But, truthfully, when it comes to puff pastry, you're better off buying it than trying to make it yourself. Shhhh.

WHY YOU NEED TO LEARN IT

One of the great things about puff pastry, what the French call pate feuilletee, is that no one makes it at home. There are two reasons.

First, perfectly good commercial puff pastries are available at most supermarkets and specialty stores. We recommend brands that use butter rather than other shortenings: The taste is better, and because butter melts at a lower temperature than we are (86 degrees for butter versus 98.6 degrees for us), it leaves a much cleaner mouth feel.

Second, it's just too hard and time-consuming for most people: Puff pastry is what's called a laminated dough because it's layered. Like other laminated doughs, such as croissants, it's made by placing a brick of butter on top of a sheet of regular dough. Unlike other laminated doughs, however, puff pastry has no yeast, and its rising occurs naturally because of the way it's made: The sides of the dough are folded over the top, encasing the butter. Both ends are folded into the middle, then one side is folded over on the other, creating five layers of dough separated by four layers of butter. After chilling, this process is repeated several times, increasing the numbers of layers geometrically to the many hundreds.

When puff pastry is baked, the butter melts, separating those hundreds of layers of dough. At the same time, the water in the butter turns to steam which, in turn, pushes all those hundreds of layers apart, causing the dough to rise and, in the process, creating a light, flaky, buttery, brown and crunchy final product.

STEPS TO FOLLOW

Regardless of what you're using it for, here are some guidelines to follow when handling puff pastry:

1. It needs to stay cold. If the butter begins to melt before it goes into the oven, the dough can turn to mush.

2. Any fillings should be at room temperature.

3. When cutting unbaked puff pastry, use a very sharp knife so you don't mash the layers into one another.

4. Puff pastry can rise up to eight times its initial thickness. If you want a thinner finished product, roll out the dough before baking. Alternately, poke the dough all over with a fork (called docking) before baking.

5. Puff pastry can be filled before or after cooking.

6. Puff pastry takes anywhere from 20 to 30 minutes to bake for smaller items, or 40 to 50 minutes for larger items, usually at about 400 degrees. You'll know when it's done because it'll be golden brown and beautifully risen.

Puff pastry options

Here are just a few terrific uses to which you can put puff pastry (for others, consult the Internet or any standard baking book):

Pot pies. Toss cubes of cooked meat and aromatic vegetables with seasoned, thickened broth. Spoon into individual ramekins, top with puff pastry and bake until done.

Turnovers. Cut puff pastry into 4- to 6-inch squares. Rub the edges with egg wash, then place a dollop of fruit filling in one corner. Fold the opposite corner over to make a triangle, then press down the edges to seal and bake until done (photo 1). (Alternately, use the pot pie filling to make savory turnovers. These are great for snacks or carried lunches.)

Palmiers. Spread duxelles (finely diced mushrooms and onions, seasoned and sauteed until dry) over a puff pastry sheet. Roll opposite sides toward the middle, like a scroll, then cut into thin slices. Lay on a sheet tray and bake until golden brown. These make terrific hors d'oeuvres.

TAKE A POUNDCAKE ... WHEN GOOD ISN'T GOOD ENOUGH, USE THIS CLASSIC DESSERT (AND BREAK THE BREAD HABIT) TO BUILD UNEXPECTED DELIGHTS

Way, way, way down, near the bottom of the "List of Very Interesting Foods," you'll find poundcake. So-called because, traditionally, it was made from one pound each of butter, sugar, eggs and flour, its texture is nonthreatening, its flavor rather polite. No one can argue with poundcake. Indeed, it is its very ordinariness that makes it so useful in the kitchen.

WHY YOU NEED TO LEARN IT

One thing I always tell my students is that everything can be better, that they should ask themselves always: "What else can I do with this dish? How can I improve it?" Poundcake is a great tool for this exercise. Because it is, by its very nature, a rather unassuming, somewhat plain thing, it lends itself perfectly to being transformed into something else, into becoming an ingredient in a far more interesting dish.

PUTTING YOUR SKILLS TO WORK

Traditional poundcake (pg. 330)

STEPS TO FOLLOW

Start with poundcake. You can use your favorite recipe or just go to the market and pick one out. (One caveat: Check the label and try to get one that has only natural ingredients. See, I'm watching out for you!)

By the way, you'll notice that many of these ideas are simply substituting poundcake for bread. This makes perfect sense because, in terms of ingredients, they're pretty similar except for the sugar. After you read it, imagine what other ideas you can come up with.

One last note: Many of the ideas for this piece came from a recent conversation I had with my friend Melina Kelson, chef, Kendall College colleague and certified master baker.

HOW TO MAKE A CLASSIC

Here's eight ways to gild the lily—that is, creative suggestions on what to do with poundcake. You can use your own favorite poundcake recipe, or buy a ready-made cake at the grocery. Or better still—try this one.

Toad in the hole (photo 1)

Another great brunch item. Use a biscuit cutter or knife to carve out a 3-inch hole in the center of a poundcake slice. Fry the slice

Photo 1

and the hole in butter or, better yet, bacon fat. In a separate pan or pot, fry or poach an egg the way you like it and set it in the center of the slice. Break the yolk and dunk the hole piece inside. Yum. Oh, and don't forget the bacon and coffee.

PCPB&J

Make everyone's favorite sweet sandwiches—peanut butter and jelly or peanut butter and banana— on slices of poundcake. You can even do a supersweet Monte Cristo: Make a sandwich of pound-cake, sliced ham and cheese, then dunk both sides into an egg mixture like you used for the French toast (only leave out the cinnamon and vanilla). Fry it in butter until golden-brown on both sides. Serve with your favorite jelly on the side.

▶

TAKE A POUNDCAKE *(continued)*

Croutons

Cut poundcake into ¾-inch cubes and bake in a 350-degree oven until golden, about 10 to 15 minutes. Try them on a salad that has some sweet component such as a honey or maple syrup vinaigrette or dried or fresh fruit. They are perfect for chilled fruit soup come summer: Puree some peaches or melons with just enough orange juice and Champagne—equal amounts of those two—to make a soupy consistency, season with salt and a touch of white pepper, chill, then serve garnished with croutons and mint sprigs. They'll also go great on ice cream.

Apple charlotte (photo 2)

Here's a nod to Auguste Escoffier, the father of French classical cuisine: Cut thin slices of poundcake and butter them or dip in melted butter. Line buttered ramekins with the slices and pack full with apples sauteed in butter with cinnamon and lemon zest. Put a round, buttered poundcake slice on top. Bake in a 375-degree oven until golden-brown, 10-15 minutes.

French toast (photo 3)

One of the best things in life just got better. Never made French toast? Whisk 2 eggs with about ½ cup of milk, a teaspoon of vanilla and a sprinkling of cinnamon. Dunk ½-inch-thick slices of poundcake in egg mixture and fry in butter over medium heat until golden brown. Flip and repeat. Serve with syrup, jam, sour cream—anything you like.

Rum balls

Moisten untoasted crumbs with rum, then roll into balls. Dip the rum balls into tempered or coating chocolate, then roll in sprinkles. If you want to be really trendy, put a stick in each one for rum ball lollipops.

Trifle

Crumble some poundcake in a bowl or sundae dish. Pour over some melted but still cold ice cream. Garnish with fresh berries and, if you're so inclined, a splash of liqueur that's flavored like your berries.

Crumbs

If you have stale or dried-out cake, crumble it relatively finely, then toss in a hot, dry skillet to toast. Use to garnish ice cream, frosted cakes or other desserts.

Photo 2

Photo 3

TRADITIONAL POUNDCAKE

Originally, poundcakes had 1 pound each of the four major ingredients. Because many home cooks don't have kitchen scales, we've converted everything to more usable amounts. (You should really get a kitchen scale, though; they're very handy.)

PREP TIME: 20 MINUTES

BAKE: 1 HOUR, 15 MINUTES

YIELD: 3 CAKES, 36 SERVINGS

1 pound butter

2¼ cups sugar

9 eggs

2 tablespoons vanilla

4 cups cake flour

1. Heat oven to 350 degrees. Cream butter in a stand mixer with paddle attachment until light and airy, about 5 minutes. Add sugar; cream, 6-8 minutes.

2. With mixer running, add eggs one at a time until incorporated. Scrape down sides occasionally while adding eggs to ensure complete incorporation. Beat in the vanilla.

3. Add flour; mix until just combined. Divide batter among three greased loaf pans; bake until done, about 1 hour 15 minutes.

NUTRITION INFORMATION PER SERVING: 214 calories, 12g fat, 7g saturated fat, 80mg cholesterol, 25g carbohydrates, 3g protein, 19mg sodium, 0g fiber

RECIPE INDEX

PHOTO CREDITS

Presents for the cook
Fila, Bob, December 20, 2006

Cooking tips to make life better in the kitchen
Trafelet, Bonnie, January 25, 2012

6 essentials to make you a better cook
Photo 1, Photo 2: Fila, Bob, January 25, 2012
Photo 3: Tercha, Michael, January 25, 2012

Sharpening your knife skills
Fila, Bob, May 11, 2005

Steeling yourself
Dziekan, John, March 28, 2007

Learning the best cuts
Fila, Bob, June 8, 2005

Twice the dice
Garcia, Alex, July 25, 2007

Mastering the perfect diced onion
Fila, Bob, July 6, 2005

There's another way to slice it
Fila, Bob, November 8, 2006; food styling by Lisa Schumacher

Tricks for tackling ripe summer fruit
Fila, Bob, July 20, 2005

Sharpening your skills on a whole bird
Fila, Bob, January 4, 2006; food styling by Lisa Schumacher

Spatchcocking makes cooking a bird quicker
Fila, Bob, May 25, 2005

Chicken takes a romantic turn
Fila, Bob, December 26, 2007; food styling by Corrine Kozlak

Orange supremes add elegant touch
Fila, Bob, January 18, 2006; food styling by Corrine Kozlak

Fillet your way to dinner
Fila, Bob, August 16, 2006; food styling by Lisa Schumacher

More than one way to chop a nut
Trafelet, Bonnie, December 17, 2008

You'll flip for this sauteing skill
Fila, Bob, June 22, 2005

Come into the fold
Fila, Bob, December 7, 2005; food styling by Corrine Kozlak

Stir-frying puts some sizzle in a cook's repertoire
Fila, Bob, January 25, 2006; food styling by Lisa Schumacher

Building a better burger
Fila, Bob, July 30, 2008; food styling by Jennifer Lussow

Stuffing pork chops in no time
Fila, Bob, November 9, 2005; food styling by Lisa Schumacher

Braise away the winter blues
Hogan, Bill, February 28, 2007

Praising braising
Fila, Bob, March 1, 2006; food styling by Lisa Schumacher

Take one roast, tie up in knots
Fila, Bob, April 12, 2006; food styling by Corrine Kozlak

Smoky sensation
Dziekan, John, June 7, 2006

To brine is divine
Fila, Bob, July 5, 2006; food styling by Lisa Schumacher

Running hot and cold
Fila, Bob, September 13, 2006; food styling by Lisa Schumacher

French elegance, on the double
Dziekan, John, August 31, 2005; food styling by Mark Graham

Don't fear the mussels
Fila, Bob, March 15, 2006, food styling by Lisa Schumacher

CIY (cure it yourself)
Garcia, Alex, October 19, 2011; food styling by Corrine Kozlak

Bathed in simplicity
Fila, Bob, September 5, 2007

Poaching perfection
Hogan, Bill, October 3, 2007, food styling by Lisa Schumacher

Fricassee elevates humble chicken
Hogan, Bill, March 23, 2011, food styling by Lisa Schumacher

Frenching 101
Fila, Bob, October 31, 2007; food styling by Lisa Schumacher

A toast to bringing out flavor
Trafelet, Bonnie, April 30, 2008; food styling by Corrine Kozlak

Listen for the whistling
Hogan, Bill, May 4, 2011, food styling by Corrine Kozlak

Sticking with it
Fila, Bob, June 21, 2006; food styling by Lisa Schumacher

Grilling wizardry applies to veggies too
Fila, Bob, August 30, 2006; food styling by Lisa Schumacher